1000

GRAPHIC ELEMENTS
SPECIAL DETAILS FOR DISTINCTIVE DESIGNS
WILSON HARVEY: LONDON

ROCKPORT

0001 0002 0003 0004 0005 0006 0007 0008 0009 0010 0011 0012 0013 0014 0015 0016 0017 0018 0019 0020 0021 0022 0023 00
0051 0052 0053 0054 0055 0056 0057 0058 0059 0060 0061 0062 0063 0064 0065 0066 0067 0068 0069 0070 0071 0072 0073 00
0101 0102 0103 0104 0105 0106 0107 0108 0109 0110 0111 0112 0113 0114 0115 0116 0117 0118 0119 0120 0121 0122 0123 01
0151 0152 0153 0154 0155 0156 0157 0158 0159 0160 0161 0162 0163 0164 0165 0166 0167 0168 0169 0170 0171 0172 0173 01
0201 0202 0203 0204 0205 0206 0207 0208 0209 0210 0211 0212 0213 0214 0215 0216 0217 0218 0219 0220 0221 0222 0223 02
0251 0252 0253 0254 0255 0256 0257 0258 0259 0260 0261 0262 0263 0264 0265 0266 0267 0268 0269 0270 0271 0272 0273 02
0301 0302 0303 0304 0305 0306 0307 0308 0309 0310 0311 0312 0313 0314 0315 0316 0317 0318 0319 0320 0321 0322 0323 03
0351 0352 0353 0354 0355 0356 0357 0358 0359 0360 0361 0362 0363 0364 0365 0366 0367 0368 0369 0370 0371 0372 0373 03
0401 0402 0403 0404 0405 0406 0407 0408 0409 0410 0411 0412 0413 0414 0415 0416 0417 0418 0419 0420 0421 0422 0423 04
0451 0452 0453 0454 0455 0456 0457 0458 0459 0460 0461 0462 0463 0464 0465 0466 0467 0468 0469 0470 0471 0472 0473 04
0501 0502 0503 0504 0505 0506 0507 0508 0509 0510 0511 0512 0513 0514 0515 0516 0517 0518 0519 0520 0521 0522 0523 05
0551 0552 0553 0554 0555 0556 0557 0558 0559 0560 0561 0562 0563 0564 0565 0566 0567 0568 0569 0570 0571 0572 0573 05
0601 0602 0603 0604 0605 0606 0607 0608 0609 0610 0611 0612 0613 0614 0615 0616 0617 0618 0619 0620 0621 0622 0623 06
0651 0652 0653 0654 0655 0656 0657 0658 0659 0660 0661 0662 0663 0664 0665 0666 0667 0668 0669 0670 0671 0672 0673 06
0701 0702 0703 0704 0705 0706 0707 0708 0709 0710 0711 0712 0713 0714 0715 0716 0717 0718 0719 0720 0721 0722 0723 07
0751 0752 0753 0754 0755 0756 0757 0758 0759 0760 0761 0762 0763 0764 0765 0766 0767 0768 0769 0770 0771 0772 0773 07
0801 0802 0803 0804 0805 0806 0807 0808 0809 0810 0811 0812 0813 0814 0815 0816 0817 0818 0819 0820 0821 0822 0823 08
0851 0852 0853 0854 0855 0856 0857 0858 0859 0860 0861 0862 0863 0864 0865 0866 0867 0868 0869 0870 0871 0872 0873 08
0901 0902 0903 0904 0905 0906 0907 0908 0909 0910 0911 0912 0913 0914 0915 0916 0917 0918 0919 0920 0921 0922 0923 09
0951 0952 0953 0954 0955 0956 0957 0958 0959 0960 0961 0962 0963 0964 0965 0966 0967 0968 0969 0970 0971 0972 0973 09

1000

GRAPHIC ELEMENTS

SPECIAL DETAILS FOR DISTINCTIVE DESIGNS

WILSON HARVEY: LONDON

25 0026 0027 0028 0029 0030 0031 0032 0033 0034 0035 0036 0037 0038 0039 0040 0041 0042 0043 0044 0045 0046 0047 0048 0049
75 0076 0077 0078 0079 0080 0081 0082 0083 0084 0085 0086 0087 0088 0089 0090 0091 0092 0093 0094 0095 0096 0097 0098 0099
25 0126 0127 0128 0129 0130 0131 0132 0133 0134 0135 0136 0137 0138 0139 0140 0141 0142 0143 0144 0145 0146 0147 0148 0149 0150
75 0176 0177 0178 0179 0180 0181 0182 0183 0184 0185 0186 0187 0188 0189 0190 0191 0192 0193 0194 0195 0196 0197 0198 0199 0200
25 0226 0227 0228 0229 0230 0231 0232 0233 0234 0235 0236 0237 0238 0239 0240 0241 0242 0243 0244 0245 0246 0247 0248 0249 0250
75 0276 0277 0278 0279 0280 0281 0282 0283 0284 0285 0286 0287 0288 0289 0290 0291 0292 0293 0294 0295 0296 0297 0298 0299 0300
25 0326 0327 0328 0329 0330 0331 0332 0333 0334 0335 0336 0337 0338 0339 0340 0341 0342 0343 0344 0345 0346 0347 0348 0349 0350
75 0376 0377 0378 0379 0380 0381 0382 0383 0384 0385 0386 0387 0388 0389 0390 0391 0392 0393 0394 0395 0396 0397 0398 0399 0400
25 0426 0427 0428 0429 0430 0431 0432 0433 0434 0435 0436 0437 0438 0439 0440 0441 0442 0443 0444 0445 0446 0447 0448 0449 0450
75 0476 0477 0478 0479 0480 0481 0482 0483 0484 0485 0486 0487 0488 0489 0490 0491 0492 0493 0494 0495 0496 0497 0498 0499 0500
25 0526 0527 0528 0529 0530 0531 0532 0533 0534 0535 0536 0537 0538 0539 0540 0541 0542 0543 0544 0545 0546 0547 0548 0549 0550
75 0576 0577 0578 0579 0580 0581 0582 0583 0584 0585 0586 0587 0588 0589 0590 0591 0592 0593 0594 0595 0596 0597 0598 0599 0600
25 0626 0627 0628 0629 0630 0631 0632 0633 0634 0635 0636 0637 0638 0639 0640 0641 0642 0643 0644 0645 0646 0647 0648 0649 0650
75 0676 0677 0678 0679 0680 0681 0682 0683 0684 0685 0686 0687 0688 0689 0690 0691 0692 0693 0694 0695 0696 0697 0698 0699 0700
25 0726 0727 0728 0729 0730 0731 0732 0733 0734 0735 0736 0737 0738 0739 0740 0741 0742 0743 0744 0745 0746 0747 0748 0749 0750
75 0776 0777 0778 0779 0780 0781 0782 0783 0784 0785 0786 0787 0788 0789 0790 0791 0792 0793 0794 0795 0796 0797 0798 0799 0800
25 0826 0827 0828 0829 0830 0831 0832 0833 0834 0835 0836 0837 0838 0839 0840 0841 0842 0843 0844 0845 0846 0847 0848 0849 0850
75 0876 0877 0878 0879 0880 0881 0882 0883 0884 0885 0886 0887 0888 0889 0890 0891 0892 0893 0894 0895 0896 0897 0898 0899 0900
25 0926 0927 0928 0929 0930 0931 0932 0933 0934 0935 0936 0937 0938 0939 0940 0941 0942 0943 0944 0945 0946 0947 0948 0949 0950
75 0976 0977 0978 0979 0980 0981 0982 0983 0984 0985 0986 0987 0988 0989 0990 0991 0992 0993 0994 0995 0996 0997 0998 0999 1000

+ ART DIRECTOR
PAUL BURGESS

+ DESIGN
BEN WOOD

+ ARTWORK
PETE USHER

+ RESEARCH AND JUDGING
PAUL BURGESS
BEN WOOD
DAN ELLIOTT
GRAHAM FARR
ALUN STEEL

+ ALL ADDITIONAL PHOTOGRAPHY
PHIL COOK

+ FONTS
DIN + BELL

First published in the United States of America by
Rockport Publishers, Inc.
33 Commercial Street
Gloucester, Massachusetts 01930-5089
Telephone: (978) 282-9590
Fax: (978) 283-2742
www.rockpub.com

DESIGNED AT WILSON HARVEY: LONDON

10 9 8 7 6 5 4   ISBN 1-59253-077-X

PRINTED IN CHINA

Illustrator, Photoshop, InDesign, and
Pagemaker are all registered trademarks
of Adobe.

INTRODUCTION

0001 0002 0003 0004 0005 0006 0007 0008 0009 0010 0011 0012 0013
0041 0042 0043 0044 0045 0046 0047 0048 0049 0050 0051 0052 0053
0081 0082 0083 0084 0085 0086 0087 0088 0089 0090 0091 0092 0093
0121 0122 0123 0124 0125 0126 0127 0128 0129 0130 0131 0132 0133
0161 0162 0163 0164 0165 0166 0167 0168 0169 0170 0171 0172 0173
0201 0202 0203 0204 0205 0206 0207 0208 0209 0210 0211 0212 0213
0241 0242 0243 0244 0245 0246 0247 0248 0249 0250 0251 0252 0253
0281 0282 0283 0284 0285 0286 0287 0288 0289 0290 0291 0292 0293
0321 0322 0323 0324 0325 0326 0327 0328 0329 0330 0331 0332 0333
0361 0362 0363 0364 0365 0366 0367 0368 0369 0370 0371 0372
0401 0402 0403 0404 0405 0406 0407 0408 0409 0410 0411 0412
0441 0442 0443 0444 0445 0446 0447 0448 0449 0450 0451 0452 0453
0481 0482 0483 0484 0485 0486 0487 0488 0489 0490 0491 0492 0493
0521 0522 0523 0524 0525 0526 0527 0528 0529 0530 0531 0532
0561 0562 0563 0564 0565 0566 0567 0568 0569 0570 0571 0572 0573
0601 0602 0603 0604 0605 0606 0607 0608 0609 0610 0611 0612 0613
0641 0642 0643 0644 0645 0646 0647 0648 0649 0650 0651 0652
0681 0682 0683 0684 0685 0686 0687 0688 0689 0690 0691 0692
0721 0722 0723 0724 0725 0726 0727 0728 0729 0730 0731 0732 0733
0761 0762 0763 0764 0765 0766 0767 0768 0769 0770 0771 0772
0801 0802 0803 0804 0805 0806 0807 0808 0809 0810 0811 0812
0841 0842 0843 0844 0845 0846 0847 0848 0849 0850 0851 0852
0881 0882 0883 0884 0885 0886 0887 0888 0889 0890 0891 0892 0893
0921 0922 0923 0924 0925 0926 0927 0928 0929 0930 0931 0932 0933
0961 0962 0963 0964 0965 0966 0967 0968 0969 0970 0971 0972

KEY TO SYMBOLS+

- GRAPHIC DEVICES
- MATERIALS
- TEXT
- DIE CUTS
- ADD-ONS
- EMBOSSING
- INKS
- FORMATS
- BINDINGS

+

This book is as much about the possibilities as it is about the detail. Most projects begin with the former and arrive at the latter. The possibilities are often the justification we as designers give ourselves for all those late nights and obsessive thoughts. Possibility is what keeps us inspired, and realization is what keeps us content. Detail is the challenge that connects the two. **+** Getting the finer details to fall into place is an art form. Get it right and the project comes alive, get it wrong and the project can be a disaster. The line is fine between experimentation, exploitation, and excess, but should the design allow it, then it is a line worth exploring. **+** The work featured in this book exemplifies this exploration; 1,000 examples of work that goes the extra inch or, in some cases, the extra mile. At first glance, many seem to have started life with the perfect brief, almost to the point where the budget seems as flexible as the concepts produced—a design utopia you dream of but never experience firsthand. However, many of these solutions have emerged from hard-fought battles and persuasive designers doing whatever they can to progress their possibilities. In many cases, it's true to say "if you have nothing, the possibilities are endless"—a bad brief, a low budget, or a vague client might actually be the perfect platform to realizing those possibilities. **+** With today's ever-expanding repertoire of finishing techniques, materials, and processes, there are plenty of excuses to innovate. Some might argue that "everything's been designed before," but here are 1,000 pieces of work that beg to differ. There are common themes and processes, but each piece is as unique as the client it represents and the information it contains, a testament to the designer's possibilities. This collection is also hard proof that it doesn't always work. While there are 1,000 pieces on display here, there are plenty more on the cutting room floor. What's left is an inspiring collection. It shows the work of those seeking to push the boundaries and others who concentrate on using more standard approaches with equally stunning success. **+** If there's one common thread throughout this book, it's the desire to realize new possibilities, and for us it's inspiring to see so many designers with the courage to push those possibilities to the limit.   Paul Burgess, Ben Wood, and all at Wilson Harvey

27 0028 0029 0030 0031 0032 0033 0034 0035 0036 0037 0038 0039 0040
67 0068 0069 0070 0071 0072 0073 0074 0075 0076 0077 0078 0079 0080
07 0108 0109 0110 0111 0112 0113 0114 0115 0116 0117 0118 0119 0120
47 0148 0149 0150 0151 0152 0153 0154 0155 0156 0157 0158 0159 0160
87 0188 0189 0190 0191 0192 0193 0194 0195 0196 0197 0198 0199 0200
27 0228 0229 0230 0231 0232 0233 0234 0235 0236 0237 0238 0239 0240
67 0268 0269 0270 0271 0272 0273 0274 0275 0276 0277 0278 0279 0280
07 0308 0309 0310 0311 0312 0313 0314 0315 0316 0317 0318 0319 0320
47 0348 0349 0350 0351 0352 0353 0354 0355 0356 0357 0358 0359 0360
87 0388 0389 0390 0391 0392 0393 0394 0395 0396 0397 0398 0399 0400
27 0428 0429 0430 0431 0432 0433 0434 0435 0436 0437 0438 0439 0440
67 0468 0469 0470 0471 0472 0473 0474 0475 0476 0477 0478 0479 0480
07 0508 0509 0510 0511 0512 0513 0514 0515 0516 0517 0518 0519 0520
47 0548 0549 0550 0551 0552 0553 0554 0555 0556 0557 0558 0559 0560
87 0588 0589 0590 0591 0592 0593 0594 0595 0596 0597 0598 0599 0600
27 0628 0629 0630 0631 0632 0633 0634 0635 0636 0637 0638 0639 0640
67 0668 0669 0670 0671 0672 0673 0674 0675 0676 0677 0678 0679 0680
07 0708 0709 0710 0711 0712 0713 0714 0715 0716 0717 0718 0719 0720
47 0748 0749 0750 0751 0752 0753 0754 0755 0756 0757 0758 0759 0760
87 0788 0789 0790 0791 0792 0793 0794 0795 0796 0797 0798 0799 0800
27 0828 0829 0830 0831 0832 0833 0834 0835 0836 0837 0838 0839 0840
67 0868 0869 0870 0871 0872 0873 0874 0875 0876 0877 0878 0879 0880
07 0908 0909 0910 0911 0912 0913 0914 0915 0916 0917 0918 0919 0920
47 0948 0949 0950 0951 0952 0953 0954 0955 0956 0957 0958 0959 0960
87 0988 0989 0990 0991 0992 0993 0994 0995 0996 0997 0998 0999 1000

_01

PRINTING TECHNIQUES

SCREEN PRINTING
HAND RENDERING
LETTERPRESS
VARNISHES
OVERPRINTING

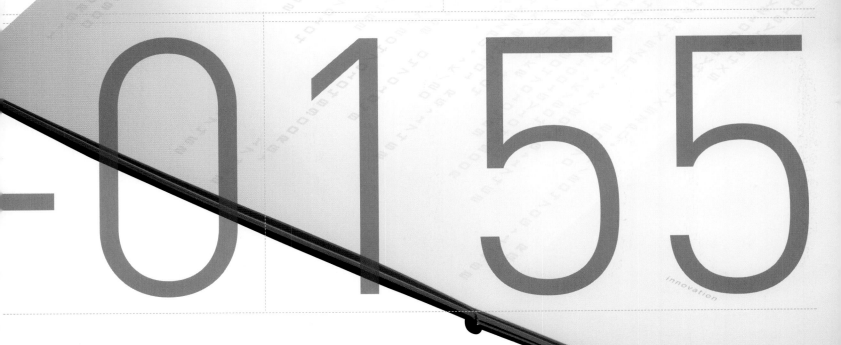

-0155

innovation

75031

COMMON STOCK
PAR VALUE
$0.01 PER SHARE

JANUS CAPITAL
Group INC.

INCORPORATED UNDER THE LAWS OF THE STATE OF DELAWARE

NUMBER
JNS

THIS IS TO CERTIFY THAT

IS THE OWNER OF

FULLY PAID AND NON-ASSESSABLE SHARES OF THE COMMON STOCK OF

Janus Capital Group Inc., transferable on the books of the Corporation
hereof in person or by duly authorized attorney upon
properly endorsed. This Certificate and the
all the terms, conditions and
Bylaws of the Co
with

"GET UP TO NO GOOD AT THE CHRISTMAS PARTY AND STILL LOOK
(For a truly angelic look, punch out the 'glow in the dark' halo and place it

MERRY CHRISTMAS
from everyone at
ONE O'CLOCK GUN

You're comin' with
up one morning...

Romantic comedy adventure set in Brighton.
...a Townie Boy and Funk Girl on a blind date
EP to score some drugs and overhear a murder
robbery being planned by two hit men...

PhotoaboutCore

0002 TEMPLIN BRINK DESIGN USA	☀◌🖐↑	**0003** ONE O'CLOCK GUN DESIGN CONSULTANTS SCOTLAND	☰◌↑
0004 CRUSH DESIGN UK	+🖉◌🖐↑	**0005** SCANDINAVIAN DESIGN GROUP DENMARK	◌T↑

0006 **SCANDINAVIAN DESIGN GROUP**
DENMARK

0007 **PRECURSOR**
UK

0008 **MODE**
UK

0009 **PRECURSOR**
UK

The Mill.
New York.

The Mill.
435 Hudson Street
New York NY 10014
Telephone (212) 520 3150
www.mill.co.uk

Sale at Viaduct
6–20 July 2002
Up to 50% off selected items
10–15% off all orders

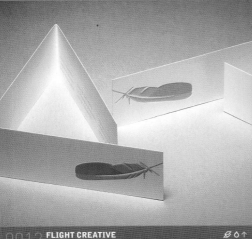

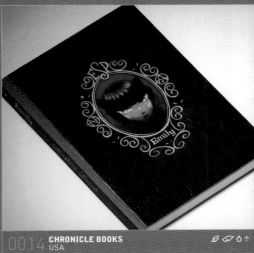

0012 FLIGHT CREATIVE
AUSTRALIA

0013 LLOYDS GRAPHIC DESIGN AND
COMMUNICATION
NEW ZEALAND

0014 CHRONICLE BOOKS
USA

0015 WALLACE CHURCH
USA

0016 TEMPLIN BRINK DESIGN
USA

0017 TEMPLIN BRINK DESIGN
USA

0018 HAND MADE GROUP
ITALY

0019 HGV FELTON
UK

0020 POINT BLANK DESIGN
UK

0021 UNTITLED
UK

0022 SAMPSONMAY
UK

0023 HESSE DESIGN GMBH
GERMANY

0024 SCANDINAVIAN DESIGN GROUP
DENMARK

11.12.2002
horst hörtner linz
ars electronica center
»futurelab«
19:30 uhr. aula

12.02.2003
peter bexte berl
curator, autor, the
»transitstrecken«
19:30 uhr. aula

heinz und gisela friederichs
stiftungsprofessur

interaktive videoinstallationen/environmental-medienprojekte
prof. masaki fujihata

hochschule für gestaltung offenbach am main
schlossstraße 31, aula, beginn 19:30 uhr

0027 **EGBG**
THE NETHERLANDS

0028 **SK VISUAL**
USA

0029 **MADE THOUGHT**
UK

0030 **FELDER GRAFIKDESIGN**
AUSTRIA

0031 **V06**
BRAZIL

0032 **SHIH DESIGN**
TAIWAN

0033 **WEBB & WEBB**
UK

0034 **THE WORKS DESIGN COMMUNICATIONS**
CANADA

0035 **FIELD DESIGN CONSULTANTS**
UK

0036 **THE PHOENIX STUDIO**
USA

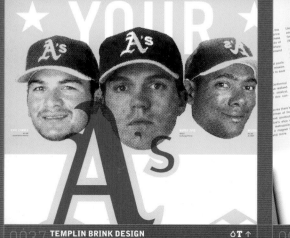

From Vernal Pool to Metropolis

0037 **TEMPLIN BRINK DESIGN**
USA

0038 **TEMPLIN BRINK DESIGN**
USA

0039 **CRUSH DESIGN**
UK

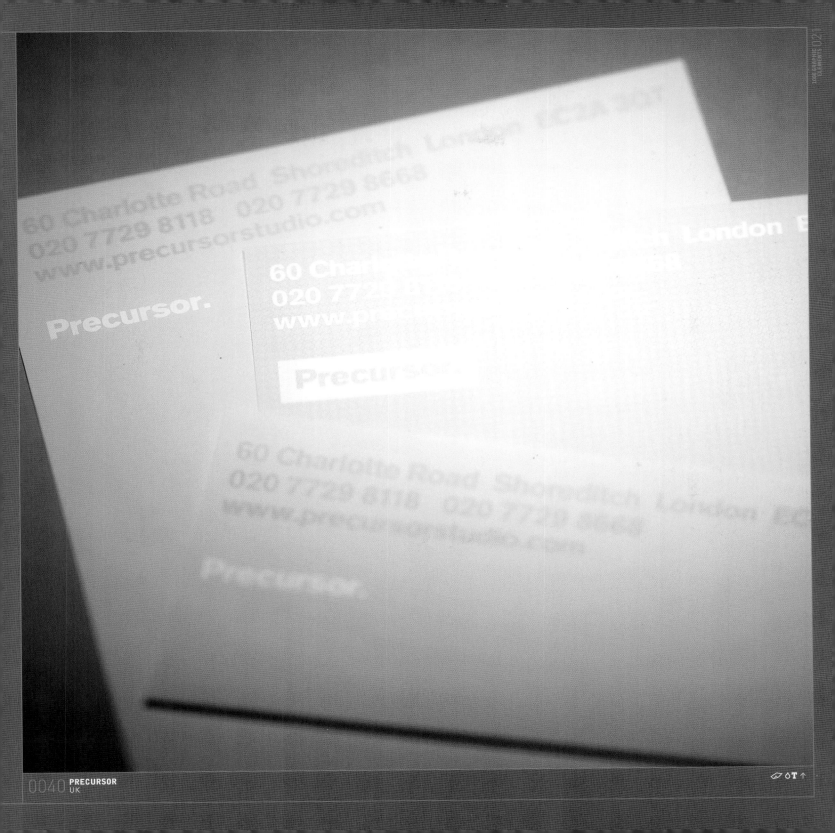

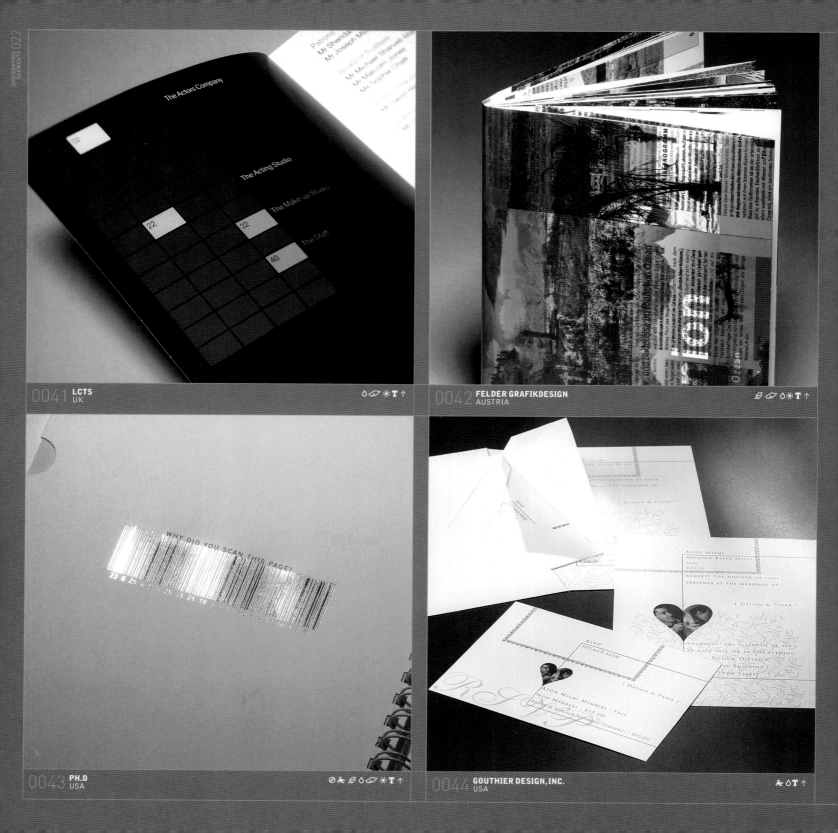

0041 LCTS
UK

0042 FELDER GRAFIKDESIGN
AUSTRIA

0043 PH.D
USA

0044 GOUTHIER DESIGN, INC.
USA

WHY DID YOU SCAN THIS PAGE?

twelve:ten

Cover 4 col. + Matt laminate + Spot varnish
Origination tool Apple Mac
Construction tool Komori Lithrone
Avg. age of operatives = 27
Avg. Daily hot beverage intake = 4.3 cups

Dimensions 277 mm x 210mm
Front Colour Mix C34 M0 Y100 K79
Publication Font FF Din Medium
Office Hours = 50 + After Hours = 70

Graphica

03

IMMENSE
HIDDEN
BETWEEN
SLEEVES

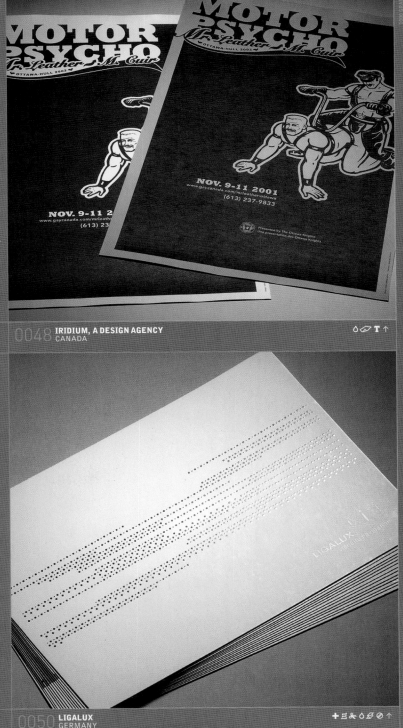

0047 **LIGALUX**
GERMANY   ◊ ⬚ **T** ↑

0048 **IRIDIUM, A DESIGN AGENCY**
CANADA   ◊ ⬚ **T** ↑

0049 **FORTYFOUR DESIGN**
AUSTRALIA   ＋◊ ⬚ ↑

0050 **LIGALUX**
GERMANY   ＋☰☆◊∅◊↑

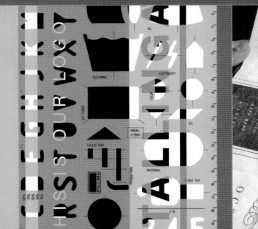

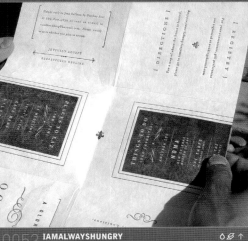

0052 **LAVA**
THE NETHERLANDS ◇ ✳ **T** ↑

0053 **IAMALWAYSHUNGRY**
USA ◇ ⬡ ↑

0054 **DINNICK & HOWELLS**
CANADA ◇ ↑

0055 **RIORDON DESIGN**
CANADA ◇ ⬡ ⬡ ↑

0056 **R2 DESIGN**
PORTUGAL ◇ ⬡ ⬡ ↑

0057 **NIKLAUS TROXLER DESIGN**
SWITZERLAND ◇ ⬡ ⬡ **T** ↑

0058 **JASON & JASON**
ISRAEL ◇ ↑

0059 **SCANDINAVIAN DESIGN GROUP**
DENMARK ◇ **T** ⬡ ↑

0060 **GRAPHISCHE FORMGEBUNG,**
HERBERT ROHSIEPE
GERMANY ◇ ⬡ ↑

0061 **THOMPSON**
UK

0062 **PROJECT 88**
UK

0063 **WILSON HARVEY**
UK

0064 **LAYFIELD**
AUSTRALIA

STEVEN AND JULIE SWIRES
ARE DELIGHTED TO ANNOUNCE THE BIRTH
OF DANIEL STEVEN

Wholesale, Dark Fibre & Internet Markets
Europe, Latin America & Asia-Pacific
5 new studies

...d Administration

CENTRE STAFFING:

The permanent staff of the Centre has been ma...

...level commensurate with efficient operatio...

...e financial resources of the Centre...

...hart Chief Exe...

...Com...

0067 **MARIUS FAHRNER DESIGN**
GERMANY

0068 **HAND MADE GROUP**
ITALY

0069 **....,STAAT**
THE NETHERLANDS

0070 **LIPPA PEARCE DESIGN**
UK

0071 R2 DESIGN
PORTUGAL

ONY OURSLER THE INFLUENCE MACHINE

0072 EGGERS + DIAPER
GERMANY

0073 STARSHOT
GERMANY

0074 MOTIVE DESIGN RESEARCH
USA

0075 YAEL MILLER DESIGN
USA

0076 EMERY VINCENT DESIGN
AUSTRALIA

0077 KOLEGRAM DESIGN
CANADA

северный олень

1 2 3 4 5 6 7 8 9 10

0078 DESIGN DEPOT CREATIVE BUREAU
RUSSIA

0079 UNDERWARE
THE NETHERLANDS

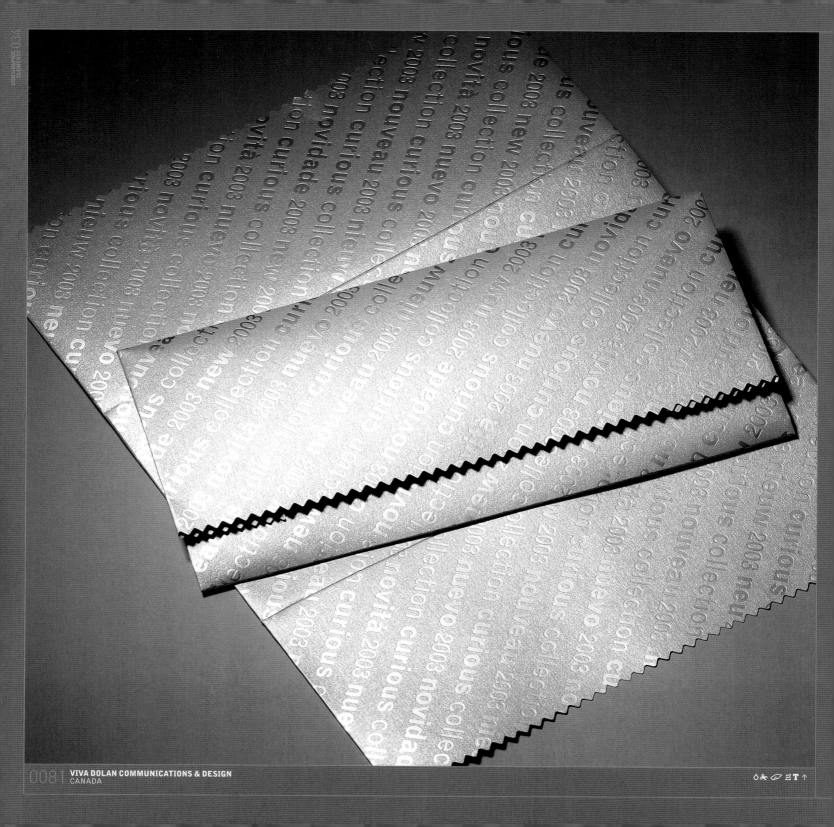

High Definition.
The Mill invite you to a private v...
the newly opened high-definitio...
There will also be an exclusive pre-Canne...
of commercials shot with Sony HDcam or...
posted in high-def at The Mill
June 18th and 19th. Open house between 7p...
Champagne and canapés
RSVP to hd@mill.co.uk

hochwertiger
treue Restauration
Winnen und

ESIGN

0082 **MADE THOUGHT**
UK

0083 **NO.PARKING**
ITALY

0084 **CHEN DESIGN ASSOCIATES**
USA

0085 **BRUKETA & ZINIC**
CROATIA

0086 **STRICHPUNKT**
GERMANY

0087 **MIRKO ILIC**
USA

0088 **SCANDINAVIAN DESIGN GROUP**
DENMARK

0089 **STRICHPUNKT**
GERMANY

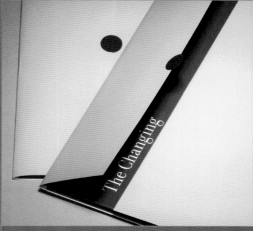

0091 FELDER GRAFIKDESIGN
AUSTRIA

0092 ALOOF DESIGN
UK

0093 KBDA
USA

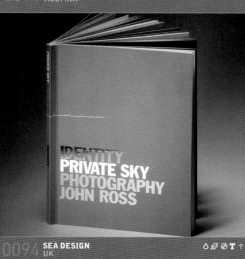

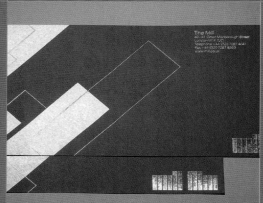

0094 SEA DESIGN
UK

0095 MADE THOUGHT
UK

0096 ANDERSON THOMAS DESIGN
USA

0097 MODE
UK

0098 SUSSNER DESIGN
USA

0099 VOICE
AUSTRALIA

AMANDA HAVEL
USA

GRAPHISCHE FORMGEBUNG, HERBERT ROHSIEPE
GERMANY

0102 **ROSE DESIGN**
UK

0103 **SCANDINAVIAN DESIGN GROUP**
DENMARK

0104 **IAMALWAYSHUNGRY**
USA

0105 **CDT DESIGN**
UK

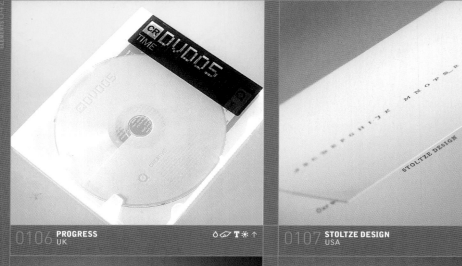

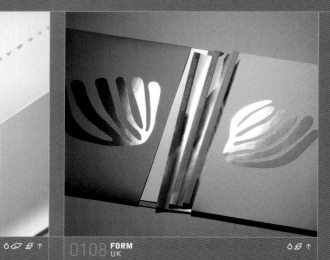

0106 PROGRESS
UK
◊☞ **T** ✳ ↑

0107 STOLTZE DESIGN
USA
◊☞ ∅ ↑

0108 FORM
UK
◊∅ ↑

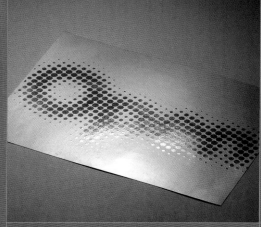

0109 STEERSMCGILLAN
UK
◊**T** ↑

0110 @RADICAL.MEDIA
USA
◊✳☞ ↑

0111 JONES DESIGN GROUP
USA
◊∅∅ ☰ ↑

0112 STEERSMCGILLAN
UK
◊**T** ↑

0113 V06
BRAZIL
◊∅☞ ↑

0114 AVE DESIGN STUDIO
USA
◊∅☞ ↑

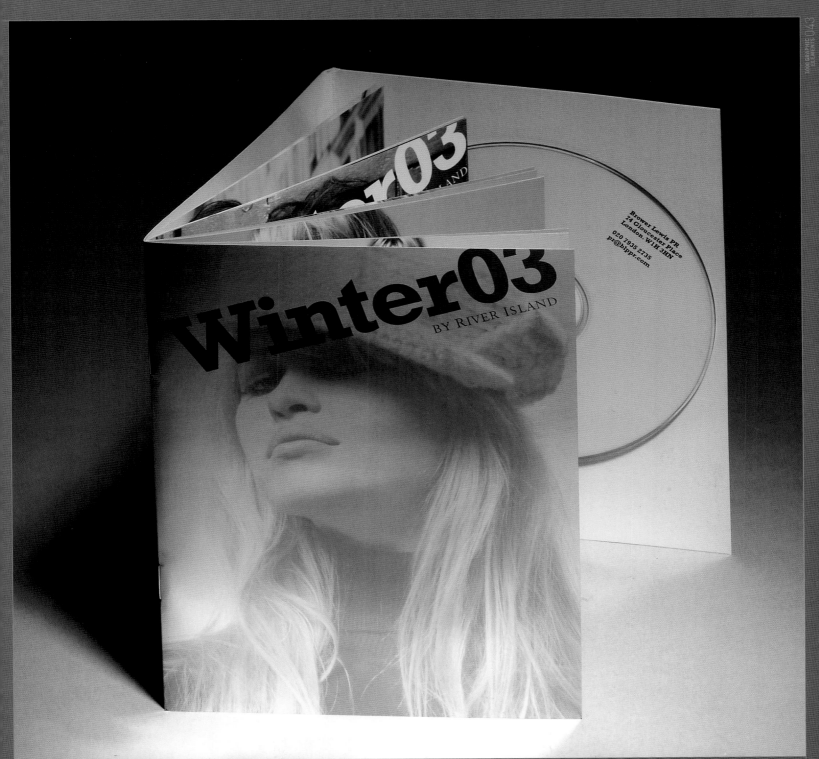

Winter03
BY RIVER ISLAND

Blower Lewis PR
74 Gloucester Place
London, W1H 3HN
020 7935 2735
pr@blpr.com

RSVP: VIA ENCLOSED
REPLY CARD

INVITATION: ADMITS ONE
ONLY PLEASE BRING IT
WITH YOU ON THE NIGHT

VISIT: THE EXHIBITION
WILL ALSO BE OPEN
FROM 10AM UNTIL 6PM
17/18/19/20/21 OCTOBER
ADMISSION FREE

INFORMATION: D&AD
+44 (0) 20 7840 1111
www.dandad.org

SPONSOR: PREMIER PAPER
DRINKS: COURTESY OF
KIRIN BEER

premierpaper

0117 **V06**
BRAZIL

0118 **PROGRESS**
UK

0119 **MIASO DESIGN**
USA

0120 **RIPE IN ASSOCIATION WITH ALCAN PRINT FINISHING**
UK

Gloss OPP Lamination
Gloss OPP (oriented polypropylene) lamination provides a wide range of uses across the whole spectrum of printed products. The properties of good gloss and strength and the advantages of low cost make it suitable for a variety of applications

Matt OPP Lamination
This Matt finish coupled with its smooth texture offers a very high quality image to brochures and book covers. Matt finishes are also particularly suited to surfaces which need to be easily read such as wall maps, but can be prone to scuffing and should be handled with care.

UV Spot Varnish
Spot varnish is a high gloss and matt UV varnish applied to selected areas of a printed image to enhance product impact or form part of the graphic design.

0121 **ROYCROFT DESIGN**
USA

0122 **THE FAMILY**
UK

0123 **IRIDIUM, A DESIGN AGENCY**
CANADA

0124 **PRECURSOR**
UK

LITTLE LOVE

AND DIE, SOMETIMES WE ARE RUNNING BLIND, SOMETIMES ONLY PAIN WE FIND, I
SEE YOU CLIMBING MOUNTAINS HIGH, I SEE YOU PAINT VANILLA SKY, I SEE THEM
SCREAM I SEE THEM CRY, I HEAR THE OLD SOULS ASKING WHY, WITH A LITTLE LOVE

SOMETIMES WE ALL WAR AND CRY, SOMETIMES WE ALL

0127 TAXI STUDIO
UK

0128 ROYCROFT DESIGN
USA

0129 URBAN MAPPING
USA

0130 CRANHAM ADVERTISING
UK

0131 ROSE DESIGN
UK

0132 FELDER GRAFIKDESIGN
AUSTRIA

0133 SUM DESIGN
UK

0134 EGBG
THE NETHERLANDS

0135 LIPPA PEARCE DESIGN
UK

0136 **ORANGESEED DESIGN**
USA

0137 **MODE**
UK

0138 **HESSE DESIGN**
GERMANY

0139 **PRECURSOR**
UK

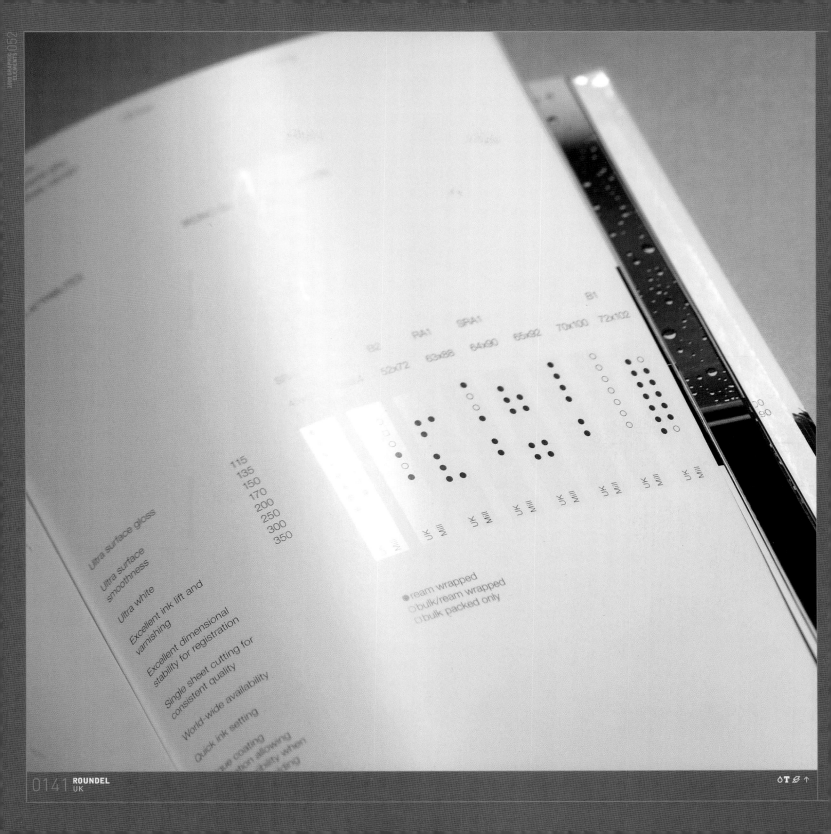

0142 SCANDINAVIAN DESIGN GROUP
DENMARK

0143 MARIUS FAHRNER DESIGN
GERMANY

0144 CAPSULE
USA

0145 LIPPA PEARCE DESIGN
UK

0146 **STEERSMCGILLAN**
UK

0147 **QUESTION DESIGN**
USA

0148 **MAIOW CREATIVE BRANDING**
UK

0149 **MONA MACDONALD DESIGN**
USA

0150 **ELMWOOD**
UK

0151 **11D – ELEVEN DESIGN**
DENMARK

0152 **WILSON HARVEY**
UK

0153 **MAIOW CREATIVE BRANDING**
UK

0154 **TRICKETT & WEBB**
UK

0001 0002 0003 0004 0005 0006 0007 0008 0009 0010 0011 0012 0013 0014 0015 0016 0017 0018 0019 0020 0021 0022 0023 0024 0025
0041 0042 0043 0044 0045 0046 0047 0048 0049 0050 0051 0052 0053 0054 0055 0056 0057 0058 0059 0060 0061 0062 0063 0064 0065
0081 0082 0083 0084 0085 0086 0087 0088 0089 0090 0091 0092 0093 0094 0095 0096 0097 0098 0099 0100 0101 0102 0103 0104 0105
0121 0122 0123 0124 0125 0126 0127 0128 0129 0130 0131 0132 0133 0134 0135 0136 0137 0138 0139 0140 0141 0142 0143 0144 0145
0161 0162 0163 0164 0165 0166 0167 0168 0169 0170 0171 0172 0173 0174 0175 0176 0177 0178 0179 0180 0181 0182 0183 0184 0185
0201 0202 0203 0204 0205 0206 0207 0208 0209 0210 0211 0212 0213 0214 0215 0216 0217 0218 0219 0220 0221 0222 0223 0224 0225
0241 0242 0243 0244 0245 0246 0247 0248 0249 0250 0251 0252 0253 0254 0255 0256 0257 0258 0259 0260 0261 0262 0263 0264 0265
0281 0282 0283 0284 0285 0286 0287 0288 0289 0290 0291 0292 0293 0294 0295 0296 0297 0298 0299 0300 0301 0302 0303 0304 0305
0321 0322 0323 0324 0325 0326 0327 0328 0329 0330 0331 0332 0333 0334 0335 0336 0337 0338 0339 0340 0341 0342 0343 0344 0345
0361 0362 0363 0364 0365 0366 0367 0368 0369 0370 0371 0372 0373 0374 0375 0376 0377 0378 0379 0380 0381 0382 0383 0384 0385
0401 0402 0403 0404 0405 0406 0407 0408 0409 0410 0411 0412 0413 0414 0415 0416 0417 0418 0419 0420 0421 0422 0423 0424 0425
0441 0442 0443 0444 0445 0446 0447 0448 0449 0450 0451 0452 0453 0454 0455 0456 0457 0458 0459 0460 0461 0462 0463 0464 0465
0481 0482 0483 0484 0485 0486 0487 0488 0489 0490 0491 0492 0493 0494 0495 0496 0497 0498 0499 0500 0501 0502 0503 0504 0505
0521 0522 0523 0524 0525 0526 0527 0528 0529 0530 0531 0532 0533 0534 0535 0536 0537 0538 0539 0540 0541 0542 0543 0544 0545
0561 0562 0563 0564 0565 0566 0567 0568 0569 0570 0571 0572 0573 0574 0575 0576 0577 0578 0579 0580 0581 0582 0583 0584 0585
0601 0602 0603 0604 0605 0606 0607 0608 0609 0610 0611 0612 0613 0614 0615 0616 0617 0618 0619 0620 0621 0622 0623 0624 0625
0641 0642 0643 0644 0645 0646 0647 0648 0649 0650 0651 0652 0653 0654 0655 0656 0657 0658 0659 0660 0661 0662 0663 0664 0665
0681 0682 0683 0684 0685 0686 0687 0688 0689 0690 0691 0692 0693 0694 0695 0696 0697 0698 0699 0700 0701 0702 0703 0704 0705
0721 0722 0723 0724 0725 0726 0727 0728 0729 0730 0731 0732 0733 0734 0735 0736 0737 0738 0739 0740 0741 0742 0743 0744 0745
0761 0762 0763 0764 0765 0766 0767 0768 0769 0770 0771 0772 0773 0774 0775 0776 0777 0778 0779 0780 0781 0782 0783 0784 0785
0801 0802 0803 0804 0805 0806 0807 0808 0809 0810 0811 0812 0813 0814 0815 0816 0817 0818 0819 0820 0821 0822 0823 0824 0825
0841 0842 0843 0844 0845 0846 0847 0848 0849 0850 0851 0852 0853 0854 0855 0856 0857 0858 0859 0860 0861 0862 0863 0864 0865
0881 0882 0883 0884 0885 0886 0887 0888 0889 0890 0891 0892 0893 0894 0895 0896 0897 0898 0899 0900 0901 0902 0903 0904 0905
0921 0922 0923 0924 0925 0926 0927 0928 0929 0930 0931 0932 0933 0934 0935 0936 0937 0938 0939 0940 0941 0942 0943 0944 0945
0961 0962 0963 0964 0965 0966 0967 0968 0969 0970 0971 0972 0973 0974 0975 0976 0977 0978 0979 0980 0981 0982 0983 0984 0985

0156-

7 0028 0029 0030 0031 0032 0033 0034 0035 0036 0037 0038 0039 0040
7 0068 0069 0070 0071 0072 0073 0074 0075 0076 0077 0078 0079 0080
7 0108 0109 0110 0111 0112 0113 0114 0115 0116 0117 0118 0119 0120
7 0148 0149 0150 0151 0152 0153 0154 0155 0156 0157 0158 0159 0160
7 0188 0189 0190 0191 0192 0193 0194 0195 0196 0197 0198 0199 0200
7 0228 0229 0230 0231 0232 0233 0234 0235 0236 0237 0238 0239 0240
7 0268 0269 0270 0271 0272 0273 0274 0275 0276 0277 0278 0279 0280
7 0308 0309 0310 0311 0312 0313 0314 0315 0316 0317 0318 0319 0320
7 0348 0349 0350 0351 0352 0353 0354 0355 0356 0357 0358 0359 0360
7 0388 0389 0390 0391 0392 0393 0394 0395 0396 0397 0398 0399 0400
7 0428 0429 0430 0431 0432 0433 0434 0435 0436 0437 0438 0439 0440
7 0468 0469 0470 0471 0472 0473 0474 0475 0476 0477 0478 0479 0480
7 0508 0509 0510 0511 0512 0513 0514 0515 0516 0517 0518 0519 0520
7 0548 0549 0550 0551 0552 0553 0554 0555 0556 0557 0558 0559 0560
7 0588 0589 0590 0591 0592 0593 0594 0595 0596 0597 0598 0599 0600
7 0628 0629 0630 0631 0632 0633 0634 0635 0636 0637 0638 0639 0640
7 0668 0669 0670 0671 0672 0673 0674 0675 0676 0677 0678 0679 0680
7 0708 0709 0710 0711 0712 0713 0714 0715 0716 0717 0718 0719 0720
7 0748 0749 0750 0751 0752 0753 0754 0755 0756 0757 0758 0759 0760
7 0788 0789 0790 0791 0792 0793 0794 0795 0796 0797 0798 0799 0800
7 0828 0829 0830 0831 0832 0833 0834 0835 0836 0837 0838 0839 0840
7 0868 0869 0870 0871 0872 0873 0874 0875 0876 0877 0878 0879 0880
7 0908 0909 0910 0911 0912 0913 0914 0915 0916 0917 0918 0919 0920
7 0948 0949 0950 0951 0952 0953 0954 0955 0956 0957 0958 0959 0960
7 0988 0989 0990 0991 0992 0993 0994 0995 0996 0997 0998 0999 1000

_02

MANIPULATED
SURFACES

EMBOSSING
PERFORATION
FOIL BLOCKING
SPECIAL INKS
METALLICS

Journey

-0340

E

65

PEACE
Nobel Prize 100th Anniversary

PHYSICS
Nobel Prize 100th Anniversary

0156 **HGV FELTON**
UK

0157 **KINETIC SINGAPORE**
SINGAPORE

0158 **CRUSH DESIGN**
UK

0159 **WEBB & WEBB**
UK

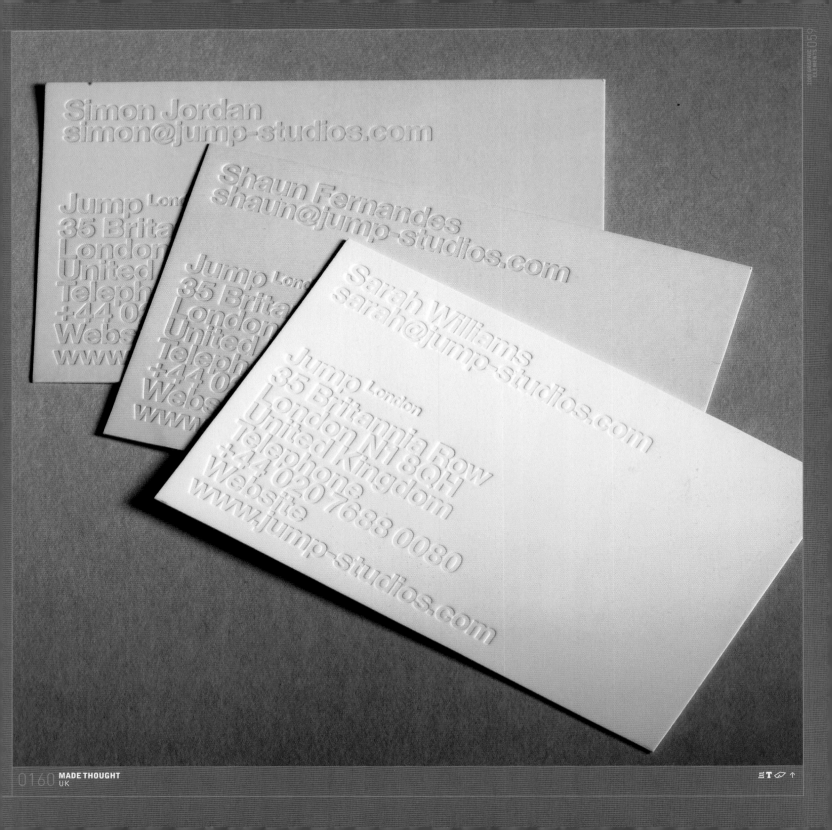

Simon Jordan
simon@jump-studios.com

Jump London
35 Brita
London
United
Teleph
+44 0
Webs
www

Shaun Fernandes
shaun@jump-studios.com

Jump London
35 Brita
London
United
Teleph
+44 0
Webs
www

Sarah Williams
sarah@jump-studios.com

Jump London
35 Britannia Row
London N1 8QH
United Kingdom
Telephone
+44 020 7688 0080
Website
www.jump-studios.com

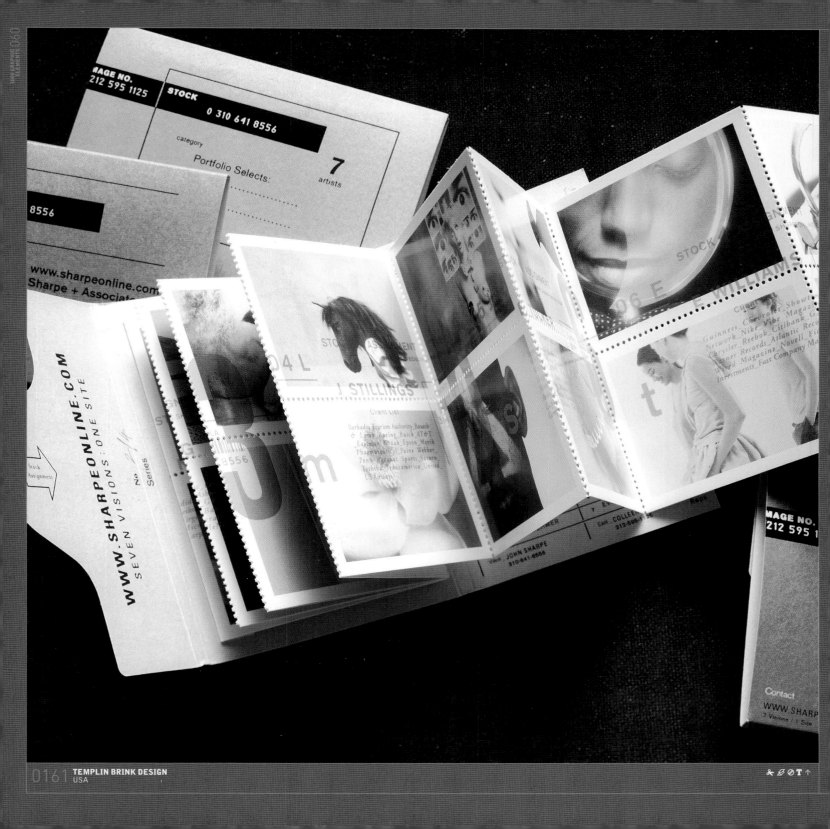

0162 **GIORGIO DAVANZO DESIGN**
USA

0163 **BBM & D**
USA

0164 **STARSHOT**
GERMANY

0165 **TEMPLIN BRINK DESIGN**
USA

0166 **PHILLIPS**
UK

0167 **ERBE DESIGN**
USA

the cats' home

SHAW HEAD FARM
BECKWITHSHAW HARROGATE
NORTH YORKSHIRE HG3 1QU
TEL 01423 561 897

0168 **JASON & JASON**
ISRAEL

0169 **LAYFIELD**
AUSTRALIA

0170 **MARIUS FAHRNER DESIGN**
GERMANY

0171 **WALLACE CHURCH**
USA

(touching)

touching hearts...
to honor our friends this holiday season we have made a donation
to the Blind Babies Foundation of America

Wallace Church, Inc.

0172 **KONTRAPUNKT**
SLOVENIA

0173 **AFTERHOURS CREATIVE**
USA

CLEARDATA.NET

0174 **FORM**
UK

Form®

47 Tabernacle Street
London EC2A 4AA, UK
Telephone: +44 (0)20 7014 1430
Fax: +44 (0)20 7014 1431
ISDN: +44 (0)20 7014 1432
Email: studio@form.uk.com
Web: www.form.uk.com

SENOK™
TEA FOR THE SENSES

SENOK™
TEA FOR THE SENSES

SENOK™
TEA FOR THE SENSES

Landy Pen

126 S Spokane Street | Seattle WA 98124
P **206.903.0858** | 1 877.736.6583 | F 206.624.3026
lpen@senoktea.com | www.senoktea.com

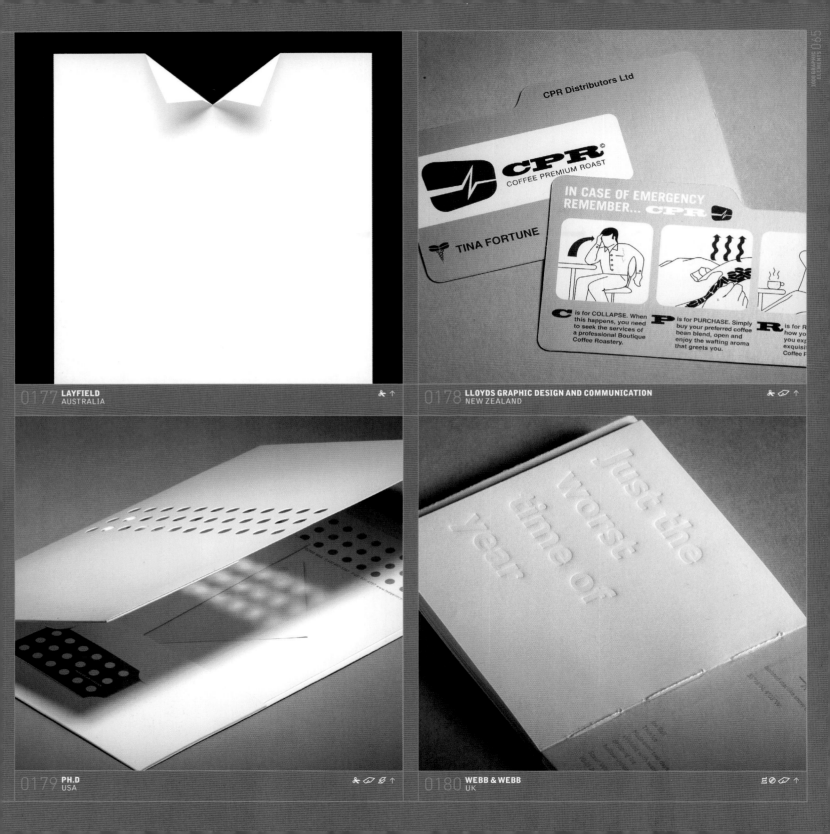

CPR Distributors Ltd

CPR©
COFFEE PREMIUM ROAST

TINA FORTUNE

IN CASE OF EMERGENCY
REMEMBER... **CPR**

C is for COLLAPSE. When this happens, you need to seek the services of a professional Boutique Coffee Roastery.

P is for PURCHASE. Simply buy your preferred coffee bean blend, open and enjoy the wafting aroma that greets you.

R is for R... how yo... you exp... exquisi... Coffee P...

Just the worst time of year

0177 **LAYFIELD**
AUSTRALIA

0178 **LLOYDS GRAPHIC DESIGN AND COMMUNICATION**
NEW ZEALAND

0179 **PH.D**
USA

0180 **WEBB & WEBB**
UK

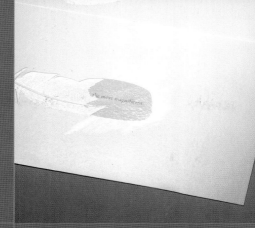

0181 **LIPPA PEARCE DESIGN**
UK

0182 **FLIGHT CREATIVE**
AUSTRALIA

0183 **FIBRE**
UK

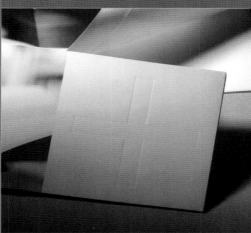

0184 **DOSSIERCREATIVE**
CANADA

0185 **NAVY BLUE**
UK

0186 **ULTRA DESIGN**
BRAZIL

0187 **BISQIT DESIGN**
UK

0188 **PH.D**
USA

0189 **LIPPA PEARCE DESIGN**
UK

0191 DINNICK & HOWELLS
CANADA

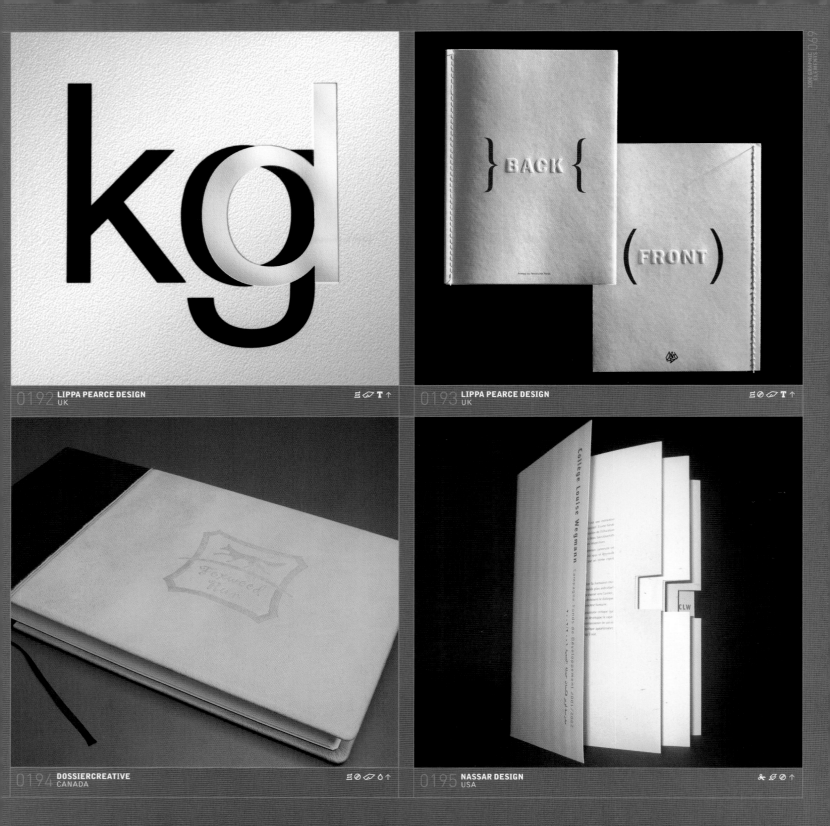

0192 **LIPPA PEARCE DESIGN**
UK

0193 **LIPPA PEARCE DESIGN**
UK

0194 **DOSSIERCREATIVE**
CANADA

0195 **NASSAR DESIGN**
USA

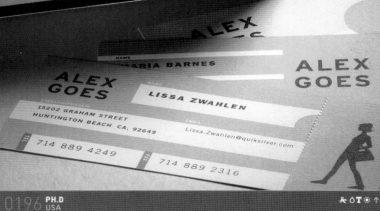

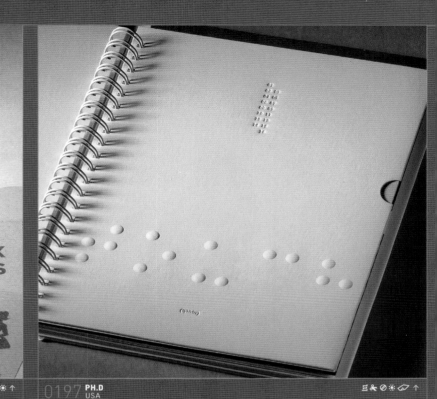

REFLECTIONS

02

CPC for Functional Communication Surfaces

under the Australian Government's
...ness Program

0202 **BWA DESIGN**
UK

0203 **LIPPA PEARCE DESIGN**
UK

0204 **BARCELLONA**
USA

0205 **NYC COLLEGE OF TECHNOLOGY**
USA

0206 **CHRONICLE BOOKS**
USA

0207 **EMERY VINCENT DESIGN**
AUSTRALIA

0208 **ZIP DESIGN**
UK

0209 **GRAPEFRUIT DESIGN**
ROMANIA

0210 **JULIA TAM DESIGN**
USA

0211 BWA DESIGN
UK

0212 EMPIRE DESIGN STUDIO
USA

SAVE THE DATE
12/04/01

The Educational Foundation for the Fashion Industries
Annual Awards Dinner Honoring

Calvin Klein

R. Brad Martin
Chairman and Chief Executive Officer of Saks Incorporated

A Benefit for the Fashion Institute of Technology's
Student Scholarship and Educational Development Fund

For more information call
The Educational Foundation for the Fashion Industries
212 217.7820

The Educational Foundation
for the Fashion Industries
Seventh Avenue at 27th Street
Room C 204, New York, NY 1010

0213 CASERTA DESIGN COMPANY
USA

0214 CHRONICLE BOOKS
USA

EMERY VINCENT DESIGN
AUSTRALIA

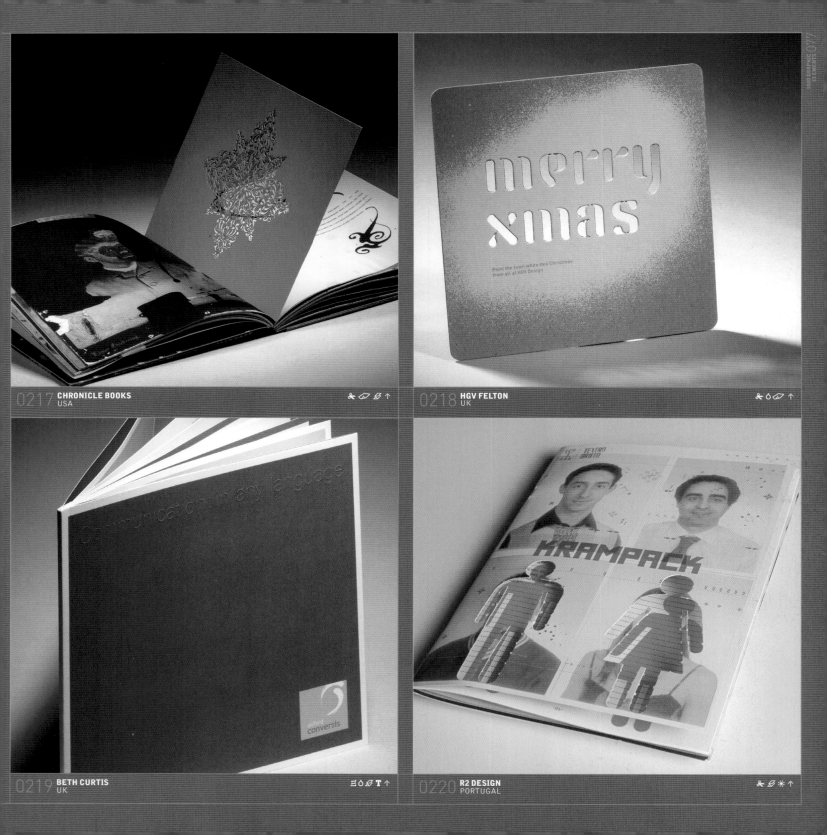

0217 **CHRONICLE BOOKS**
USA

0218 **HGV FELTON**
UK

merry xmas

Paint the town white this Christmas
from all at HGV Design

0219 **BETH CURTIS**
UK

Communication in any language

conversis

0220 **R2 DESIGN**
PORTUGAL

KRAMPACK

0221 **LAVA**
THE NETHERLANDS

0222 **BLACKCOFFEE**
USA

0223 **IRIDIUM, A DESIGN AGENCY**
CANADA

0224 **IRIDIUM, A DESIGN AGENCY**
CANADA

0225 **HORNALL ANDERSON DESIGN WORKS**
USA

0226 **IRIDIUM, A DESIGN AGENCY**
CANADA

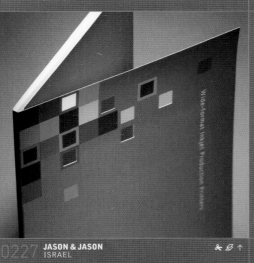

0227 **JASON & JASON**
ISRAEL

0228 **NET#WORK BBDO**
SOUTH AFRICA

0229 **GEE + CHUNG DESIGN**
USA

Works by Peter Meacock
Central Workshop

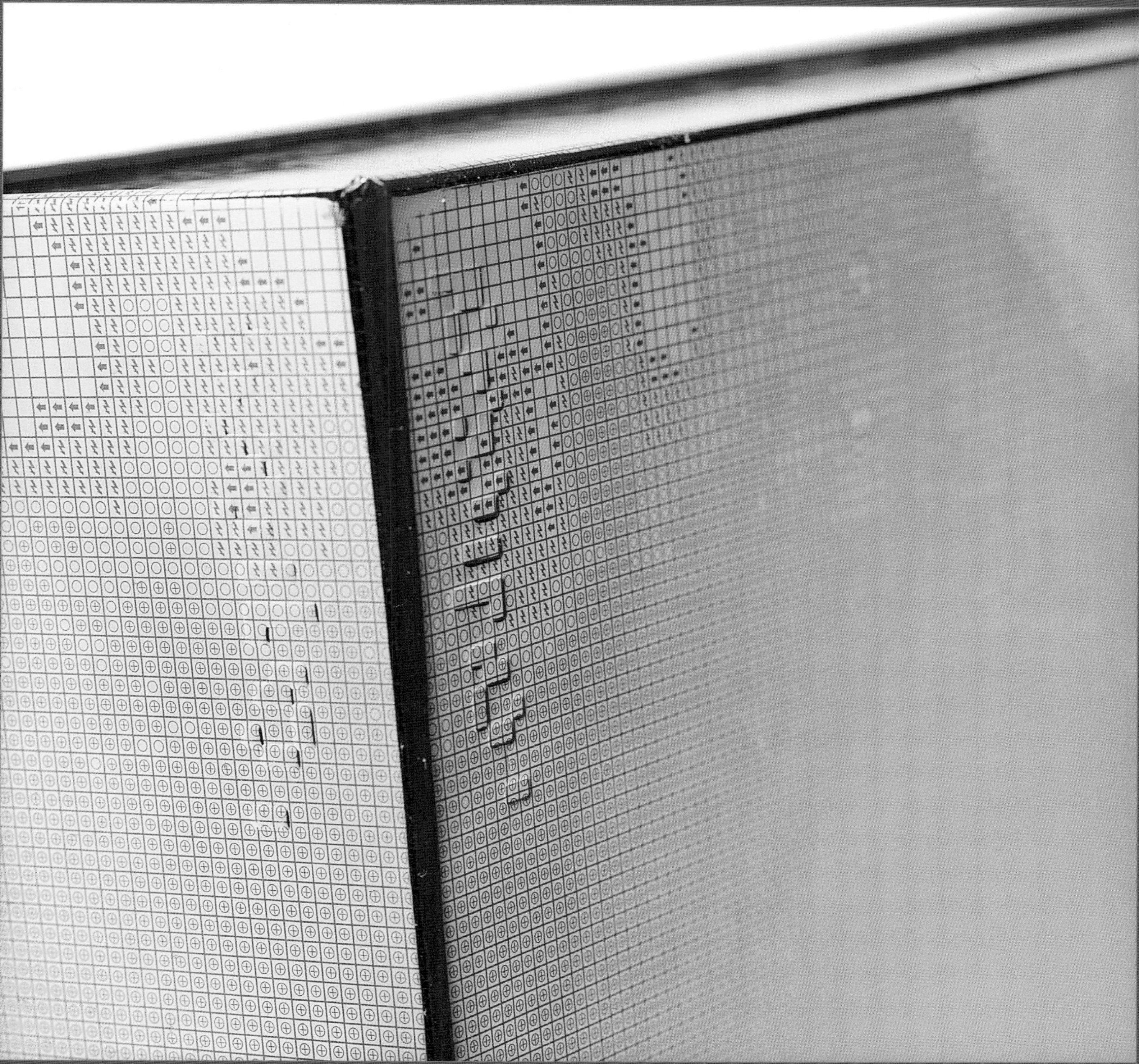

0231 **MODE**
UK

people. innovation. design.

ef

esther franklin

showroom...
ground floor
29–30 elvaston mews
london SW7 5HZ

phone
+44 (0)207 584 4344
fax
+44 (0)207 584 5355

studio...
5 lansdowne court
bath road
maidenhead
berkshire SL6 0AH.

phone/fax
+44 (0)1628 770 619
mobile
+44 (0)7887 566 474

email
esther@estherfranklin.co.uk
website
www.estherfranklin.co.uk

Cooperative Research Centre
for Functional Communication Surfaces
HERE
RUB
ANNUAL REPORT
under the Australian Government's

0232	**BNIM ARCHITECTS** USA	
0233	**MADE THOUGHT** UK	
0234	**FORTYFOUR DESIGN** AUSTRALIA	
0235	**XAX CREATIVE** USA	

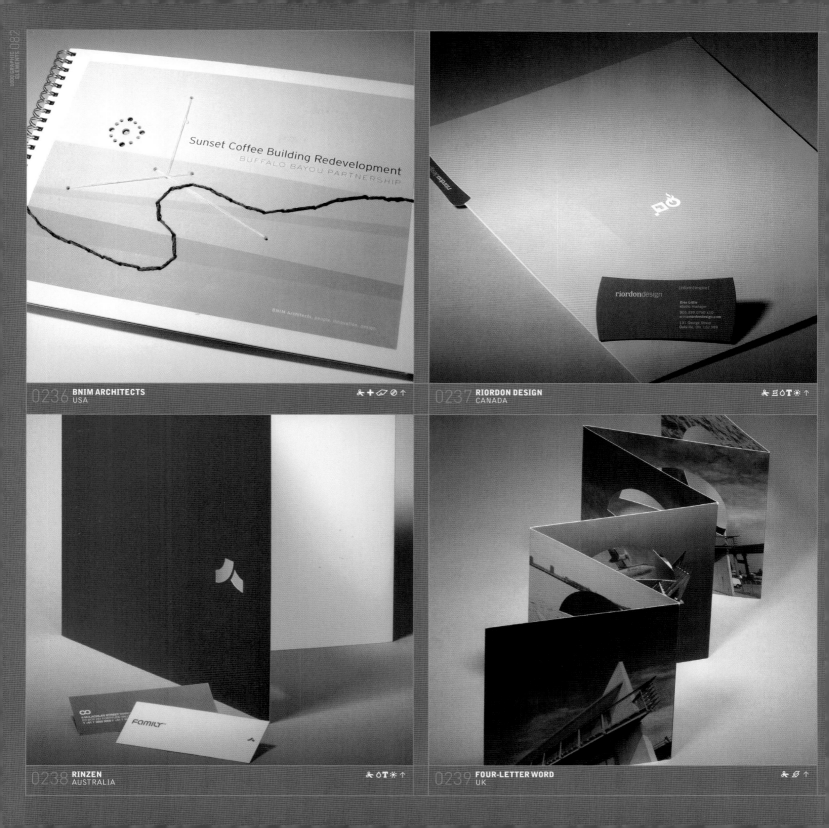

0236 **BNIM ARCHITECTS**
USA

0237 **RIORDON DESIGN**
CANADA

0238 **RINZEN**
AUSTRALIA

0239 **FOUR-LETTER WORD**
UK

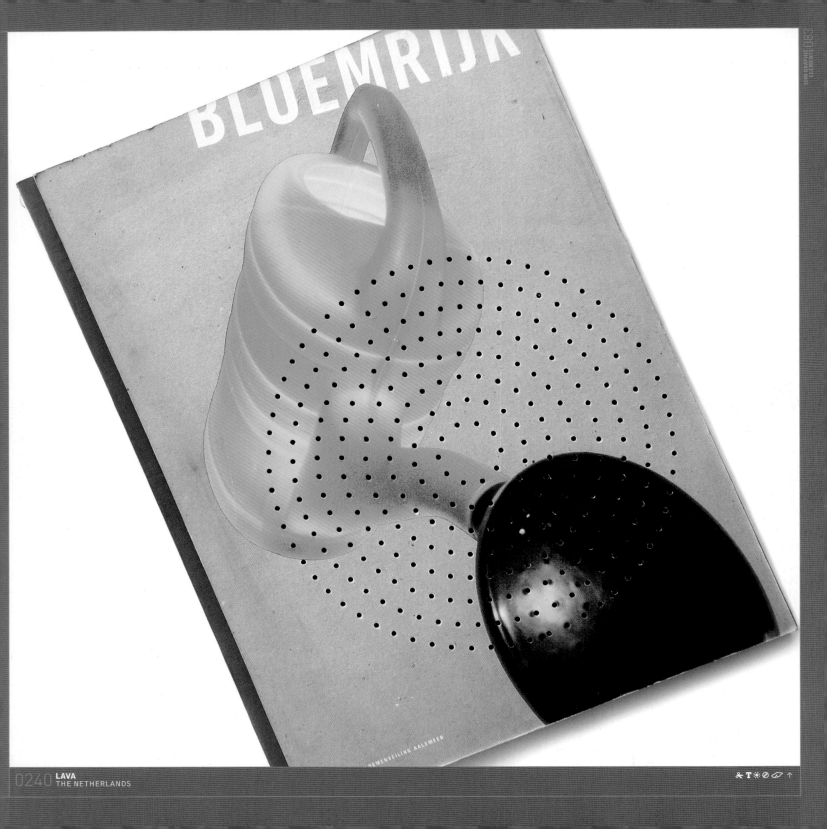

BLUEMRIJK

BRUKETA & ZINIC
CROATIA

0242 KINETIC SINGAPORE
SINGAPORE

0243 PLUS DESIGN
USA

0244 BELYEA
USA

0245 PROGRESS
UK

0246 KINETIC SINGAPORE
SINGAPORE

0247 PROGRESS
UK

0248 THE FAMILY
UK

0249 SCANDINAVIAN DESIGN GROUP
DENMARK

0250 KINETIC SINGAPORE
SINGAPORE

THUIS IN AMSTERDAM

0251 **KESSELS KRAMER**
THE NETHERLANDS

ALISON POPP
Designer
alison@bbkstudio.com

YANG K
Prin
yang@bbkstu

BBK STUDIO
648 Monroe Ave NW Suite 212
Grand Rapids Michigan 49503
616 459 4444 x109
616 459 4477 fax

BBK STUDIO
648 Monroe Ave NW Suite 212
Grand Rapids Michigan 49503
616 459 4444 x104
616 459 4477 fax

BBK STUDIO
648 Monroe Ave NW Suite 212
Grand Rapids Michigan 49503
616 459 4444
616 459 4477 fax
www.bbkstudio.com

0252 **BBK STUDIO**
USA

MAKE A SCENE. SEASONS GREETINGS FROM HILL&KNOWLTON

0253 **BISQIT DESIGN**
UK

KERYX BIOPHARMACEUTICALS, INC.

0254 **JASON & JASON**
ISRAEL

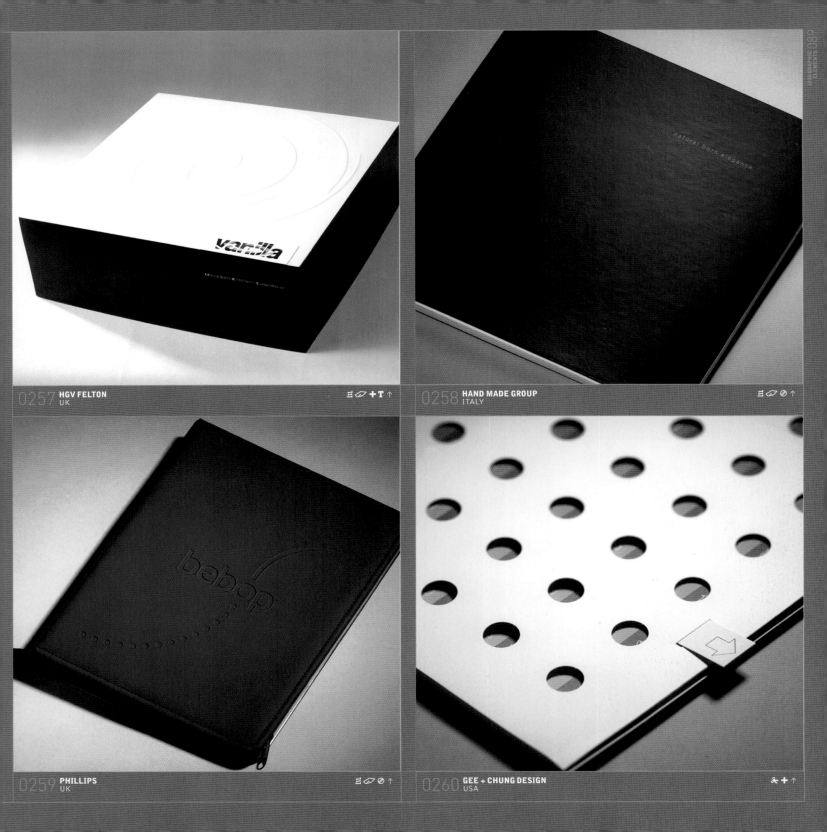

0257 **HGV FELTON**
UK

0258 **HAND MADE GROUP**
ITALY

0259 **PHILLIPS**
UK

0260 **GEE + CHUNG DESIGN**
USA

portfolio-cph

[address] Løngangstræde 37B / DK-1468 Copenhagen K
[phone] +45 3393 6670 / [fax] +45 3393 6680 / www.**portfolio-cph**.dk
[mail] pernille@portfolio-cph.dk / [mail] heidi@portfolio-cph.dk

Hasse Nielse

0262 **PHILLIPS**
UK

0263 **PHILLIPS**
UK

0264 **GEE + CHUNG DESIGN**
USA

0265 **FAUXPAS**
SWITZERLAND

0266 **MOTIVE DESIGN RESEARCH**
USA

0267 **STRICHPUNKT**
GERMANY

0268 **ALOOF DESIGN**
UK

0269 **ANDERSON THOMAS DESIGN**
USA

0270 **MIRES**
USA

0271 **STRUKTUR DESIGN**
UK

0272 **MIRES**
USA

0273 **JASON & JASON**
ISRAEL

0274 **THE FAMILY**
UK

GEORGINAGOODMAN

12/14 Shepherd Street, M...

7JF

GEORGINAGOODMAN

12/14 Shepherd Street, Mayfair, London W...

t +44 20 7499 8599

f +44 20 7...

GEORGINAGOODMAN

0277 CAPSULE
USA

0278 FELDER GRAFIKDESIGN
AUSTRIA

0279 KINETIC SINGAPORE
SINGAPORE

0280 SCANDINAVIAN DESIGN GROUP
DENMARK

0281 **IRIDIUM, A DESIGN AGENCY**
CANADA

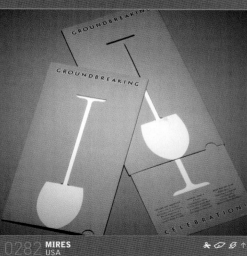

0282 **MIRES**
USA

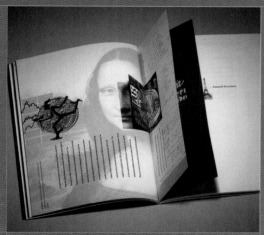

0283 **UNA (AMSTERDAM) DESIGNERS**
THE NETHERLANDS

0284 **KOLEGRAM DESIGN**
CANADA

0285 **KOLEGRAM DESIGN**
CANADA

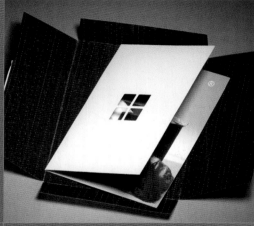

0286 **KOLEGRAM DESIGN**
CANADA

0287 **BEAULIEU CONCEPTS GRAPHIQUES**
CANADA

0288 **ADDUCI STUDIOS**
USA

0289 **TRICKETT & WEBB**
UK

RIPE IN ASSOCIATION WITH ALCAN PRINT FINISHING

SKIN BIOLOGY CENTER

S·B·C

DR. MED. VOLKER STEINKRAUS

0296 **MARIUS FAHRNER DESIGN**
GERMANY

0297 **METAL**
USA

CAMDEN
Living Excellence

04

tigé

SOLUTIONS

0298 **DESIGN 5**
USA

0299 **JASON & JASON**
ISRAEL

0292 **MORTENSON DESIGN**
USA

0293 **TRACY DESIGN**
USA

0294 **PRECURSOR**
UK

0295 **MORTENSON DESIGN**
USA

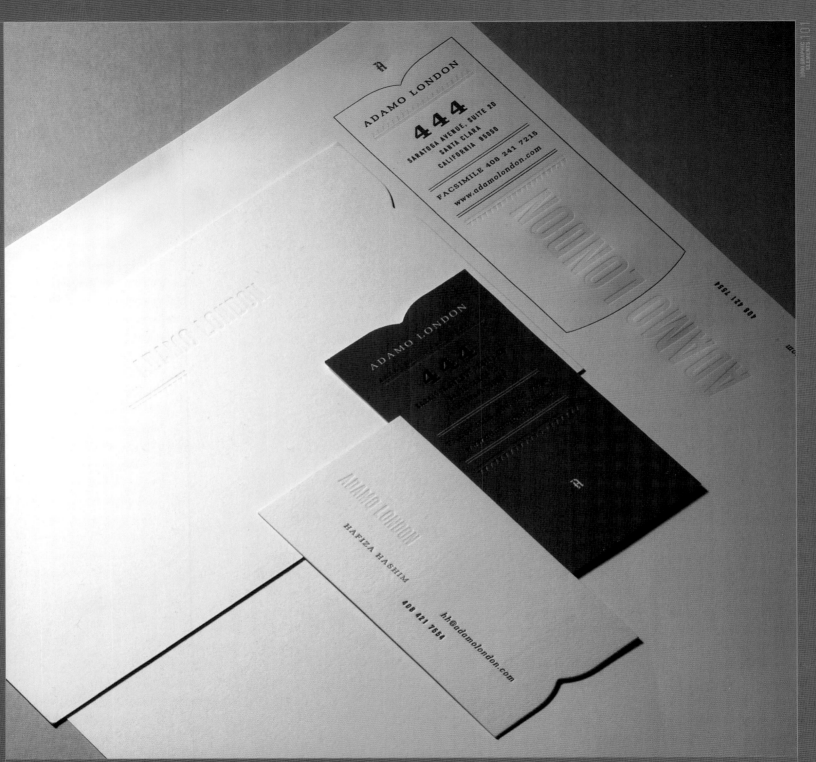

ADAMO LONDON

444

SARATOGA AVENUE, SUITE 20
SANTA CLARA
CALIFORNIA 95050

FACSIMILE 408 241 7215
www.adamolondon.com

ADAMO LONDON

HAFIZA HASHIM

hh@adamolondon.com
408 421 7554

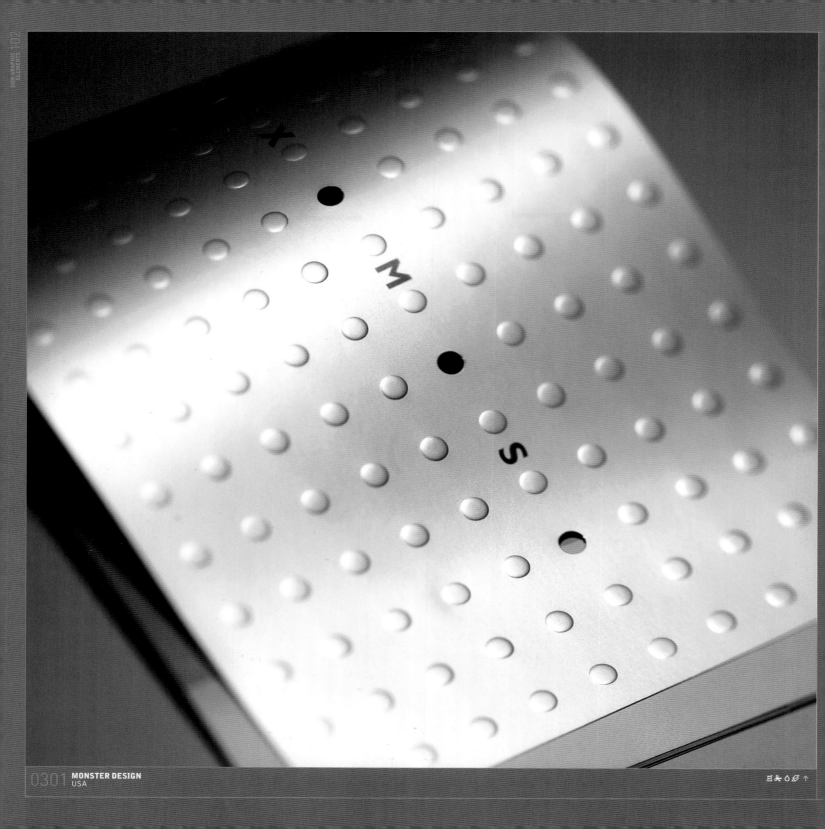

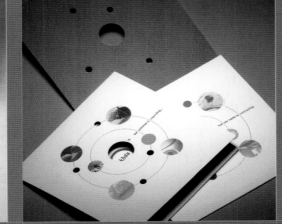

0302	**NETSUCCESS** USA		0303	**KBDA** USA		0304	**DESIGN 5** USA

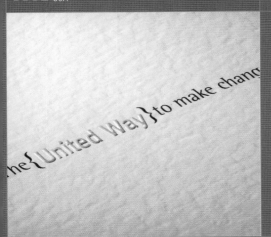

0305	**DESIGN 5** USA		0306	**JOHNSON BANKS** UK		0307	**LIGALUX** GERMANY

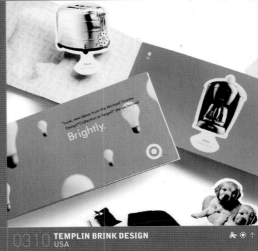

0308	**LIPPA PEARCE DESIGN** UK		0309	**JASON & JASON** ISRAEL		0310	**TEMPLIN BRINK DESIGN** USA

0311 **AND PARTNERS**
USA

0312 **MIRIELLO GRAFICO**
USA

0313 **SALTERBAXTER**
UK

0314 **IRIDIUM, A DESIGN AGENCY**
CANADA

WHAT DOES PROGRESS SOUND LIKE?

IRIDIUM, A DESIGN AGENCY
CANADA

0317 **MIRKO ILIC**
USA

0318 **BUREAU GRAS**
THE NETHERLANDS

0319 **IE DESIGN**
USA

0320 **PLUS DESIGN**
USA

| 0321 | **MARIUS FAHRNER DESIGN**
GERMANY | | 0322 | **IE DESIGN**
USA | | 0323 | **IRIDIUM, A DESIGN AGENCY**
CANADA |

| 0324 | **CINCODEMAYO DESIGN**
MEXICO | | 0325 | **FELDER GRAFIKDESIGN**
AUSTRIA | | 0326 | **IE DESIGN**
USA |

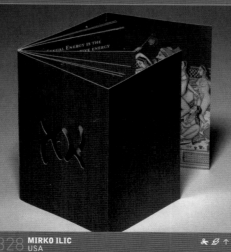

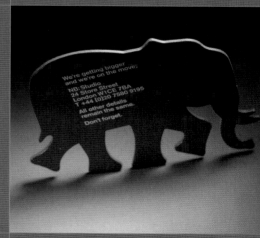

| 0327 | **BRAD TERRES DESIGN**
USA | | 0328 | **MIRKO ILIC**
USA | | 0329 | **NB:STUDIO**
UK |

0332 **HANS DESIGN**
USA

0333 **THE WORKS DESIGN COMMUNICATIONS**
CANADA

0334 **PH.D**
USA

0335 **....STAAT**
THE NETHERLANDS

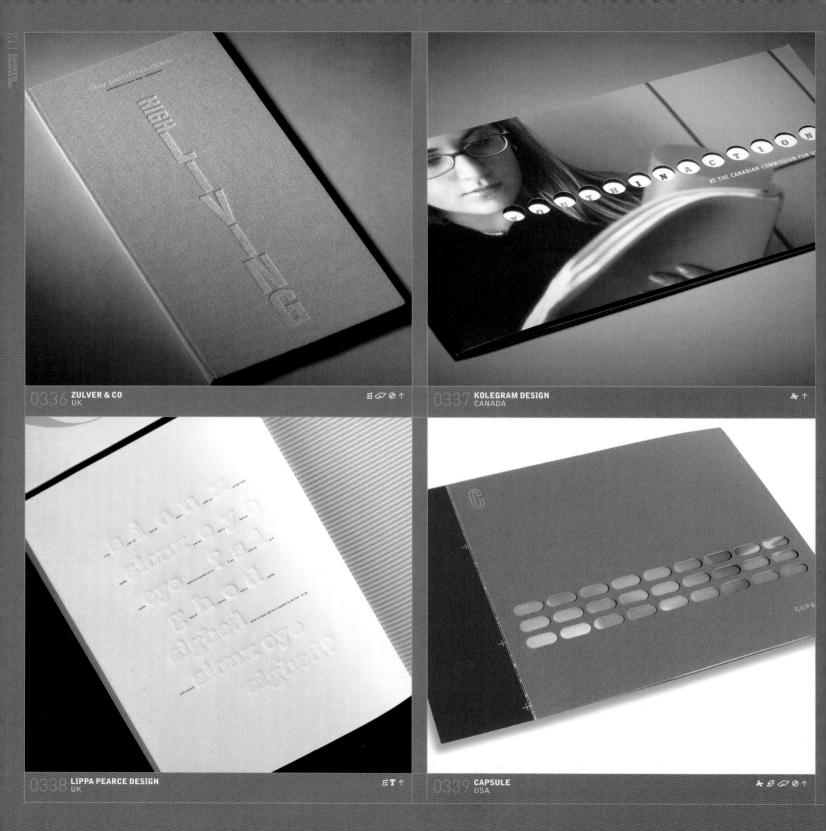

0336 **ZULVER & CO**
UK

0337 **KOLEGRAM DESIGN**
CANADA

0338 **LIPPA PEARCE DESIGN**
UK

0339 **CAPSULE**
USA

SPECTACLE
10 09 03
(see for yourself)

63 FA
SA
CAL

0001 0002 0003 0004 0005 0006 0007 0008 0009 0010 0011 0012 0013 0014 0015 0016 0017 0018 0019 0020 0021 0022 0023 0024 0025
0041 0042 0043 0044 0045 0046 0047 0048 0049 0050 0051 0052 0053 0054 0055 0056 0057 0058 0059 0060 0061 0062 0063 0064 0065
0081 0082 0083 0084 0085 0086 0087 0088 0089 0090 0091 0092 0093 0094 0095 0096 0097 0098 0099 0100 0101 0102 0103 0104 0105
0121 0122 0123 0124 0125 0126 0127 0128 0129 0130 0131 0132 0133 0134 0135 0136 0137 0138 0139 0140 0141 0142 0143 0144 0145
0161 0162 0163 0164 0165 0166 0167 0168 0169 0170 0171 0172 0173 0174 0175 0176 0177 0178 0179 0180 0181 0182 0183 0184 0185
0201 0202 0203 0204 0205 0206 0207 0208 0209 0210 0211 0212 0213 0214 0215 0216 0217 0218 0219 0220 0221 0222 0223 0224 0225
0241 0242 0243 0244 0245 0246 0247 0248 0249 0250 0251 0252 0253 0254 0255 0256 0257 0258 0259 0260 0261 0262 0263 0264 0265
0281 0282 0283 0284 0285 0286 0287 0288 0289 0290 0291 0292 0293 0294 0295 0296 0297 0298 0299 0300 0301 0302 0303 0304 0305
0321 0322 0323 0324 0325 0326 0327 0328 0329 0330 0331 0332 0333 0334 0335 0336 0337 0338 0339 0340 0341 0342 0343 0344 0345
0361 0362 0363 0364 0365 0366 0367 0368 0369 0370 0371 0372 0373 0374 0375 0376 0377 0378 0379 0380 0381 0382 0383 0384 0385
0401 0402 0403 0404 0405 0406 0407 0408 0409 0410 0411 0412 0413 0414 0415 0416 0417 0418 0419 0420 0421 0422 0423 0424 0425
0441 0442 0443 0444 0445 0446 0447 0448 0449 0450 0451 0452 0453 0454 0455 0456 0457 0458 0459 0460 0461 0462 0463 0464 0465
0481 0482 0483 0484 0485 0486 0487 0488 0489 0490 0491 0492 0493 0494 0495 0496 0497 0498 0499 0500 0501 0502 0503 0504 0505
0521 0522 0523 0524 0525 0526 0527 0528 0529 0530 0531 0532 0533 0534 0535 0536 0537 0538 0539 0540 0541 0542 0543 0544 0545
0561 0562 0563 0564 0565 0566 0567 0568 0569 0570 0571 0572 0573 0574 0575 0576 0577 0578 0579 0580 0581 0582 0583 0584 0585
0601 0602 0603 0604 0605 0606 0607 0608 0609 0610 0611 0612 0613 0614 0615 0616 0617 0618 0619 0620 0621 0622 0623 0624 0625
0641 0642 0643 0644 0645 0646 0647 0648 0649 0650 0651 0652 0653 0654 0655 0656 0657 0658 0659 0660 0661 0662 0663 0664 0665
0681 0682 0683 0684 0685 0686 0687 0688 0689 0690 0691 0692 0693 0694 0695 0696 0697 0698 0699 0700 0701 0702 0703 0704 0705
0721 0722 0723 0724 0725 0726 0727 0728 0729 0730 0731 0732 0733 0734 0735 0736 0737 0738 0739 0740 0741 0742 0743 0744 0745
0761 0762 0763 0764 0765 0766 0767 0768 0769 0770 0771 0772 0773 0774 0775 0776 0777 0778 0779 0780 0781 0782 0783 0784 0785
0801 0802 0803 0804 0805 0806 0807 0808 0809 0810 0811 0812 0813 0814 0815 0816 0817 0818 0819 0820 0821 0822 0823 0824 0825
0841 0842 0843 0844 0845 0846 0847 0848 0849 0850 0851 0852 0853 0854 0855 0856 0857 0858 0859 0860 0861 0862 0863 0864 0865
0881 0882 0883 0884 0885 0886 0887 0888 0889 0890 0891 0892 0893 0894 0895 0896 0897 0898 0899 0900 0901 0902 0903 0904 0905
0921 0922 0923 0924 0925 0926 0927 0928 0929 0930 0931 0932 0933 0934 0935 0936 0937 0938 0939 0940 0941 0942 0943 0944 0945
0961 0962 0963 0964 0965 0966 0967 0968 0969 0970 0971 0972 0973 0974 0975 0976 0977 0978 0979 0980 0981 0982 0983 0984 0985

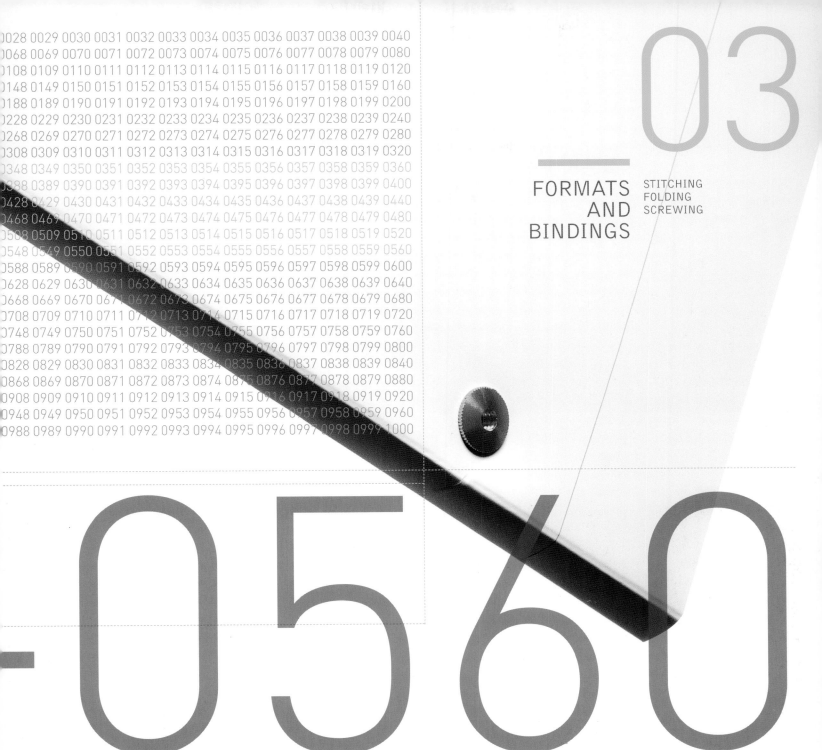

0028 0029 0030 0031 0032 0033 0034 0035 0036 0037 0038 0039 0040
0068 0069 0070 0071 0072 0073 0074 0075 0076 0077 0078 0079 0080
0108 0109 0110 0111 0112 0113 0114 0115 0116 0117 0118 0119 0120
0148 0149 0150 0151 0152 0153 0154 0155 0156 0157 0158 0159 0160
0188 0189 0190 0191 0192 0193 0194 0195 0196 0197 0198 0199 0200
0228 0229 0230 0231 0232 0233 0234 0235 0236 0237 0238 0239 0240
0268 0269 0270 0271 0272 0273 0274 0275 0276 0277 0278 0279 0280
0308 0309 0310 0311 0312 0313 0314 0315 0316 0317 0318 0319 0320
0348 0349 0350 0351 0352 0353 0354 0355 0356 0357 0358 0359 0360
0388 0389 0390 0391 0392 0393 0394 0395 0396 0397 0398 0399 0400
0428 0429 0430 0431 0432 0433 0434 0435 0436 0437 0438 0439 0440
0468 0469 0470 0471 0472 0473 0474 0475 0476 0477 0478 0479 0480
0508 0509 0510 0511 0512 0513 0514 0515 0516 0517 0518 0519 0520
0548 0549 0550 0551 0552 0553 0554 0555 0556 0557 0558 0559 0560
0588 0589 0590 0591 0592 0593 0594 0595 0596 0597 0598 0599 0600
0628 0629 0630 0631 0632 0633 0634 0635 0636 0637 0638 0639 0640
0668 0669 0670 0671 0672 0673 0674 0675 0676 0677 0678 0679 0680
0708 0709 0710 0711 0712 0713 0714 0715 0716 0717 0718 0719 0720
0748 0749 0750 0751 0752 0753 0754 0755 0756 0757 0758 0759 0760
0788 0789 0790 0791 0792 0793 0794 0795 0796 0797 0798 0799 0800
0828 0829 0830 0831 0832 0833 0834 0835 0836 0837 0838 0839 0840
0868 0869 0870 0871 0872 0873 0874 0875 0876 0877 0878 0879 0880
0908 0909 0910 0911 0912 0913 0914 0915 0916 0917 0918 0919 0920
0948 0949 0950 0951 0952 0953 0954 0955 0956 0957 0958 0959 0960
0988 0989 0990 0991 0992 0993 0994 0995 0996 0997 0998 0999 1000

_03

FORMATS
AND
BINDINGS

STITCHING
FOLDING
SCREWING

-0560

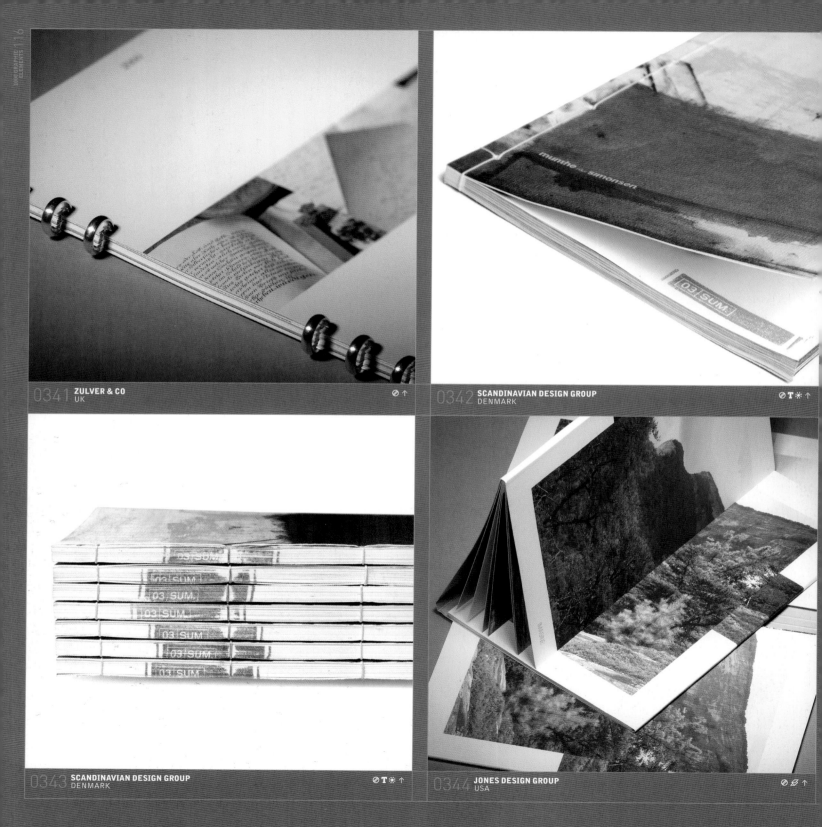

0341 **ZULVER & CO**
UK
Ø ↑

0342 **SCANDINAVIAN DESIGN GROUP**
DENMARK
Ø **T** ☀ ↑

0343 **SCANDINAVIAN DESIGN GROUP**
DENMARK
Ø **T** ☀ ↑

0344 **JONES DESIGN GROUP**
USA
Ø Ø ↑

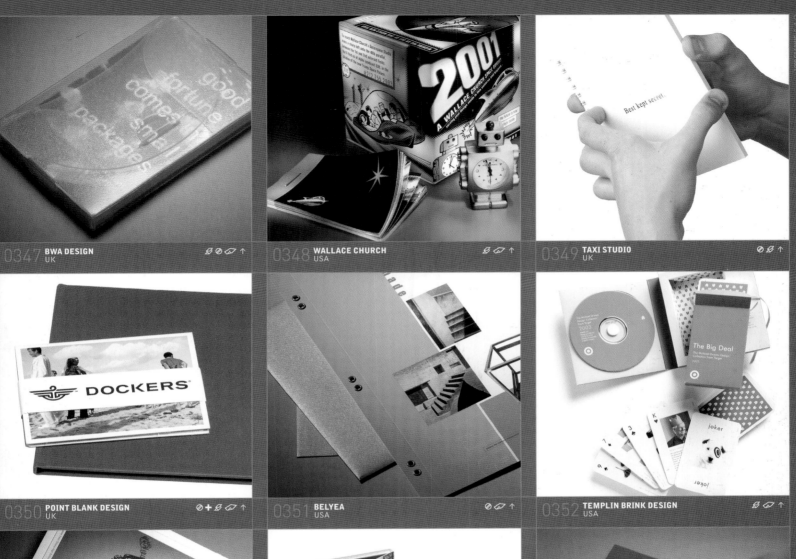

0347	**BWA DESIGN** UK	0348	**WALLACE CHURCH** USA	0349	**TAXI STUDIO** UK
0350	**POINT BLANK DESIGN** UK	0351	**BELYEA** USA	0352	**TEMPLIN BRINK DESIGN** USA
0353	**BBK STUDIO** USA	0354	**SAS** UK	0355	**IRIDIUM, A DESIGN AGENCY** CANADA

0356 **TAXI STUDIO**
UK

0357 **LEWIS COMMUNICATIONS**
USA

0358 **STOLTZE DESIGN**
USA

0359 **CRUSH DESIGN**
UK

Linear
Technology
Corporation
Annual
Report
2000

01

002

001

0362 POPCORN INITIATIVE
USA

0363 KOLEGRAM DESIGN
CANADA

0364 JASON & JASON
ISRAEL

0365 LIQUID AGENCY
USA

0366	WILSON HARVEY UK
0367	HEATHER BIANCHI DESIGN USA
0368	POINT BLANK DESIGN UK
0369	TEMPLIN BRINK DESIGN USA
0370	R2 DESIGN PORTUGAL
0371	R2 DESIGN PORTUGAL
0372	NB:STUDIO UK
0373	POINT BLANK DESIGN UK
0374	KEARNEY ROCHOLL GERMANY

0376 **FELDER GRAFIKDESIGN**
AUSTRIA

0377 **DESIGN HOCH DREI**
GERMANY

0378 **LIPPA PEARCE DESIGN**
UK

0379 **SAS**
UK

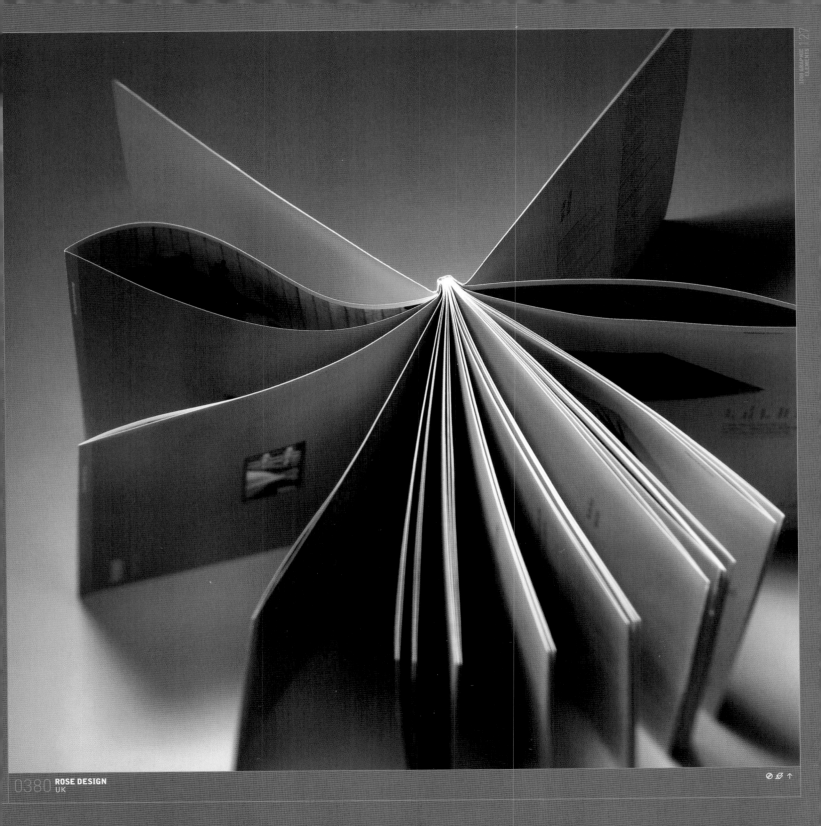

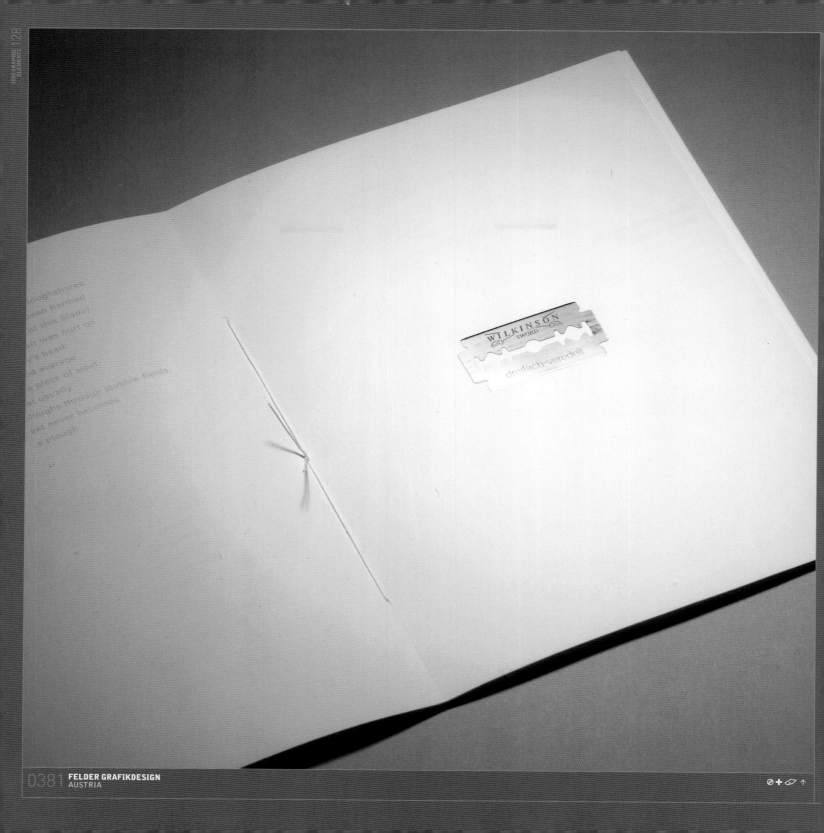

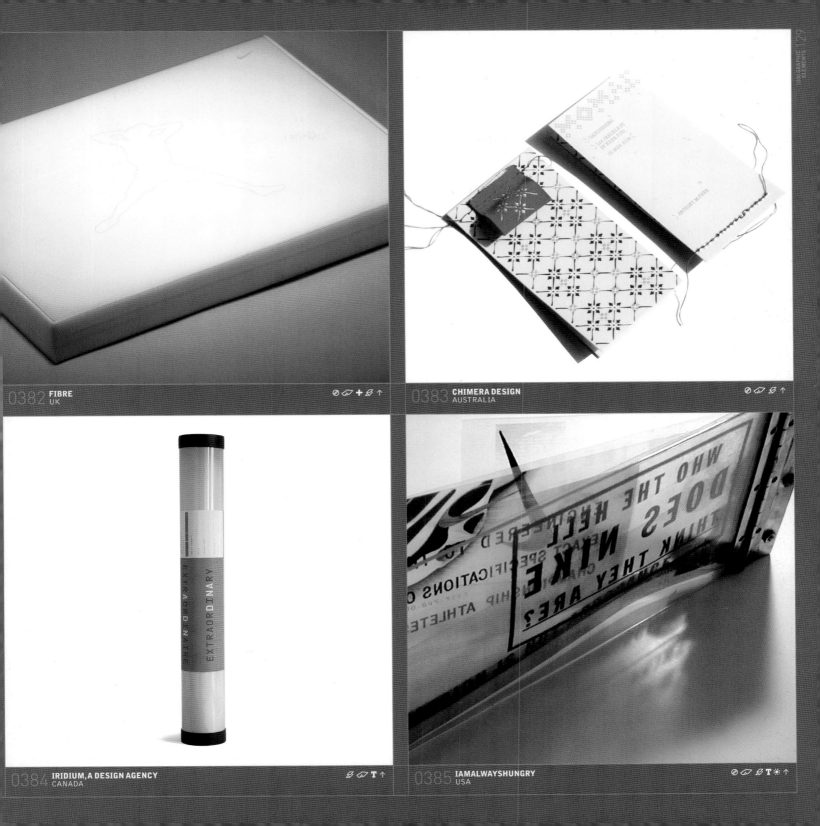

0382 **FIBRE**
UK

0383 **CHIMERA DESIGN**
AUSTRALIA

IRIDIUM, A DESIGN AGENCY
CANADA
0384

0385 **IAMALWAYSHUNGRY**
USA

PRINTING/FINISHING TECHNIQUE

CMYK

PERFORATION

MICRO-P...

PRINTING/FINISHING TECHNIQUE

CMYK + PMS

FOILBLOCKING

PRINTING/FINISHING TECHNIQUE

CMYK

SCORING

FOILBLOCKING

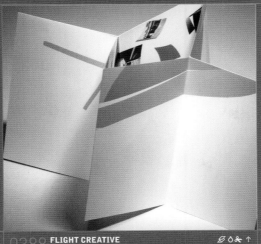

0387 **THE FORMATION**
UK

0388 **FLIGHT CREATIVE**
AUSTRALIA

0389 **GILLESPIE DESIGN**
USA

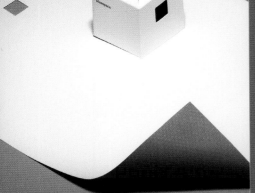

0390 **AFTERHOURS CREATIVE**
USA

0391 **FIBRE**
UK

0392 **BARCELLONA**
USA

0393 **FIBRE**
UK

0394 **RICKABAUGH GRAPHICS**
USA

0395 **IE DESIGN**
USA

0397 **OCTAVO DESIGN**
AUSTRALIA

0398 **DAWN HOSKINSON**
UK

0399 **THE WORKS DESIGN COMMUNICATIONS**
CANADA

0400 **IMAGINATION (GIC)**
UK

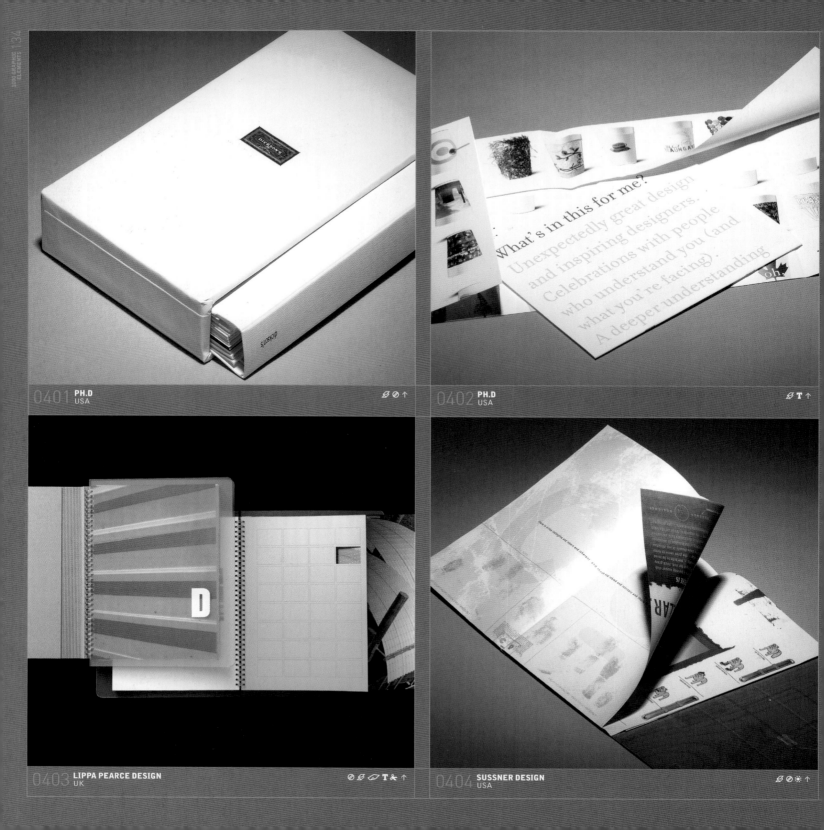

0401 **PH.D**
USA

0402 **PH.D**
USA

0403 **LIPPA PEARCE DESIGN**
UK

0404 **SUSSNER DESIGN**
USA

ACHIEVEMENT

| 0406 | **BWA DESIGN**
UK | | 0407 | **EMPIRE DESIGN STUDIO**
USA | | 0408 | **EMERY VINCENT DESIGN**
AUSTRALIA |

| 0409 | **FORM**
UK | | 0410 | **LAVA**
THE NETHERLANDS | | 0411 | **CHIMERA DESIGN**
AUSTRALIA |

| 0412 | **SHARP COMMUNICATIONS**
USA | | 0413 | **R2 DESIGN**
PORTUGAL | | 0414 | **FORM**
UK |

0417 **LLOYDS GRAPHIC DESIGN AND COMMUNICATION**
NEW ZEALAND

0418 **WILSON HARVEY**
UK

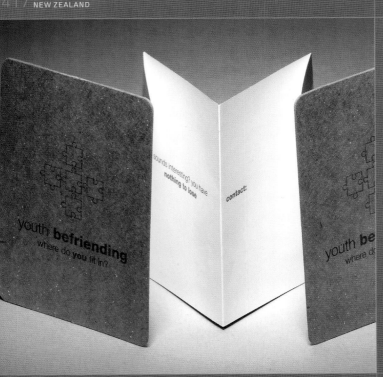

0419 **BWA DESIGN**
UK

0420 **BNIM ARCHITECTS**
USA

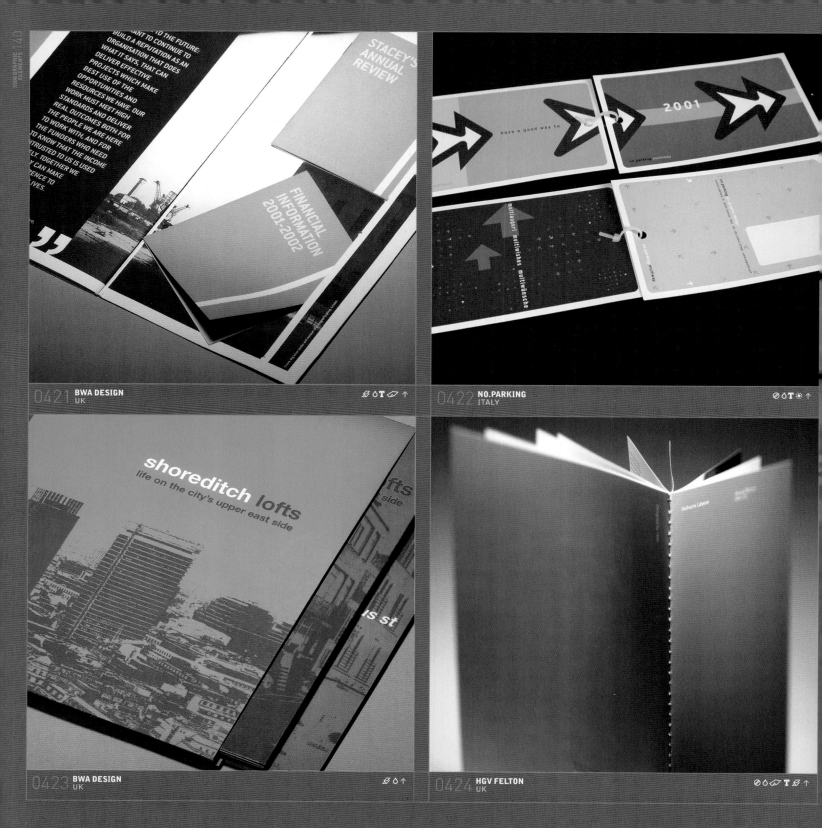

STACEY'S ANNUAL REVIEW

FINANCIAL INFORMATION 2001-2002

0421 **BWA DESIGN**
UK

0422 **NO.PARKING**
ITALY

2001

have a good way to

no parking motiway

multilagerd multiwishes multiwünsche

shoreditch lofts
life on the city's upper east side

0423 **BWA DESIGN**
UK

0424 **HGV FELTON**
UK

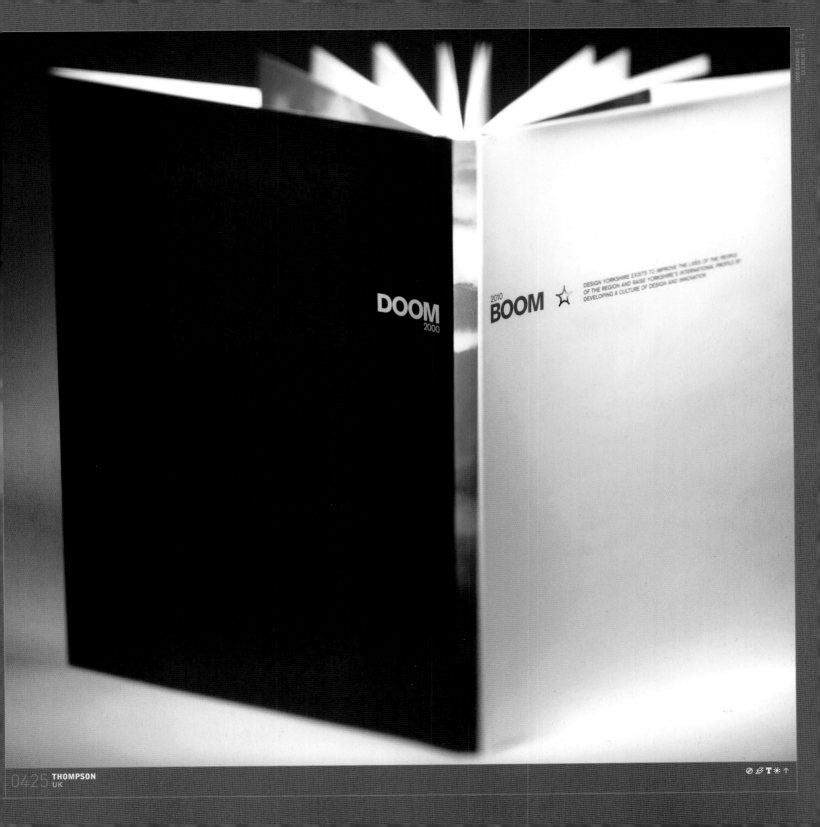

DOOM
2000

2010
BOOM ☆

DESIGN YORKSHIRE EXISTS TO IMPROVE THE LIVES OF THE PEOPLE
OF THE REGION AND RAISE YORKSHIRE'S INTERNATIONAL PROFILE BY
DEVELOPING A CULTURE OF DESIGN AND INNOVATION

0426 **THOMPSON**
UK

0427 **BLACKCOFFEE**
USA

0428 **RADLEY YELDAR**
UK

0429 **CHRONICLE BOOKS**
USA

0430 **HGV FELTON**
UK

0431 **FOXINABOX**
UK

0432 **BBK STUDIO**
USA

0433 **BIRMINGHAM INSTITUTE
OF ART & DESIGN**
UK

0434 **RINZEN**
AUSTRALIA

0437 **NASSAR DESIGN**
USA

0438 **SAMPSONMAY**
UK

0439 **SELTZER DESIGN**
USA

0440 **ZIP DESIGN**
UK

KRX-211

To fit clot models, KRX-211 has been shown to inhibit the activity of a unique kinase implicated in causing the symptoms associated with rheumatoid arthritis and septic shock.

OFFERING
PEOPLE
PROMISE AND
HOPE FOR
TOMORROW...

KRX-123

KRX-123 has demonstrated in vivo efficacy in treating hormone-resistant prostate cancer.

UNTERNEHMENSPHILOSOPHIE

OUTSIDE IS DANGE
STAY HOM

BARBARA NOAH   JOHN BAGLEY   INEKE DE LANGE
COLORGRAPHICS OPENING   SEPTEMBER 12, 2002   4:30 - 7:30 PM
freeFORM

BARBARA NOAH   JOHN BAGLEY   INEKE DE LANGE
COLORGRAPHICS OPENING   SEPTEMBER 12, 2002   4:30 - 7:30 PM
freeFORM

0441   **JASON & JASON**
ISRAEL

0442   **MARIUS FAHRNER DESIGN**
GERMANY

0443   **KESSELS KRAMER**
THE NETHERLANDS

0444   **BELYEA**
USA

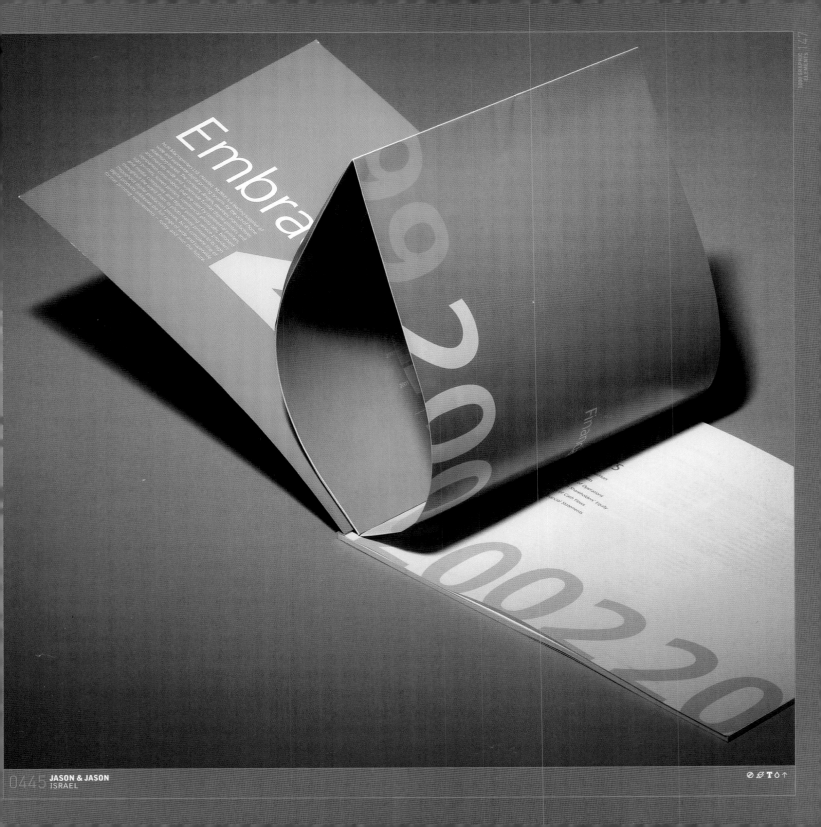

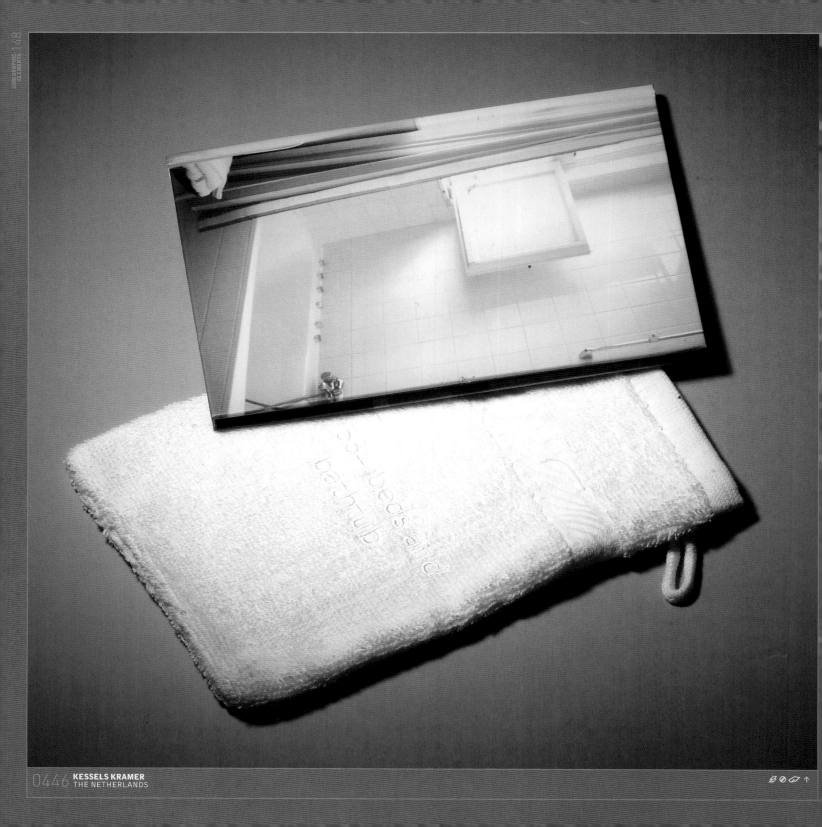

0447 **THIRTEEN**
UK

0448 **THIRTEEN**
UK

0449 **HORNALL ANDERSON DESIGN WORKS**
USA

0450 **KESSELS KRAMER**
THE NETHERLANDS

0451 **THIRTEEN**
UK

0452 **PHILLIPS**
UK

0453 **THIRTEEN**
UK

0454 **KESSELS KRAMER**
THE NETHERLANDS

0455 **HORNALL ANDERSON DESIGN WORKS**
USA

0456 **KESSELS KRAMER**
THE NETHERLANDS

0457 **KESSELS KRAMER**
THE NETHERLANDS

0458 **ORIGIN**
UK

0459 **KESSELS KRAMER**
THE NETHERLANDS

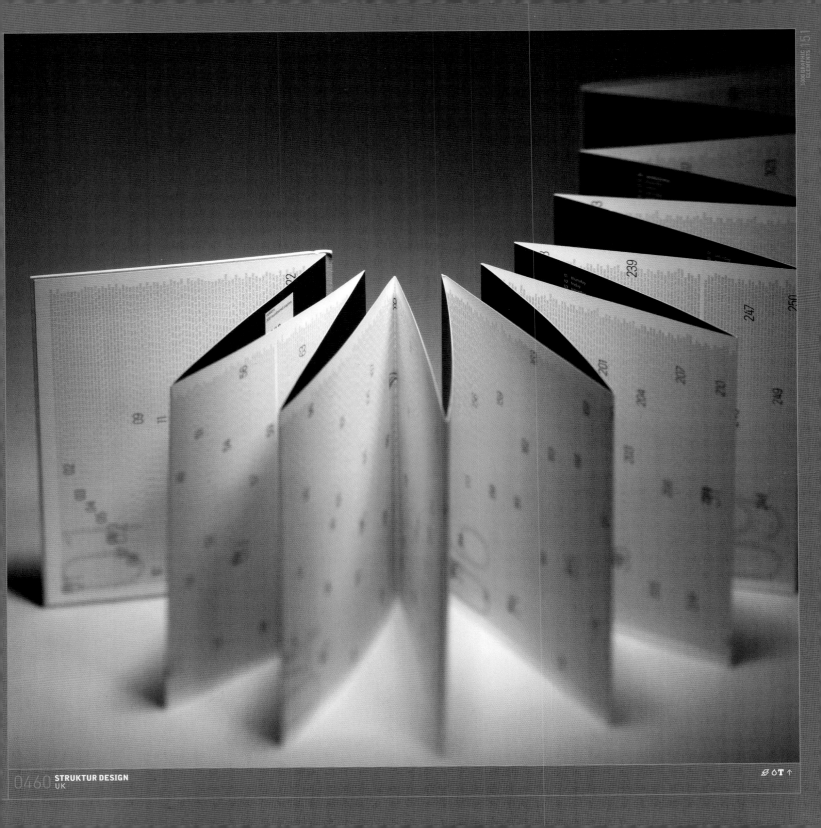

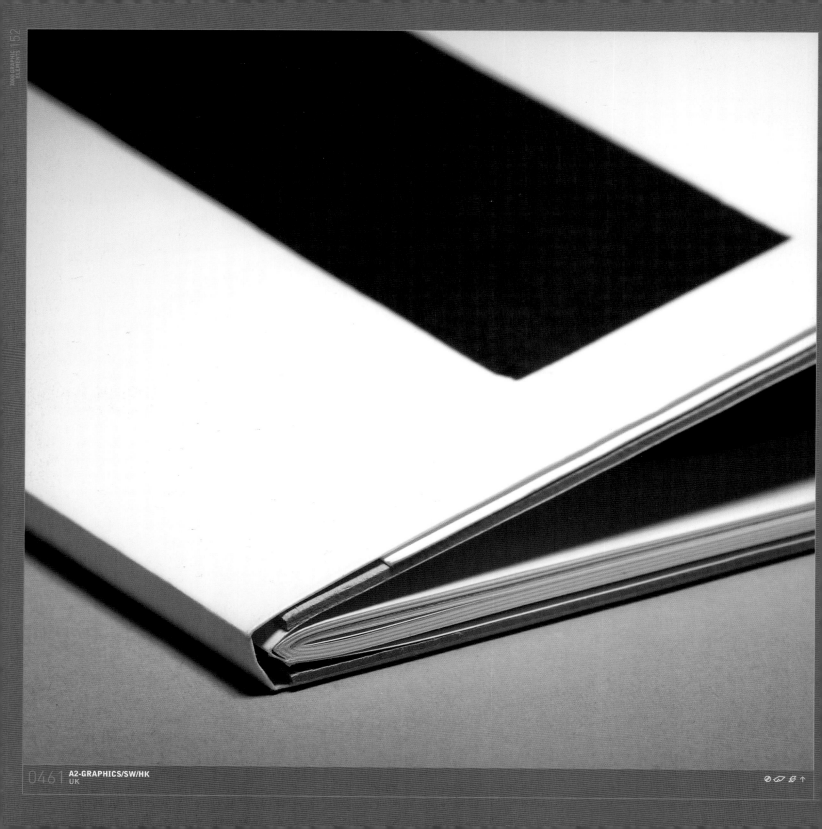

0462 **GREENFIELD/BELSER**
USA

0463 **A2-GRAPHICS/SW/HK**
UK

0464 **FELTON COMMUNICATION**
UK

0465 **COLLEGE DESIGN**
UK

0466 **HORNALL ANDERSON DESIGN WORKS**
USA

0467 **ERBE DESIGN**
USA

0468 **SCANDINAVIAN DESIGN GROUP**
DENMARK

0469 **PROGRESS**
UK

0470 **SCANDINAVIAN DESIGN GROUP**
DENMARK

0471 **Q**
GERMANY

0472 **THIRTEEN**
UK

0473 **SCANDINAVIAN DESIGN GROUP**
DENMARK

0474 **KOLEGRAM DESIGN**
CANADA

0476 **SCANDINAVIAN DESIGN GROUP**
DENMARK

0477 **SCANDINAVIAN DESIGN GROUP**
DENMARK

0478 **METAL**
USA

0479 **Q**
GERMANY

& the winner

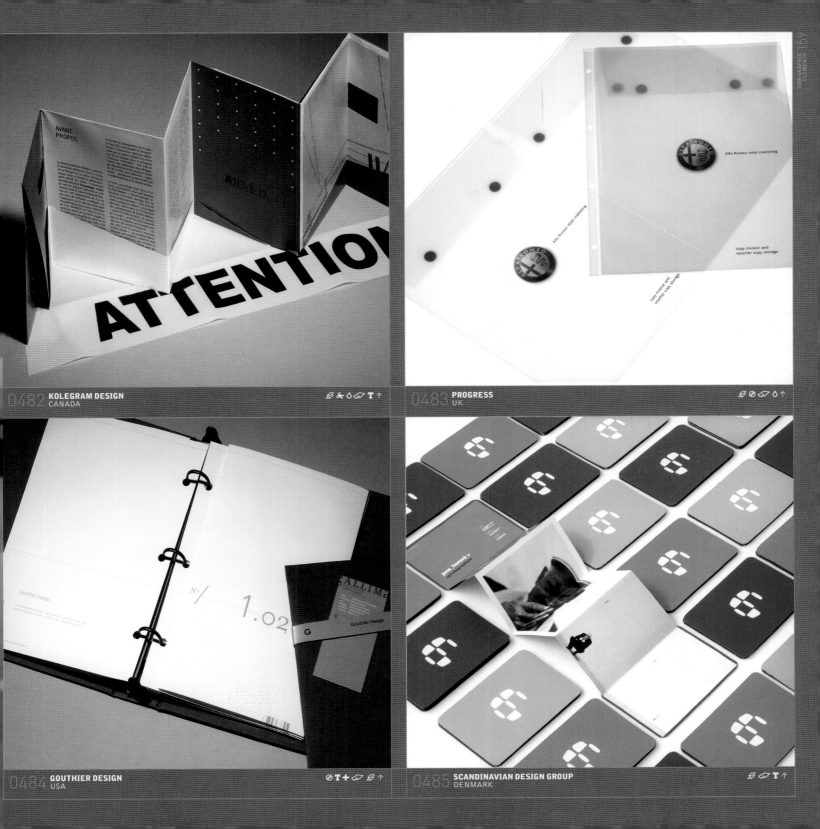

0482 **KOLEGRAM DESIGN**
CANADA

0483 **PROGRESS**
UK

0484 **GOUTHIER DESIGN**
USA

0485 **SCANDINAVIAN DESIGN GROUP**
DENMARK

0486 **ANDERSON THOMAS DESIGN**
USA

0487 **MIRES**
USA

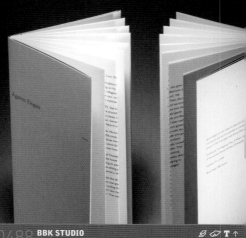

0488 **BBK STUDIO**
USA

0489 **GILLESPIE DESIGN**
USA

0490 **CAPSULE**
USA

0491 **FORM**
UK

0492 **STOLTZE DESIGN**
USA

0493 **FORM**
UK

0494 **CAPSULE**
USA

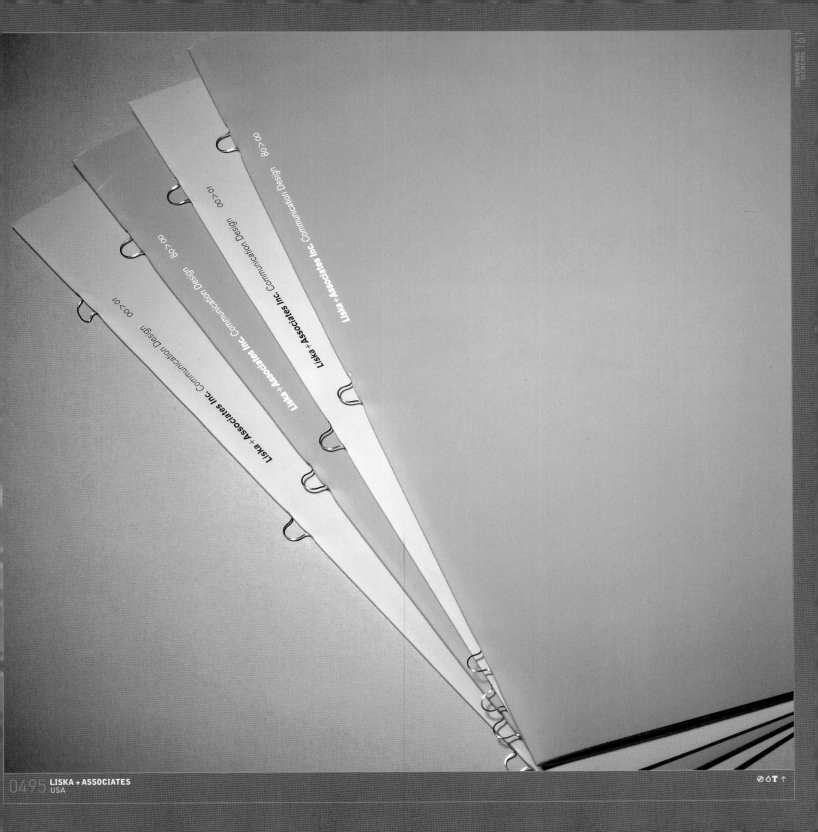

Liska + Associates Inc. Communication Design
Liska + Associates Inc. Communication Design
Liska + Associates Inc. Communication Design
Liska + Associates Inc. Communication Design

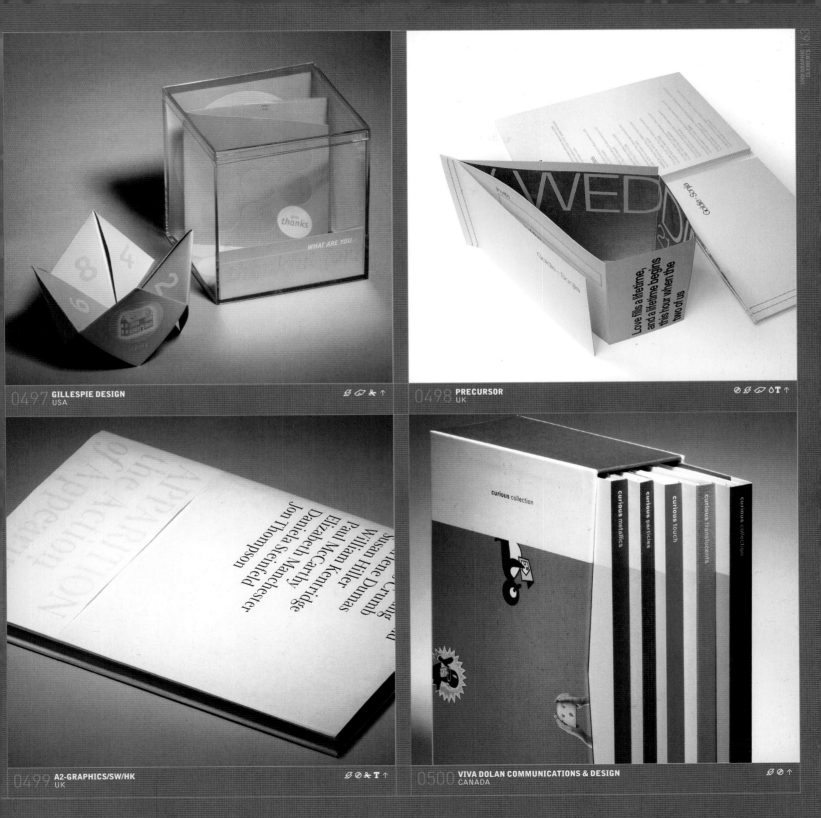

0497 GILLESPIE DESIGN
USA

thanks

WHAT ARE YOU

0498 PRECURSOR
UK

WED

invite

Goldie / Sonjia

Love fills a lifetime, and a lifetime begins this hour when the two of us

0499 A2-GRAPHICS/SW/HK
UK

APPARITION
the ACTION of
APPEAR

Susan Hiller
William Hiller
Paul Kentridge
Elizabeth McCarthy
Daniela Manfy
Jon Steinfeld
Thompson

0500 VIVA DOLAN COMMUNICATIONS & DESIGN
CANADA

curious collection

curious metallics
curious particles
curious touch
curious translucents
curious collection

0501 **CAHAN & ASSOCIATES**
USA

0502 **LEWIS COMMUNICATIONS**
USA

0503 **VIVA DOLAN COMMUNICATIONS & DESIGN**
CANADA

0504 **VIVA DOLAN COMMUNICATIONS & DESIGN**
CANADA

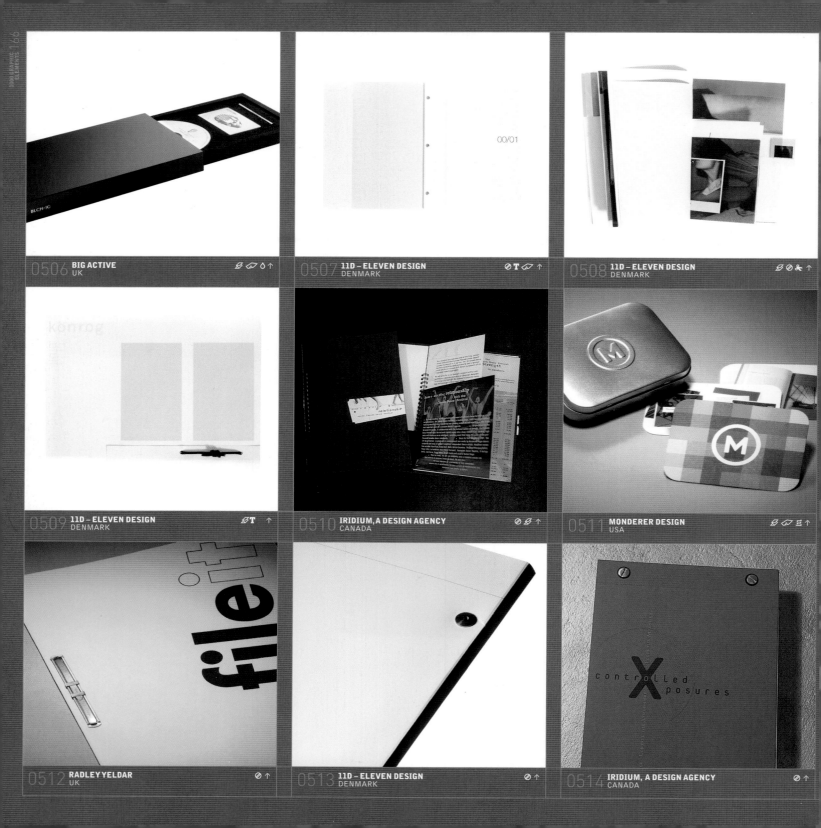

0506 **BIG ACTIVE**
UK

0507 **11D – ELEVEN DESIGN**
DENMARK

0508 **11D – ELEVEN DESIGN**
DENMARK

0509 **11D – ELEVEN DESIGN**
DENMARK

0510 **IRIDIUM, A DESIGN AGENCY**
CANADA

0511 **MONDERER DESIGN**
USA

0512 **RADLEY YELDAR**
UK

0513 **11D – ELEVEN DESIGN**
DENMARK

0514 **IRIDIUM, A DESIGN AGENCY**
CANADA

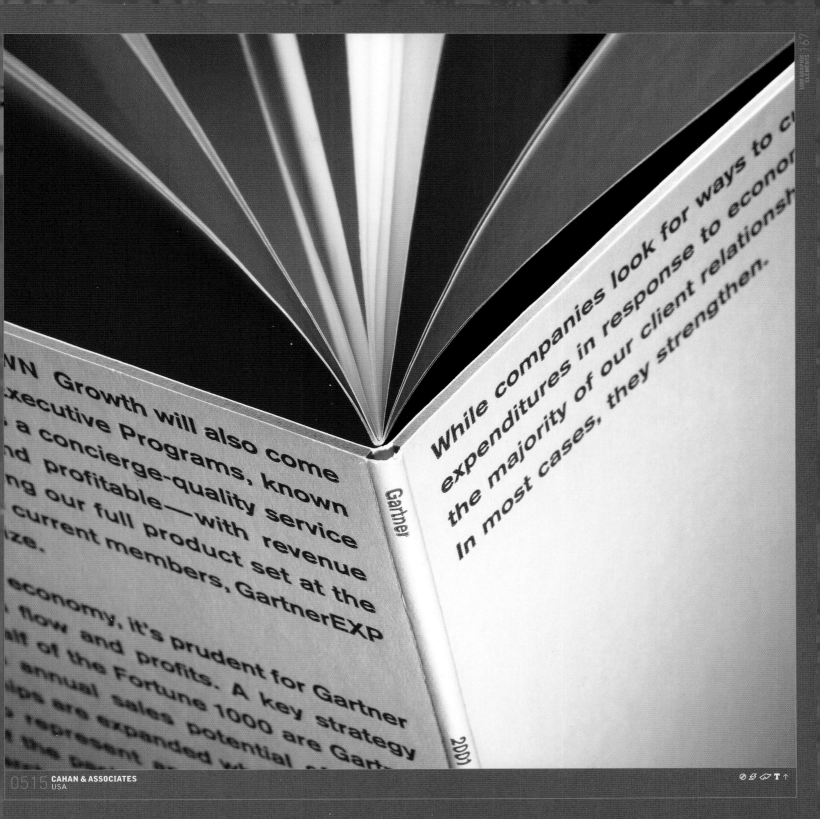

While companies look for ways to cu[t]
expenditures in response to econom[ic]
the majority of our client relationsh[ips]
In most cases, they strengthen.

NN Growth will also come

xecutive Programs, known

a concierge-quality service

nd profitable—with revenue

ng our full product set at the

current members, GartnerEXP

ze.

economy, it's prudent for Gartner

flow and profits. A key strategy

alf of the Fortune 1000 are Gart

annual sales potential

ips are expanded

represent

Gartner

2001

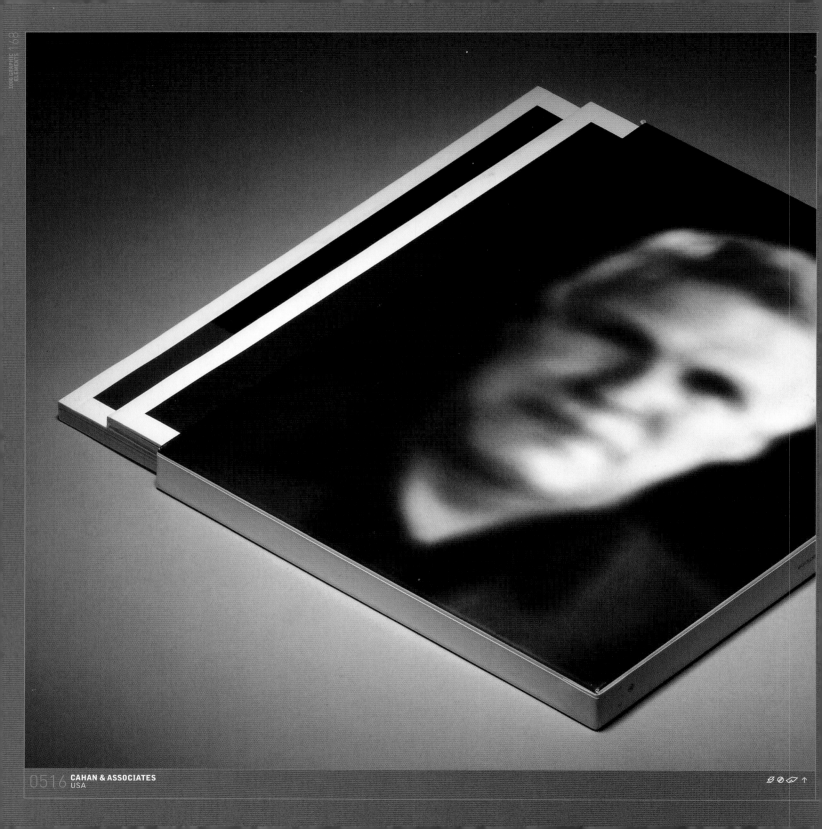

CAHAN & ASSOCIATES
USA

CAHAN & ASSOCIATES
USA

RADLEY YELDAR
UK

RADLEY YELDAR
UK

ZIGZAG DESIGN
USA

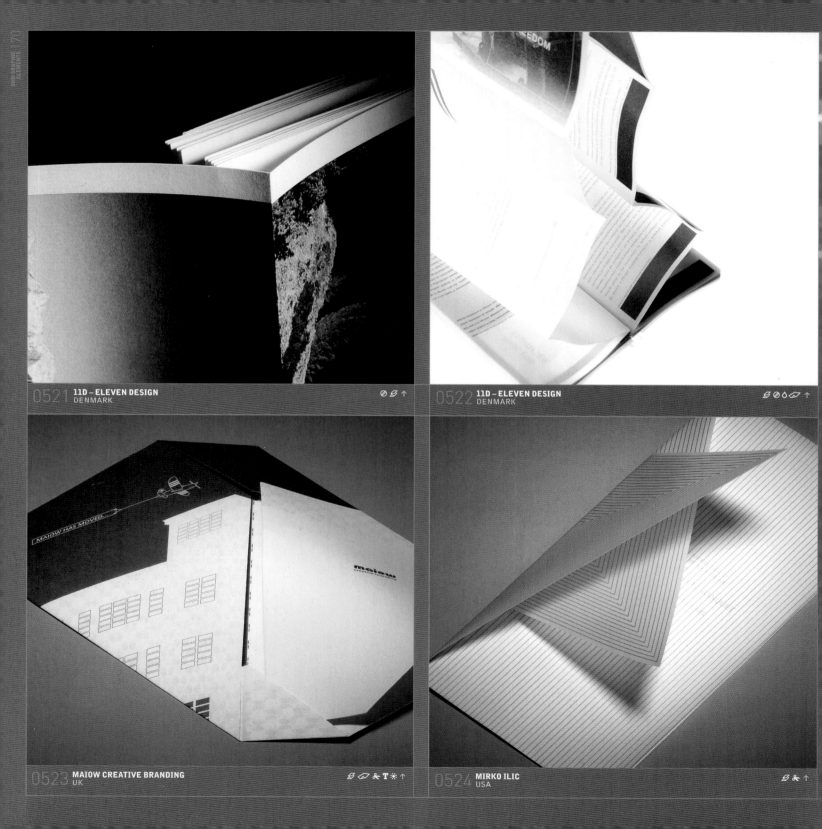

0521 **11D – ELEVEN DESIGN**
DENMARK

0522 **11D – ELEVEN DESIGN**
DENMARK

0523 **MAIOW CREATIVE BRANDING**
UK

0524 **MIRKO ILIC**
USA

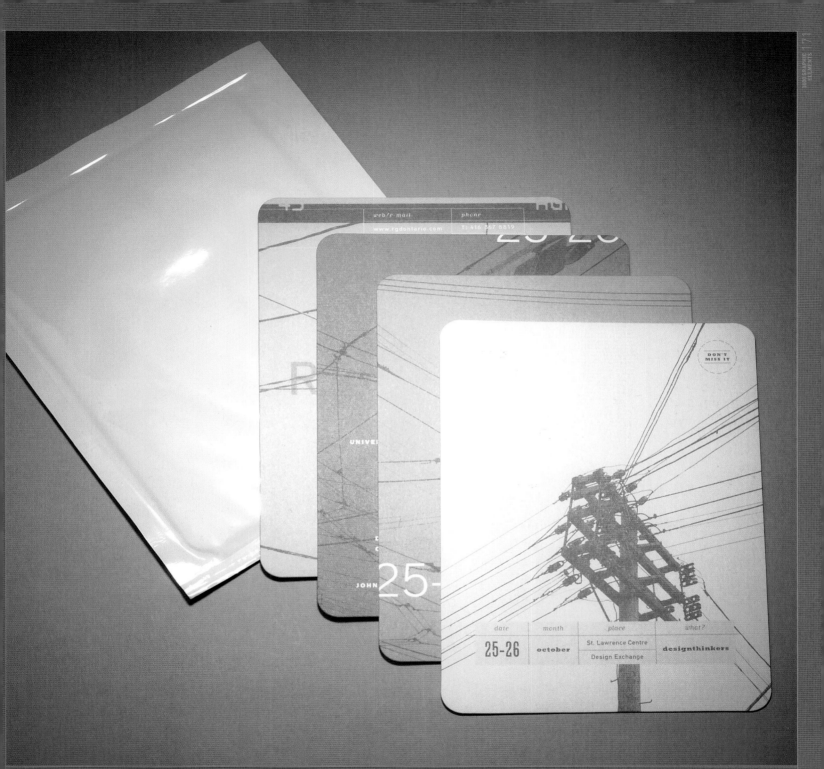

date | month | place | what?
25-26 | october | St. Lawrence Centre | designthinkers
 | | Design Exchange |

DON'T
MISS IT

web/e-mail | phone
www.rgdontario.com | T: 416 367 8819

0527	**LEWIS COMMUNICATIONS** USA

0528	**SAGE COMMUNICATION** USA

0529	**KBDA** USA

0530	**SK VISUAL** USA

0531	**LEWIS COMMUNICATIONS** USA

0532	**IMAGINATION (GIC)** UK

0533	**KOLEGRAM DESIGN** CANADA

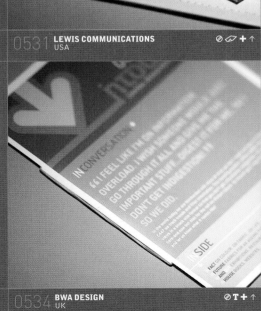

0534	**BWA DESIGN** UK

0535	**DAVID CARTER DESIGN** USA

0536 KBDA
USA

0537 MIRIELLO GRAFICO
USA

VOICE
A COLLECTION OF 10 POSTCARDS

0538 NIELINGER & ROHSIEPE
GERMANY

0539 JOHNSON BANKS
UK

Design in a global context

DESIGN IN A GLOBAL CONTEXT. Markets for UK businesses are no longer down the road but across the globe. People abroad are more likely to get excited about the idea of doing business with you if they know you're forward-thinking, modern, innovative and in tune with the world. Companies have told us so. So, the Design Council is working to demonstrate that the UK isn't a place full of dotty eccentrics who can't exploit their ideas, but about innovation and the cutting-edge design that turns those ideas into world-beaters.
Our exhibitions and events mean thousands of people around the world are getting the message, the international bonds we've formed are helping businesses find new customers, and the knowledge resources we're building are helping the UK to meet global needs.

Problem: Explaining a new flexible letting company **solved:** show what flexibility looks like, even in the logo

client: Yellow Pages **problem:** revitalising a product untouched for 15 years **solved:** let them own the colour yellow (and make it readable too)

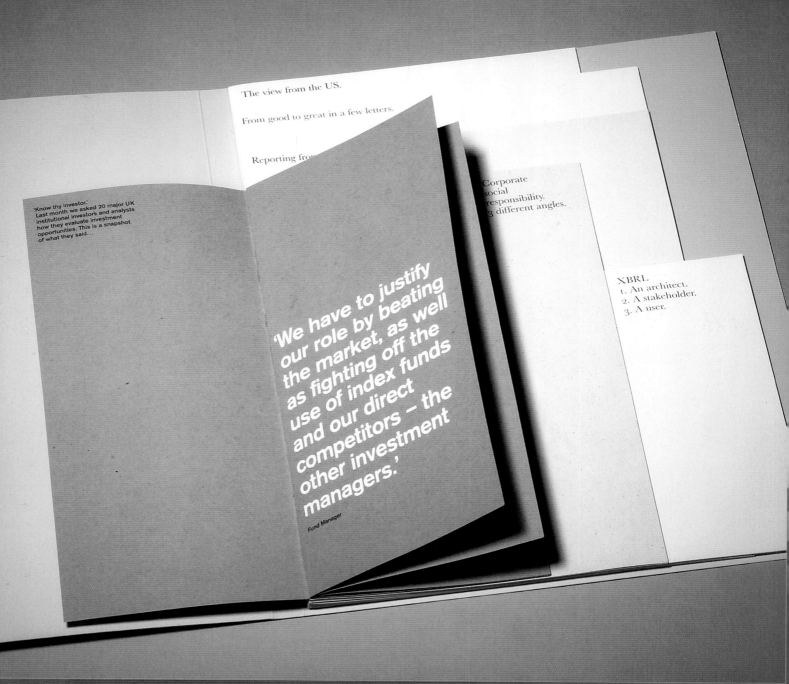

The view from the US.

From good to great in a few letters.

Reporting fro

'Know thy investor.'
Last month we asked 20 major UK
institutional investors and analysts
how they evaluate investment
opportunities. This is a snapshot
of what they said...

Corporate
social
responsibility.
3 different angles.

XBRL
1. An architect.
2. A stakeholder.
3. A user.

'We have to justify
our role by beating
the market, as well
as fighting off the
use of index funds
and our direct
competitors – the
other investment
managers.'

Fund Manager

0542 DEW GIBBONS
UK

0543 NB:STUDIO
UK

0544 NB:STUDIO
UK

0545 BUREAU GRAS
THE NETHERLANDS

Reality

01 EXPANSION

GROW THE BUSINESS
FROM 250 — 400 DEPOTS
WITHIN 5 YEARS

GROWING THE BUSINESS

RSA

HEADS
WILLEM SANDERS
KOPPEN
WILLEM SANDERS

METIS_NL

SAFE

SEALED SAFETY SEALED

K2H2 ANNUAL REPORT 2001

SCHOOLS IN THE
ARE DISTINCT

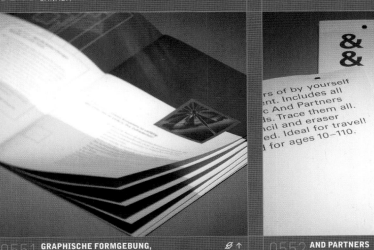

0547　**SALTERBAXTER**
UK

0548　**KOLEGRAM DESIGN**
CANADA

0549　**JOHNSON BANKS**
UK

0550　**HAND MADE GROUP**
ITALY

0551　**GRAPHISCHE FORMGEBUNG,
HERBERT ROHSIEPE**
GERMANY

0552　**AND PARTNERS**
USA

0553　**RADLEY YELDAR**
UK

0554　**NBBJ GRAPHIC DESIGN**
USA

0555　**THAT'S NICE**
USA

0556 IRIDIUM, A DESIGN AGENCY
CANADA

0557 SUM DESIGN
UK

0558 HARRIMANSTEEL
UK

0559 SALTERBAXTER
UK

PRINT FINISHING STUDIO HANDBOOK

DESIGNERS BE PROGNERS WILL BE PROSECUTED NOT

Decorative Print Finishes applied to Urban Wallscapes

ALCAN

PRINT FINISHING STUDIO HANDBOOK
DESIGNERS WILL NOT BE PROSECUTED

0001 0002 0003 0004 0005 0006 0007 0008 0009 0010 0011 0012 0013 0014 0015 0016 0017 0018 0019 0020 0021 0022 0023 0024 002
0041 0042 0043 0044 0045 0046 0047 0048 0049 0050 0051 0052 0053 0054 0055 0056 0057 0058 0059 0060 0061 0062 0063 0064 006
0081 0082 0083 0084 0085 0086 0087 0088 0089 0090 0091 0092 0093 0094 0095 0096 0097 0098 0099 0100 0101 0102 0103 0104 010
0121 0122 0123 0124 0125 0126 0127 0128 0129 0130 0131 0132 0133 0134 0135 0136 0137 0138 0139 0140 0141 0142 0143 0144 014
0161 0162 0163 0164 0165 0166 0167 0168 0169 0170 0171 0172 0173 0174 0175 0176 0177 0178 0179 0180 0181 0182 0183 0184 018
0201 0202 0203 0204 0205 0206 0207 0208 0209 0210 0211 0212 0213 0214 0215 0216 0217 0218 0219 0220 0221 0222 0223 0224 022
0241 0242 0243 0244 0245 0246 0247 0248 0249 0250 0251 0252 0253 0254 0255 0256 0257 0258 0259 0260 0261 0262 0263 0264 026
0281 0282 0283 0284 0285 0286 0287 0288 0289 0290 0291 0292 0293 0294 0295 0296 0297 0298 0299 0300 0301 0302 0303 0304 030
0321 0322 0323 0324 0325 0326 0327 0328 0329 0330 0331 0332 0333 0334 0335 0336 0337 0338 0339 0340 0341 0342 0343 0344 034
0361 0362 0363 0364 0365 0366 0367 0368 0369 0370 0371 0372 0373 0374 0375 0376 0377 0378 0379 0380 0381 0382 0383 0384 038
0401 0402 0403 0404 0405 0406 0407 0408 0409 0410 0411 0412 0413 0414 0415 0416 0417 0418 0419 0420 0421 0422 0423 0424 042
0441 0442 0443 0444 0445 0446 0447 0448 0449 0450 0451 0452 0453 0454 0455 0456 0457 0458 0459 0460 0461 0462 0463 0464 046
0481 0482 0483 0484 0485 0486 0487 0488 0489 0490 0491 0492 0493 0494 0495 0496 0497 0498 0499 0500 0501 0502 0503 0504 050
0521 0522 0523 0524 0525 0526 0527 0528 0529 0530 0531 0532 0533 0534 0535 0536 0537 0538 0539 0540 0541 0542 0543 0544 054
0561 0562 0563 0564 0565 0566 0567 0568 0569 0570 0571 0572 0573 0574 0575 0576 0577 0578 0579 0580 0581 0582 0583 0584 058
0601 0602 0603 0604 0605 0606 0607 0608 0609 0610 0611 0612 0613 0614 0615 0616 0617 0618 0619 0620 0621 0622 0623 0624 062
0641 0642 0643 0644 0645 0646 0647 0648 0649 0650 0651 0652 0653 0654 0655 0656 0657 0658 0659 0660 0661 0662 0663 0664 066
0681 0682 0683 0684 0685 0686 0687 0688 0689 0690 0691 0692 0693 0694 0695 0696 0697 0698 0699 0700 0701 0702 0703 0704 070
0721 0722 0723 0724 0725 0726 0727 0728 0729 0730 0731 0732 0733 0734 0735 0736 0737 0738 0739 0740 0741 0742 0743 0744 074
0761 0762 0763 0764 0765 0766 0767 0768 0769 0770 0771 0772 0773 0774 0775 0776 0777 0778 0779 0780 0781 0782 0783 0784 078
0801 0802 0803 0804 0805 0806 0807 0808 0809 0810 0811 0812 0813 0814 0815 0816 0817 0818 0819 0820 0821 0822 0823 0824 082
0841 0842 0843 0844 0845 0846 0847 0848 0849 0850 0851 0852 0853 0854 0855 0856 0857 0858 0859 0860 0861 0862 0863 0864 086
0881 0882 0883 0884 0885 0886 0887 0888 0889 0890 0891 0892 0893 0894 0895 0896 0897 0898 0899 0900 0901 0902 0903 0904 090
0921 0922 0923 0924 0925 0926 0927 0928 0929 0930 0931 0932 0933 0934 0935 0936 0937 0938 0939 0940 0941 0942 0943 0944 094
0961 0962 0963 0964 0965 0966 0967 0968 0969 0970 0971 0972 0973 0974 0975 0976 0977 0978 0979 0980 0981 0982 0983 0984 098

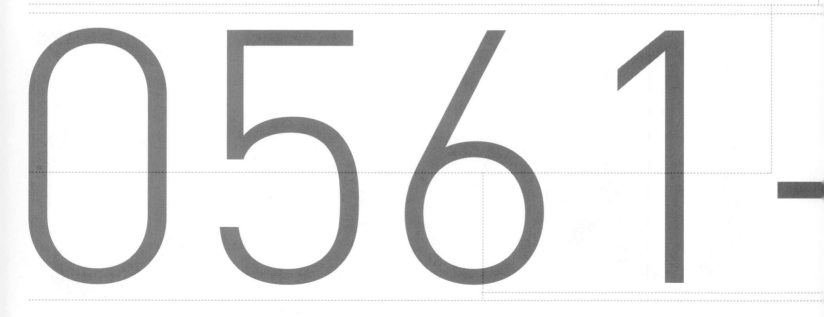

0028 0029 0030 0031 0032 0033 0034 0035 0036 0037 0038 0039 0040
0068 0069 0070 0071 0072 0073 0074 0075 0076 0077 0078 0079 0080
0108 0109 0110 0111 0112 0113 0114 0115 0116 0117 0118 0119 0120
0148 0149 0150 0151 0152 0153 0154 0155 0156 0157 0158 0159 0160
0188 0189 0190 0191 0192 0193 0194 0195 0196 0197 0198 0199 0200
0228 0229 0230 0231 0232 0233 0234 0235 0236 0237 0238 0239 0240
0268 0269 0270 0271 0272 0273 0274 0275 0276 0277 0278 0279 0280
0308 0309 0310 0311 0312 0313 0314 0315 0316 0317 0318 0319 0320
0348 0349 0350 0351 0352 0353 0354 0355 0356 0357 0358 0359 0360
0388 0389 0390 0391 0392 0393 0394 0395 0396 0397 0398 0399 0400
0428 0429 0430 0431 0432 0433 0434 0435 0436 0437 0438 0439 0440
0468 0469 0470 0471 0472 0473 0474 0475 0476 0477 0478 0479 0480
0508 0509 0510 0511 0512 0513 0514 0515 0516 0517 0518 0519 0520
0548 0549 0550 0551 0552 0553 0554 0555 0556 0557 0558 0559 0560
0588 0589 0590 0591 0592 0593 0594 0595 0596 0597 0598 0599 0600
0628 0629 0630 0631 0632 0633 0634 0635 0636 0637 0638 0639 0640
0668 0669 0670 0671 0672 0673 0674 0675 0676 0677 0678 0679 0680
0708 0709 0710 0711 0712 0713 0714 0715 0716 0717 0718 0719 0720
0748 0749 0750 0751 0752 0753 0754 0755 0756 0757 0758 0759 0760
0788 0789 0790 0791 0792 0793 0794 0795 0796 0797 0798 0799 0800
0828 0829 0830 0831 0832 0833 0834 0835 0836 0837 0838 0839 0840
0868 0869 0870 0871 0872 0873 0874 0875 0876 0877 0878 0879 0880
0908 0909 0910 0911 0912 0913 0914 0915 0916 0917 0918 0919 0920
0948 0949 0950 0951 0952 0953 0954 0955 0956 0957 0958 0959 0960
0988 0989 0990 0991 0992 0993 0994 0995 0996 0997 0998 0999 1000

_04

ADD-ONS STICKERS
RUBBER BANDS
TAGS
FOILS

2003
THE GIFT OF GOOD ART
There are many ways to solve a single problem. A thousand
paths to completing the assignment. As many possibilities
for sharing your idea as there are artists and viewers sharing
this old world. We celebrate the limitlessness of artistic
possibility with this year's calendar, a selection of the works,
of area high school students who have solved problems,
completed assignments, shared their ideas and exhibited their
work at the Holland Area Arts Council in Holland, Michigan.
Enjoy.

2003
THE GIFT OF GOOD ART
There are many ways to solve a single problem. A thousand
paths to completing the assignment. As many possibilities
for sharing your idea as there are artists and viewers sharing
this old world. We celebrate the limitlessness of artistic
possibility with this year's calendar, a selection of the works,
of area high school students who have solved problems,
completed assignments, shared their ideas and exhibited their
work at the Holland Area Arts Council in Holland, Michigan.
Enjoy.

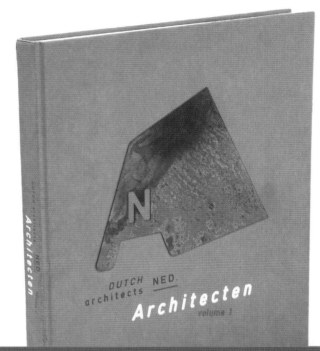

+ ✐ ⊘ T ↑

+ ⊘ T ↑

+ ✐ T ↑

+ ✐ T ↑

wem

w_ie schreibt man einen brief, liebe gruppe w_? bremen, den 01.03.2003

wenn ihr einen brief für die gruppe w_ schreiben wollt, benutzt ihr natürlich
den extra dafür vorgesehenen briefbogen. ihr legt diesen also in euren drucker
ein. beachtet: es gibt auch eine zweite seite, falls der brief etwas länger werden
sollte. benutzt in diesem fall bitte ebenfalls das dafür extra vorgesehene blatt.

was

damit nun, wenn ihr euren brief ausgedruckt ha
und ihr euch nicht jedes mal überlegen müsst,
hinkommt und wieviel leerzeilen dann folgen b
folt, gibt es diese maske die mit dem blindtext
also nur noch diesen text markieren und eure
falls ihr wert darauf legt, das eurer name auf
wort ›wer‹ steht könnt ihr am ende des brief
return drücken, bis euer name die gewünsch
zu gehen könnt ihr auch die hilfslinien einh

warum

bremen, den 01.03.2003

llt, benutzt ihr natürlich
sen also in euren drucker
brief etwas länger werden
extra vorgesehene blatt.

an seinem platz steht
noch mal die adresse

wann

wann

wie

mit freundlichem gruß,
david lindemann

wo

+T✳↑

0567 PROGRESS
UK

0568 THIRTEEN
UK

0569 LAVA
THE NETHERLANDS

leren

60 jaar IBM Nederland NV
Hugo Brandt Corstius

0570 NET#WORK BBDO
SOUTH AFRICA

0571 EMPIRE DESIGN STUDIO
USA

PUPPIES AN ADDRESS BOOK
WILLIAM WEGMAN

0572 MINGZHAM HUANG
UK

0573 NASSAR DESIGN
USA

0574 NET#WORK BBDO
SOUTH AFRICA

INVITATION

0575 R2 DESIGN
PORTUGAL

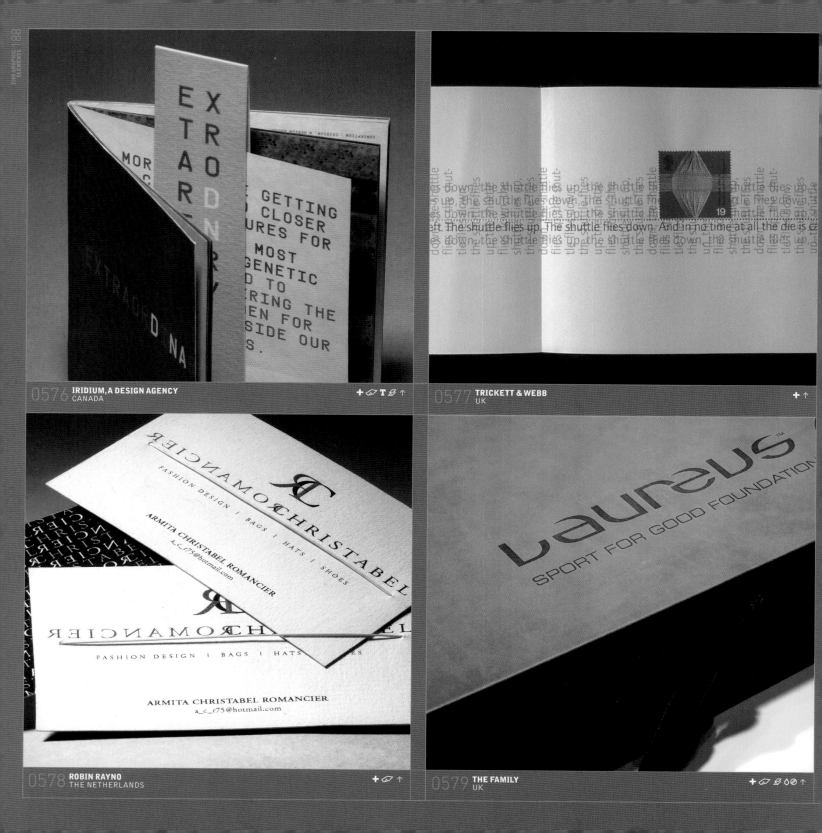

0576 **IRIDIUM, A DESIGN AGENCY**
CANADA

0577 **TRICKETT & WEBB**
UK

0578 **ROBIN RAYNO**
THE NETHERLANDS

0579 **THE FAMILY**
UK

PⱯNL

photography annual
of the netherlands

7th issue > 1996/97 >
1147 photographs
submitted > 176 photos
selected > incl. pani
award > 208 pages

PODRAVKA annual report 2000

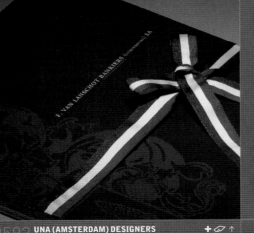

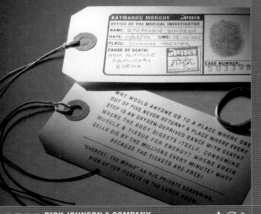

0582 UNA (AMSTERDAM) DESIGNERS
THE NETHERLANDS   + ◇ ↑

0583 RICK JOHNSON & COMPANY
USA   + ◇ ↑

0584 TEMPLIN BRINK DESIGN
USA   + ◇ T ✳ ↑

0585 NET#WORK BBDO
SOUTH AFRICA   + ◇ ↑

0586 QUESTION DESIGN
USA   + ◇ ↑

0587 LIGALUX
GERMANY   + ◇ ↑

0588 CIRCULO SOCIAL
MEXICO   + ◇ T ↑

0589 THE WORKS DESIGN COMMUNICATIONS
CANADA   + ◇ ◪ ↑

0590 SCANDINAVIAN DESIGN GROUP
DENMARK   + ◇ ◪ ↑

0592 **THE FAMILY**
UK
+ 🖋 ✏ T ↑

0593 **HAND MADE GROUP**
ITALY
+ 🖋 ✏ ↑

0594 **MARIUS FAHRNER DESIGN**
GERMANY
+ ✏ ✂ ↑

0595 **AND PARTNERS**
USA
+ ✏ T ↑

0597 **LIPPA PEARCE DESIGN**
UK

0598 **POPCORN INITIATIVE**
USA

0599 **TEMPLIN BRINK DESIGN**
USA

0600 **AND PARTNERS**
USA

0601 **BLACKCOFFEE**
USA

0602 **BNIM ARCHITECTS**
USA

0603 **RIORDON DESIGN**
CANADA

0604 **LIPPA PEARCE DESIGN**
UK

0605 **RIORDON DESIGN**
CANADA

2003
THE GIFT OF GOOD ART
There are many ways to solve a single problem. A thousand paths to completing the assignment. As many possibilities for sharing your idea as there are artists and viewers sharing this old world. We celebrate the limitlessness of artistic possibility with this year's calendar, a selection of the works of area high school students who have solved problems, completed assignments, shared their ideas and exhibited their work at the Holland Area Arts Council, in Holland, Michigan.
Enjoy.

BBK STUDIO
USA

0607 **UNA (AMSTERDAM) DESIGNERS**
THE NETHERLANDS

+ ✎ T ↑

0608 **LIGALUX**
GERMANY

+ ✎ ↑

0609 **FORM**
UK

+ ☀ ↑

0610 **GOUTHIER DESIGN**
USA

+ ✎ ◊T ↑

0611 GOUTHIER DESIGN
USA

0612 WALLACE CHURCH
USA

0613 QUESTION DESIGN
USA

0614 ZIGZAG DESIGN
USA

0615 LIPPA PEARCE DESIGN
UK

0616 BIG ACTIVE
UK

0617 CHRONICLE BOOKS
USA

0618 JONES DESIGN GROUP
USA

0619 MARIUS FAHRNER DESIGN
GERMANY

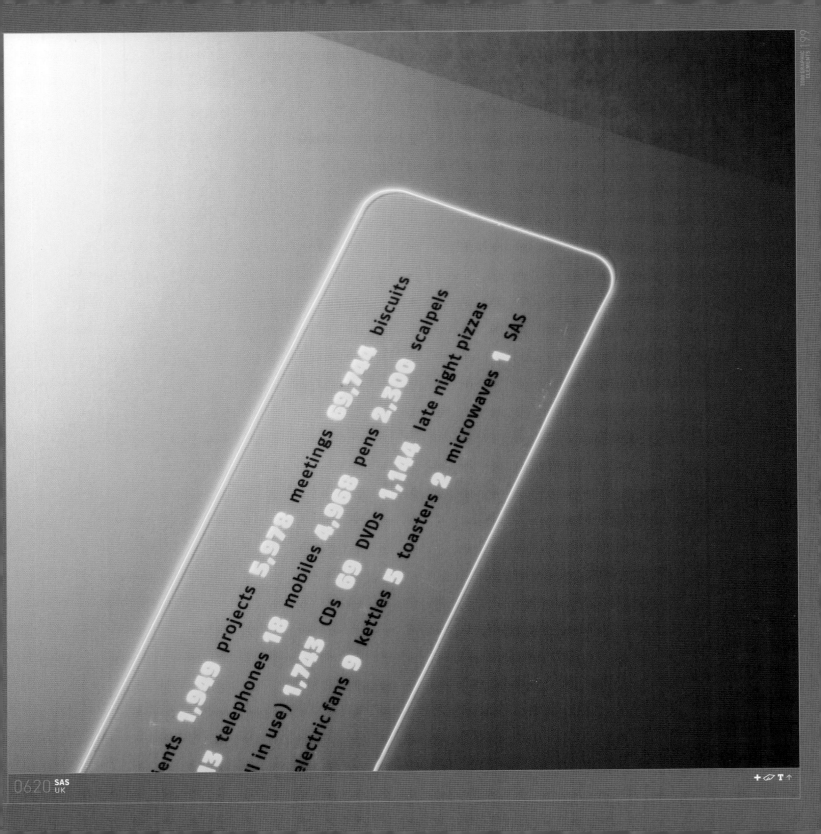

...ients **1,949** projects **5,978** meetings **69,744** biscuits

...3 telephones **18** mobiles **4,968** pens **2,300** scalpels

(all in use) **1,743** CDs **69** DVDs **1,144** late night pizzas

...electric fans **9** kettles **5** toasters **2** microwaves **1** SAS

0622　**THOMPSON**
UK

＋◇T✦↑

0623　**THE DESIGN DELL**
UK

＋◇T↑

seeing beyond
a generic genome

to identify individ
risks for cancer

0624　**NAVY BLUE**
UK

＋◇T◇↑

0625　**IE DESIGN**
USA

＋T◇↑

0626 **BECKER DESIGN**
USA

0627 **KBDA**
USA

0628 **STEERSMCGILLAN**
UK

0629 **IRIDIUM, A DESIGN AGENCY**
CANADA

0630 **JONES DESIGN GROUP**
USA

0631 **SAS**
UK

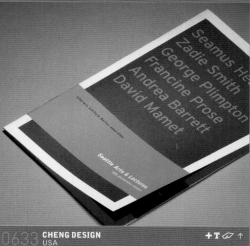

0632 **THIRTEEN**
UK

0633 **CHENG DESIGN**
USA

0634 **GOUTHIER DESIGN**
USA

ative
kroom
e positive?

er to see
s going on
switch on
e light.

Which does not illuminate either.
On the contrary:
All remains black.

cht weiter.

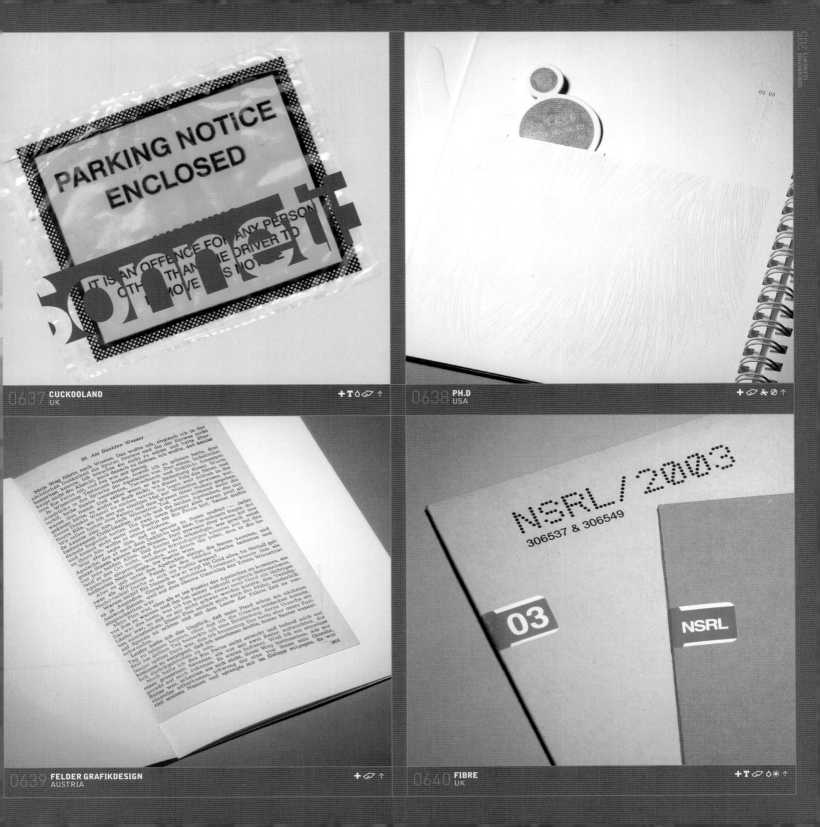

0637 **CUCKOOLAND**
UK

0638 **PH.D**
USA

0639 **FELDER GRAFIKDESIGN**
AUSTRIA

0640 **FIBRE**
UK

0642	**HAND MADE GROUP** ITALY	+ ⬦ ↑

0643	**HARRIMANSTEEL** UK	+ ↑

0644	**AFTERHOURS CREATIVE** USA	+ ↑

0645	**AFTERHOURS CREATIVE** USA	+ ↑

0646	**A2-GRAPHICS/SW/HK** UK	+ ⬦ ↑

0647	**EMSPACE DESIGN GROUP** USA	+ ↑

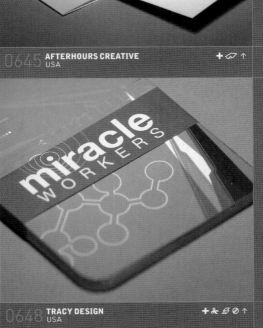

0648	**TRACY DESIGN** USA	+ ↑

0649	**GIORGIO DAVANZO DESIGN** USA	+ ↑

0650	**AFTERHOURS CREATIVE** USA	+ ↑

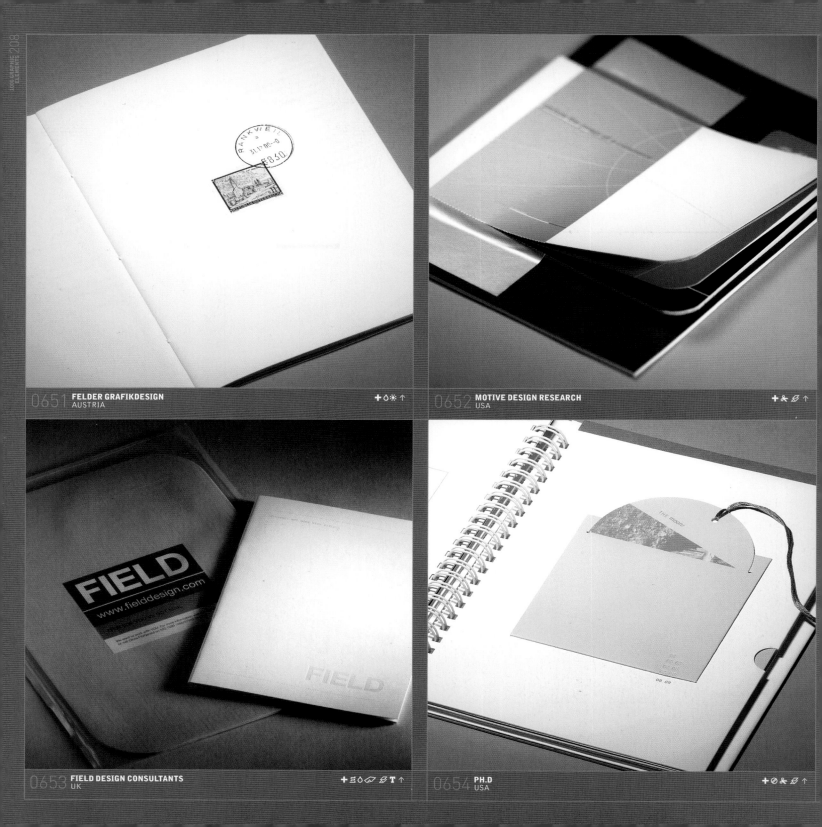

0651 **FELDER GRAFIKDESIGN**
AUSTRIA

0652 **MOTIVE DESIGN RESEARCH**
USA

0653 **FIELD DESIGN CONSULTANTS**
UK

0654 **PH.D**
USA

NIKE SHOX TL

PRODUCT CODE 305469
SIZE RUN 41.5, 14, 15
WEIGHT 400G
MIDSOLE HEIGHT 50,18

0657 **KESSELS KRAMER**
THE NETHERLANDS

0658 **CHRONICLE BOOKS**
USA

0659 **LIGALUX**
GERMANY

0660 **MOTIVE DESIGN RESEARCH**
USA

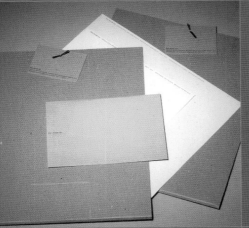

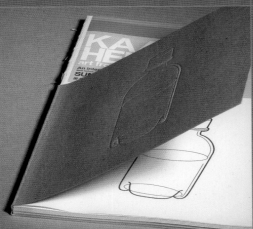

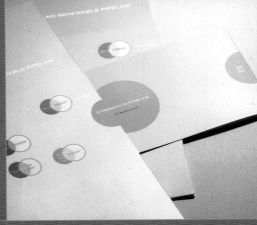

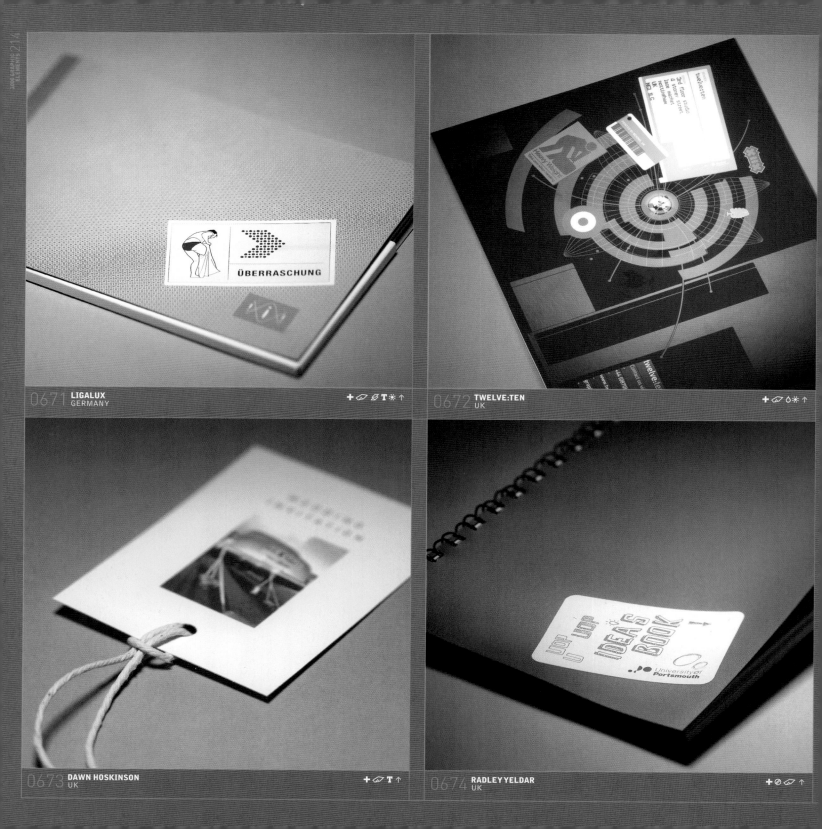

0671 **LIGALUX**
GERMANY

ÜBERRASCHUNG

0672 **TWELVE:TEN**
UK

0673 **DAWN HOSKINSON**
UK

0674 **RADLEY YELDAR**
UK

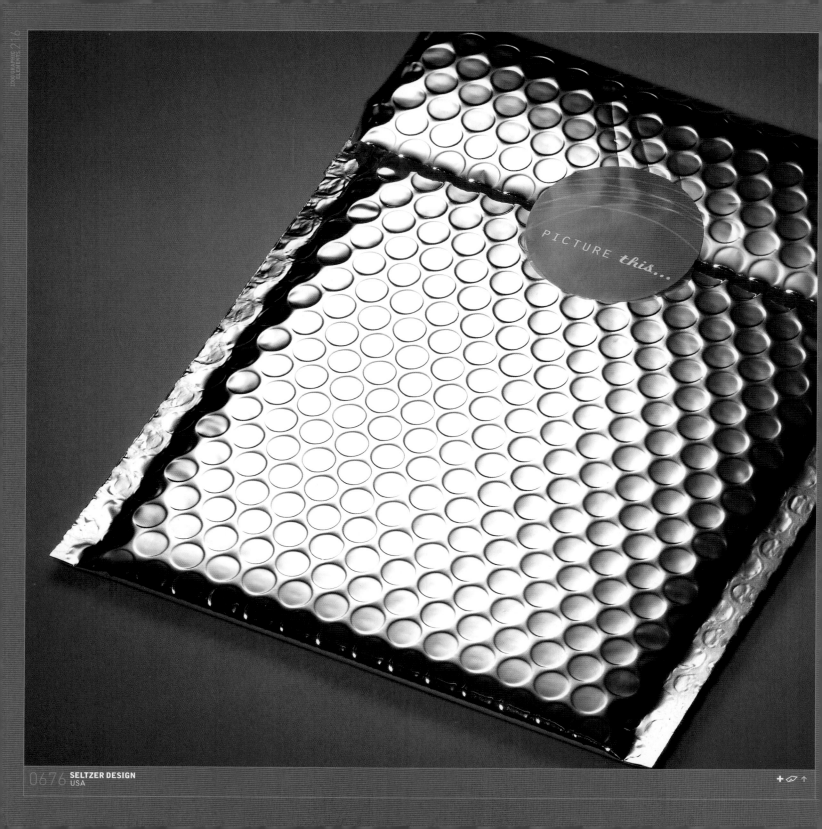

PICTURE *this...*

+ ✦ ↑

0677 **DAVID CARTER DESIGN**
USA

HAND MADE GROUP
ITALY

FELDER GRAFIKDESIGN
AUSTRIA

0680 **UNA (AMSTERDAM) DESIGNERS**
THE NETHERLANDS

0681 **SAMPSON MAY**
UK

CIRCLE K DESIGN
USA

0683 **WALLACE CHURCH**
USA

IRIDIUM, A DESIGN AGENCY
CANADA

0685 **MAGMA**
GERMANY

0001 0002 0003 0004 0005 0006 0007 0008 0009 0010 0011 0012 0013 0014 0015 0016 0017 0018 0019 0020 0021 0022 0023 0024 0025
0041 0042 0043 0044 0045 0046 0047 0048 0049 0050 0051 0052 0053 0054 0055 0056 0057 0058 0059 0060 0061 0062 0063 0064 0065
0081 0082 0083 0084 0085 0086 0087 0088 0089 0090 0091 0092 0093 0094 0095 0096 0097 0098 0099 0100 0101 0102 0103 0104 0105
0121 0122 0123 0124 0125 0126 0127 0128 0129 0130 0131 0132 0133 0134 0135 0136 0137 0138 0139 0140 0141 0142 0143 0144 0145
0161 0162 0163 0164 0165 0166 0167 0168 0169 0170 0171 0172 0173 0174 0175 0176 0177 0178 0179 0180 0181 0182 0183 0184 0185
0201 0202 0203 0204 0205 0206 0207 0208 0209 0210 0211 0212 0213 0214 0215 0216 0217 0218 0219 0220 0221 0222 0223 0224 0225
0241 0242 0243 0244 0245 0246 0247 0248 0249 0250 0251 0252 0253 0254 0255 0256 0257 0258 0259 0260 0261 0262 0263 0264 0265
0281 0282 0283 0284 0285 0286 0287 0288 0289 0290 0291 0292 0293 0294 0295 0296 0297 0298 0299 0300 0301 0302 0303 0304 0305
0321 0322 0323 0324 0325 0326 0327 0328 0329 0330 0331 0332 0333 0334 0335 0336 0337 0338 0339 0340 0341 0342 0343 0344 0345
0361 0362 0363 0364 0365 0366 0367 0368 0369 0370 0371 0372 0373 0374 0375 0376 0377 0378 0379 0380 0381 0382 0383 0384 0385
0401 0402 0403 0404 0405 0406 0407 0408 0409 0410 0411 0412 0413 0414 0415 0416 0417 0418 0419 0420 0421 0422 0423 0424 0425
0441 0442 0443 0444 0445 0446 0447 0448 0449 0450 0451 0452 0453 0454 0455 0456 0457 0458 0459 0460 0461 0462 0463 0464 0465
0481 0482 0483 0484 0485 0486 0487 0488 0489 0490 0491 0492 0493 0494 0495 0496 0497 0498 0499 0500 0501 0502 0503 0504 0505
0521 0522 0523 0524 0525 0526 0527 0528 0529 0530 0531 0532 0533 0534 0535 0536 0537 0538 0539 0540 0541 0542 0543 0544 0545
0561 0562 0563 0564 0565 0566 0567 0568 0569 0570 0571 0572 0573 0574 0575 0576 0577 0578 0579 0580 0581 0582 0583 0584 0585
0601 0602 0603 0604 0605 0606 0607 0608 0609 0610 0611 0612 0613 0614 0615 0616 0617 0618 0619 0620 0621 0622 0623 0624 0625
0641 0642 0643 0644 0645 0646 0647 0648 0649 0650 0651 0652 0653 0654 0655 0656 0657 0658 0659 0660 0661 0662 0663 0664 0665
0681 0682 0683 0684 0685 0686 0687 0688 0689 0690 0691 0692 0693 0694 0695 0696 0697 0698 0699 0700 0701 0702 0703 0704 0705
0721 0722 0723 0724 0725 0726 0727 0728 0729 0730 0731 0732 0733 0734 0735 0736 0737 0738 0739 0740 0741 0742 0743 0744 0745
0761 0762 0763 0764 0765 0766 0767 0768 0769 0770 0771 0772 0773 0774 0775 0776 0777 0778 0779 0780 0781 0782 0783 0784 0785
0801 0802 0803 0804 0805 0806 0807 0808 0809 0810 0811 0812 0813 0814 0815 0816 0817 0818 0819 0820 0821 0822 0823 0824 0825
0841 0842 0843 0844 0845 0846 0847 0848 0849 0850 0851 0852 0853 0854 0855 0856 0857 0858 0859 0860 0861 0862 0863 0864 0865
0881 0882 0883 0884 0885 0886 0887 0888 0889 0890 0891 0892 0893 0894 0895 0896 0897 0898 0899 0900 0901 0902 0903 0904 0905
0921 0922 0923 0924 0925 0926 0927 0928 0929 0930 0931 0932 0933 0934 0935 0936 0937 0938 0939 0940 0941 0942 0943 0944 0945
0961 0962 0963 0964 0965 0966 0967 0968 0969 0970 0971 0972 0973 0974 0975 0976 0977 0978 0979 0980 0981 0982 0983 0984 0985

_05

UNIQUE MATERIALS

STICKERS
RUBBER BANDS
TAGS
FOILS

_0820

test your senses

Can you recognise a real orange?
Touch each of the oranges shown above
and decide which the real one is.
The right answer is at the end of the book.

300 Group ME +

Typical.

**McCann always
wants more.**

THIS TIME IT'S BLOOD. DON'T WORRY, NOT YOURS. WE NEED NEW
BLOOD AND BELIEVE IT OR NOT, OUR EMPLOYEE REFERRAL
INITIATIVE WILL PAY FOR IT. IF YOU KNOW SOMEONE WHO'S THE
RIGHT TYPE, DONATE THEIR NAME AND NUMBER. AND PROVIDING
THE TRANSPLANT IS SUCCESSFUL, YOU'LL BE ADMINISTERED A
£300 TAX-FREE CASH INJECTION. DOESN'T SOUND TOO PAINFUL
DOES IT? HUMAN RESOURCES HAS ALL THE GORY DETAILS.

Employee Referral Initiative
McCANN-ERICKSON CENTRAL GROUP
BIRMINGHAM/LEEDS/EDINBURGH/MANCHESTER/LONDON

molten.tv

MOTIONGRAPHICS
FOR FILM AND TELEVISION

0687 **PRECURSOR**
UK

0688 **PROGRESS**
UK

0689 **PROGRESS**
UK

0690 **NB:STUDIO**
UK

0691 **DYNAMO A & D**
USA

0692 **ROUNDEL**
UK

0693 **FELDER GRAFIKDESIGN**
AUSTRIA

0694 **GRETEMAN GROUP**
USA

0695 **11D – ELEVEN DESIGN**
DENMARK

0696 **TONIC**
UK

0697 **FORM**
UK

0698 **NYC COLLEGE OF TECHNOLOGY**
USA

0699 **LIPPA PEARCE DESIGN**
UK

136 SOUTH PARK   SAN FRANCISCO CA 94107

F 415_777_8633

T 415_974_6622

SAND studios

WWW.SANDSTUDIOS.COM

JEFF WALDO SAND
PRINCIPAL / PRODUCT DEVELOPMENT

jeff@sandstudios.com
www.jeffsand.com

SAND studios

T 415_974_6622
F 415_777_8633
C 415_845_7639

136 SOUTH PARK
SAN FRANCISCO CA 94107

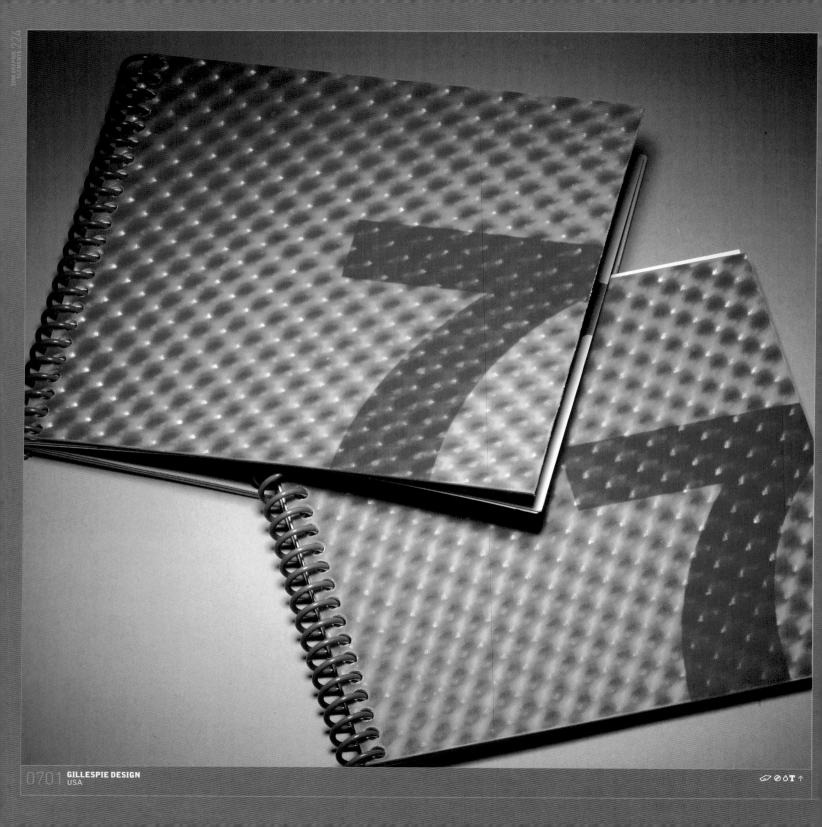

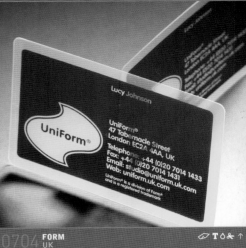

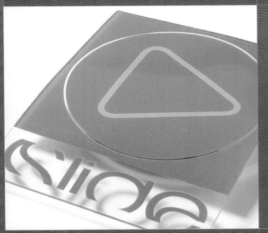

0702 **MAIOW CREATIVE BRANDING**
UK

0703 **SAS**
UK

0704 **FORM**
UK

0705 **SCANDINAVIAN DESIGN GROUP**
DENMARK

0706 **SCANDINAVIAN DESIGN GROUP**
DENMARK

0707 **WILSON HARVEY**
UK

0708 **BLOK DESIGN**
MEXICO

0709 **PROGRESS**
UK

0710 **JADE DESIGN**
UK

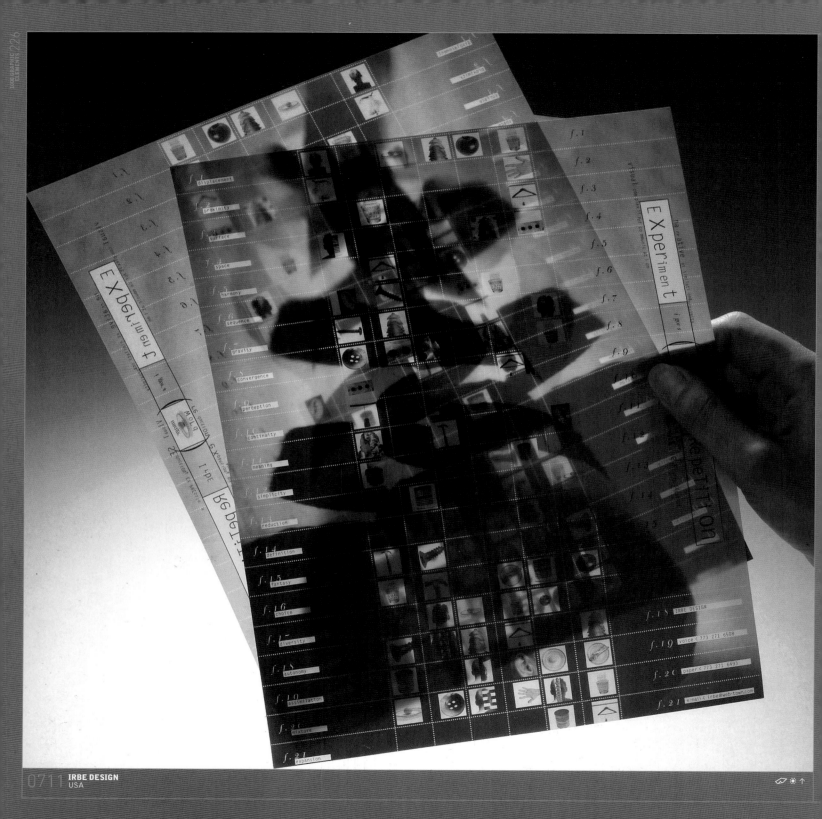

0712 **HORNALL ANDERSON DESIGN WORKS**
USA

0713 **STEERSMCGILLAN**
UK

0714 **...,STAAT**
THE NETHERLANDS

0715 **PHILLIPS**
UK

0716 **BLACKCOFFEE**
USA

0717 **PROGRESS**
UK

0718 **NB:STUDIO**
UK

0719 **STEERSMCGILLAN**
UK

0720 **WALLACE CHURCH**
USA

0721 **V06**
BRAZIL

0722 **AND PARTNERS**
USA

0723 **BLACKCOFFEE**
USA

0724 **BLACKCOFFEE**
USA

BRAND THERAPY

M
OTEL
LORIDA

Led by five of the
country's most
distinguished brand and
marketing authorities on
the Hispanic market,
this intensive one-day
session is limited to a
small, exclusive group
of senior executives.
Both consultative
and participatory, the
challenging agenda has
been structured to give
participants a significant
grasp on a little
understood, but fast
emerging population
segment. Bilingual and
bicultural, savvy and
sophisticated, the New
Hispanic Consumer in
the United States will
command tremendous
social and economic
clout in the years
to come.

Carefully structured
and highly interactive,
this distinctive gathering
will provide the essential
tools to help effectively
position participants'
brands to consumers
they will not want to
ignore.

Participants will be
invited to come to
Brand Therapy with
a map of their target
segments, message
penetration strategy
and spending power,
They will come
with the kind of
intelligence, insight and
perspective that
they need to compete
in today's complex
environment.

STAY TRUE™
CONVERSE PREMIUM: A STEP ABOVE THE TRADITIONAL. A STEP BEYOND
CONVENTION. YESTERDAY'S STYLE MADE TO TOMORROW'S STANDARDS.
PREMIUM

STAY TRUE™
CONVERSE ALL STAR
Gibson
BROUGHT TO YOU BY
TWO AMERICAN CLASSICS
® & © 2000, Gibson Guitar Corp
® & © 2000, Converse Inc.

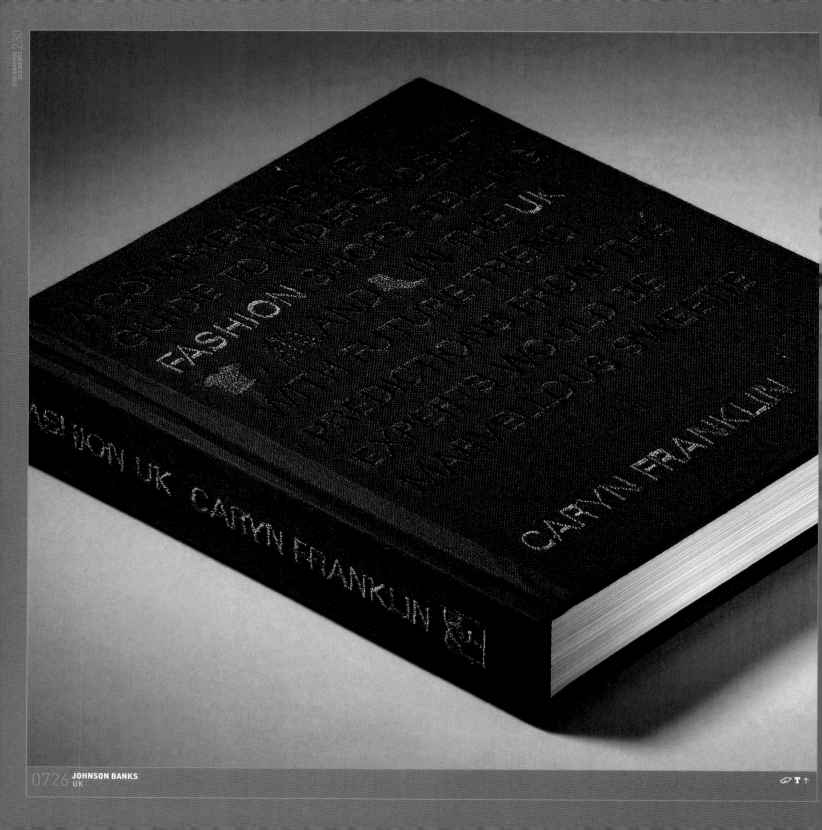

0727 **FOXINABOX**
UK

0728 **HAND MADE GROUP**
ITALY

0729 **BÜRO SCHELS FÜR GESTALTUNG**
GERMANY

0730 **NO.PARKING**
ITALY

0731 BRUKETA & ZINIC
CROATIA

0732 KBDA
USA

0733 SAS
UK

0734 COLLEGE DESIGN
UK

0735 DAVID CARTER DESIGN
USA

0736 WAGNER DESIGN
USA

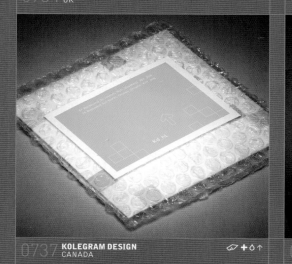

0737 KOLEGRAM DESIGN
CANADA

0738 RADLEY YELDAR
UK

0739 @RADICAL.MEDIA
USA

THIS IS NOT A LIFE SAVING DEVICE

USE ONLY UNDER ADULT SUPERVISION AND FOLLOW THE INSTRUCTIONS CAREFULLY

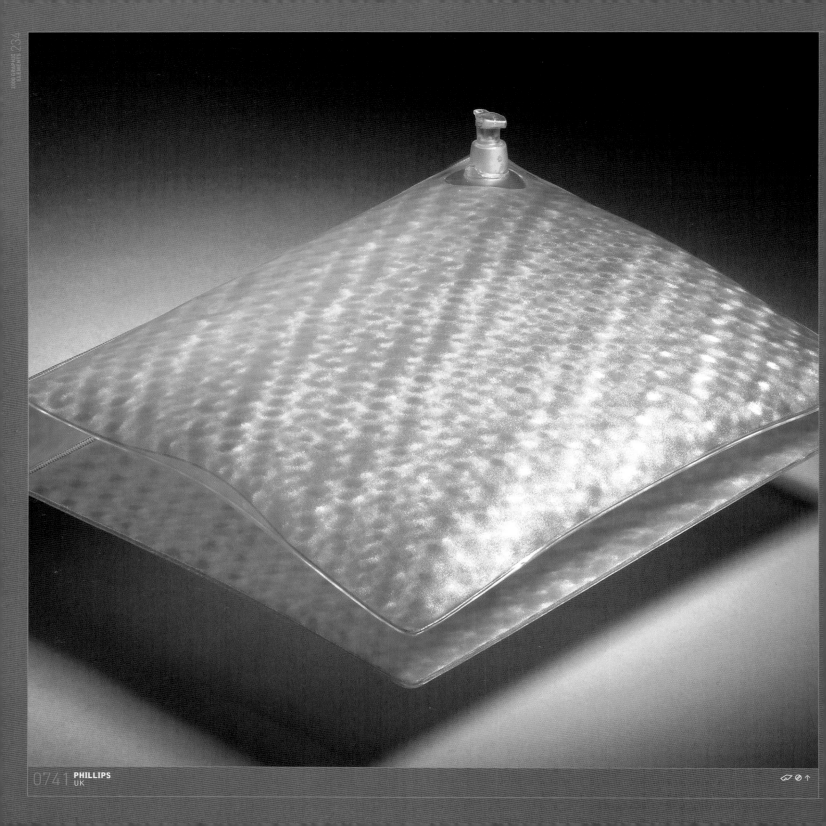

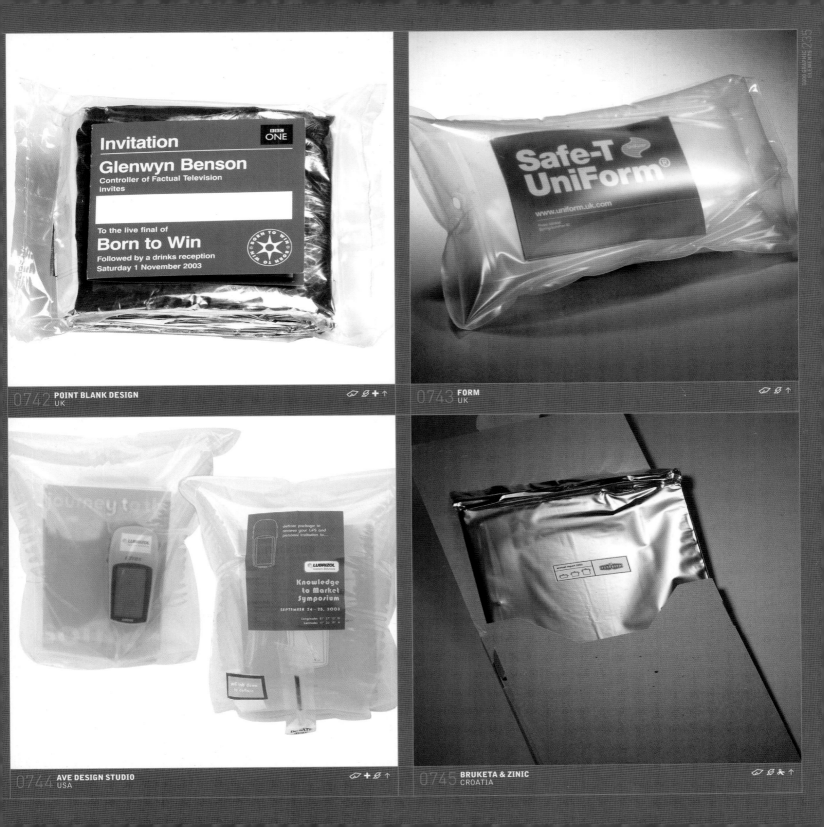

Invitation

BBC ONE

Glenwyn Benson

Controller of Factual Television
invites

To the live final of

Born to Win

Followed by a drinks reception
Saturday 1 November 2003

BORN TO WIN

Safe-T
UniForm®

www.uniform.uk.com

deflate package to
retrieve your GPS and
personal invitation to...

LUBRIZOL
Custom Solutions

**Knowledge
to Market
Symposium**

SEPTEMBER 24–25, 2003

Longitude:
Latitude:

pull tab down
to deflate

INFLATE

annual report 2002   PODRAVKA

0742 **POINT BLANK DESIGN**
UK

0743 **FORM**
UK

0744 **AVE DESIGN STUDIO**
USA

0745 **BRUKETA & ZINIC**
CROATIA

0746 PRECURSOR
UK

0747 BRUKETA & ZINIC
CROATIA

0748 EGGERS + DIAPER
GERMANY

0749 FORM
UK

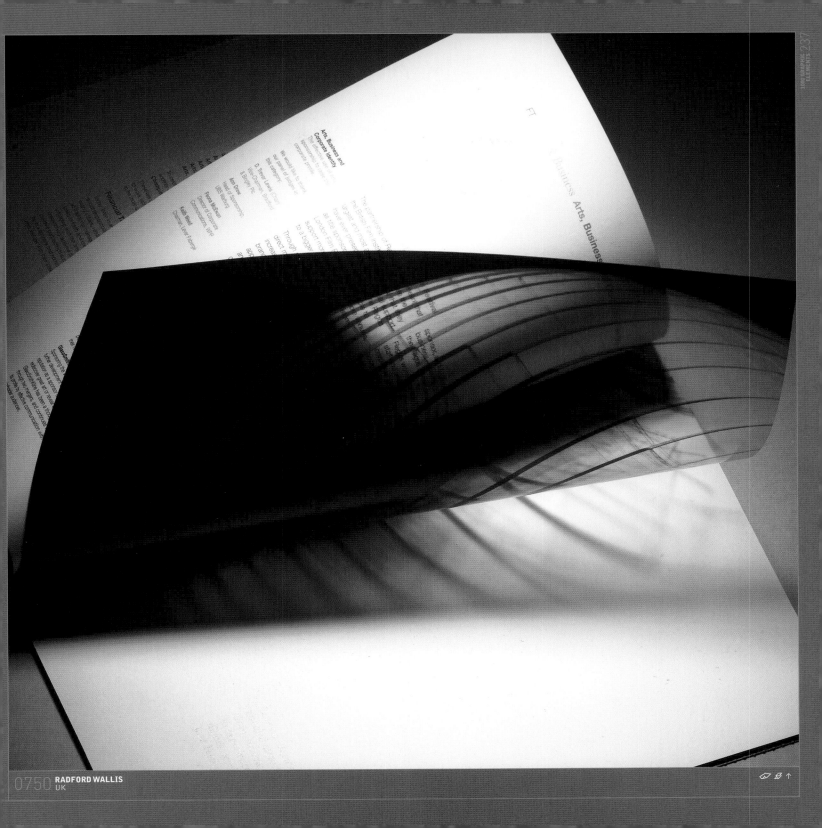

0752 **PROGRESS**
UK

0753 **REEBOK DESIGN SERVICES**
USA

0754 **PROGRESS**
UK

0755 **BELYEA**
USA

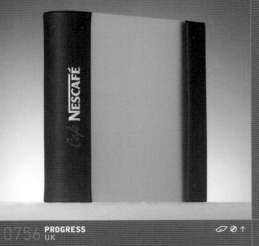

0756 **PROGRESS**
UK

0757 **PHILLIPS**
UK

0758 **EGBG**
THE NETHERLANDS

0759 **BELYEA**
USA

0760 **UNTITLED**
UK

0761 **JONES DESIGN GROUP**
USA

0762 **CARTER WONG TOMLIN**
UK

0763 **HARRIMANSTEEL**
UK

0764 **POINT BLANK DESIGN**
UK

ENJOY THE WEATHER

DOES YOUR DESIGN
AGENCY'S WORK WORK?

IT'S TIME YOU CHANGED
YOUR DESIGN AGENCY.

From January 2004 there will be a brand new design agency with over 30 years of combined experience. HGV and Felton Communication are about to merge our like-minded agencies to deliver even more lateral thinking that is logically effective. In other words, work that works.

For more details on the new agency please call Roger Felton on 020 7405 0900.

To see some of the work that has won over 100 creative and business effectiveness awards so far, visit www.hgv.co.uk and www.feltoncom.com. Our new website, www.hgvfelton.com, will be operational from the 1st January.

Can they claim over 50 top creative awards? What's more, can they back them up with 4 internationally prestigious Design Effectiveness Awards — or other business effectiveness accolades?

If not, is it time for a change.

245 GRAPHIC ELEMENTS 245

0767 **PHILLIPS**
UK

SME FOCUS

SONY

0768 **YAEL MILLER DESIGN**
USA

Le Belge
CHOCOLATIER

0769 **UNTITLED**
UK

UNTITLED

Directions for Use
1. Peel open packaging
2. Look at leaflet
3. Go to www.untitled.co.uk
4. Choose from thousands of images

©Untitled

9g

CONTEMPORARY
IMAGE
LIBRARY

WWW
UNTITLED
CO.UK

0770 **PH.D**
USA

TORRA
NCE
RRANC
E
W

DEVELOPMENTOR™

HAVE
TO
21535 HAWTHORNE BLVD, 4TH FLOOR
TORRANCE, CA 90503 (310) 543-1716
FAX (310) 543-2136   1-800-699-1932

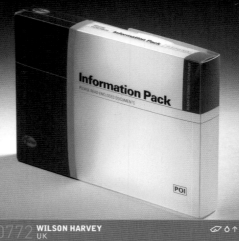

0771 **HARRIMANSTEEL**
UK

0772 **WILSON HARVEY**
UK

0773 **FORTYFOUR DESIGN**
AUSTRALIA

0774 **...,STAAT**
THE NETHERLANDS

0775 **TONIC**
UK

0776 **MAGMA**
GERMANY

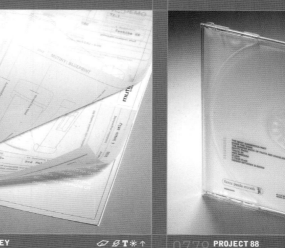

0777 **FAITH**
CANADA

0778 **WILSON HARVEY**
UK

0779 **PROJECT 88**
UK

0786 **KESSELS KRAMER**
THE NETHERLANDS

0787 **DINNICK & HOWELLS**
CANADA

0788 **CRUSH DESIGN**
UK

0789 **AFTERHOURS CREATIVE**
USA

0790 **ELMWOOD**
UK

0791 **ELMWOOD**
UK

0792 **METAL**
USA

0793 **AFTERHOURS CREATIVE**
USA

0794 **FIBRE**
UK

X-RAY FILMS

LÁMINAS RAYOS-X / RADIOGRAFIE
RÖNTGENAUFNAHMEN / FILMS RADIOGRAPHIQUE

0801 **GIORGIO DAVANZO DESIGN**
USA

greetings

greetings

giorgio davanzo design
www.davanzodesign.com

giorgio davanzo design
www.davanzodesign.com

0802 **ELMWOOD**
UK

HOT TIN ROOF

HOT TIN ROOF

HOT TIN ROOF

SARAH A. LEE

48

E:

SARAH A. LEE

48

E:

SARAH A. LEE

48

E:

0803 **SELTZER DESIGN**
USA

Mond

Erde

SONNE
celebrates new beginnings

a new year ahead

0804 **WILSON HARVEY**
UK

INNOVATION

NB:STUDIO
UK

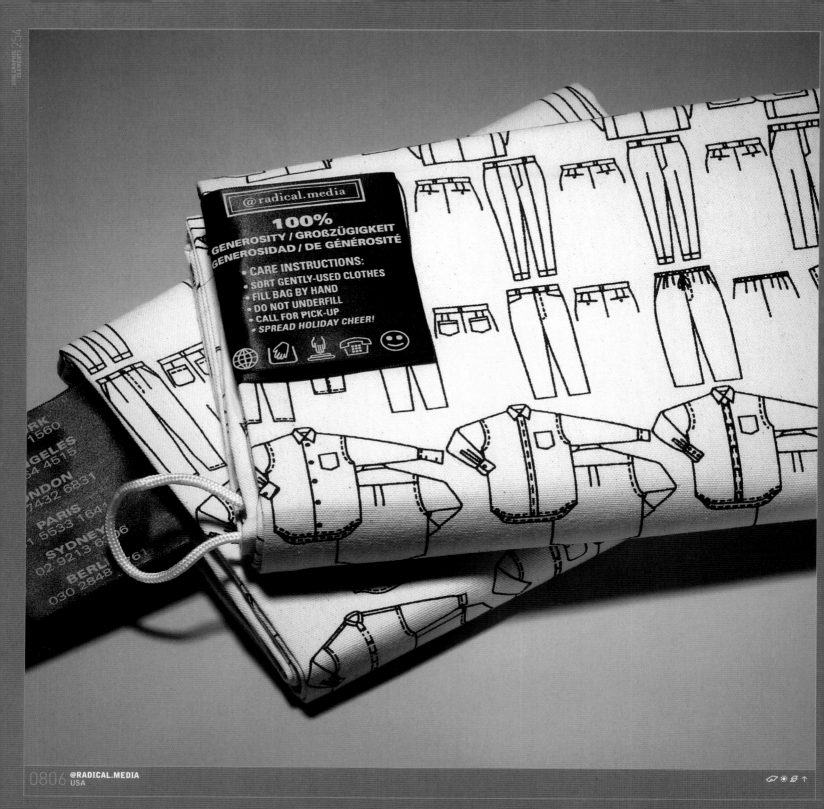

@radical.media

100%
GENEROSITY / GROßZÜGIGKEIT
GENEROSIDAD / DE GÉNÉROSITÉ

• CARE INSTRUCTIONS:
• SORT GENTLY-USED CLOTHES
• FILL BAG BY HAND
• DO NOT UNDERFILL
• CALL FOR PICK-UP
• SPREAD HOLIDAY CHEER!

0807	**MONDERER DESIGN** USA	
0808	**BBK STUDIO** USA	
0809	**BLOK DESIGN** MEXICO	

0810	**JADE DESIGN** UK	
0811	**UNTITLED** UK	
0812	**HARRIMANSTEEL** UK	

0813	**ZULVER & CO** UK	
0814	**PH.D** USA	
0815	**THE WORKS DESIGN COMMUNICATIONS** CANADA	

0816 **HGV FELTON**
UK

0817 **WEBB & WEBB**
UK

ELFEN — RYDYM WEDI SYMUD I SWYDDFA NEWYDD SBON, CROESO I CHI ALW HEIBIO UNRHYW BRYD. WE HAVE MOVED TO A NICE NEW OFFICE, FEEL FREE TO VISIT US ANYTIME.

20 HARROWBY LANE, BAE CAERDYDD/CARDI
e: post@elfen.co.u
t: 029 2048 4824 f: 029 2048 4823

0818 **ELFEN**
WALES

0819 **BISQIT DESIGN**
UK

john patrick higgins

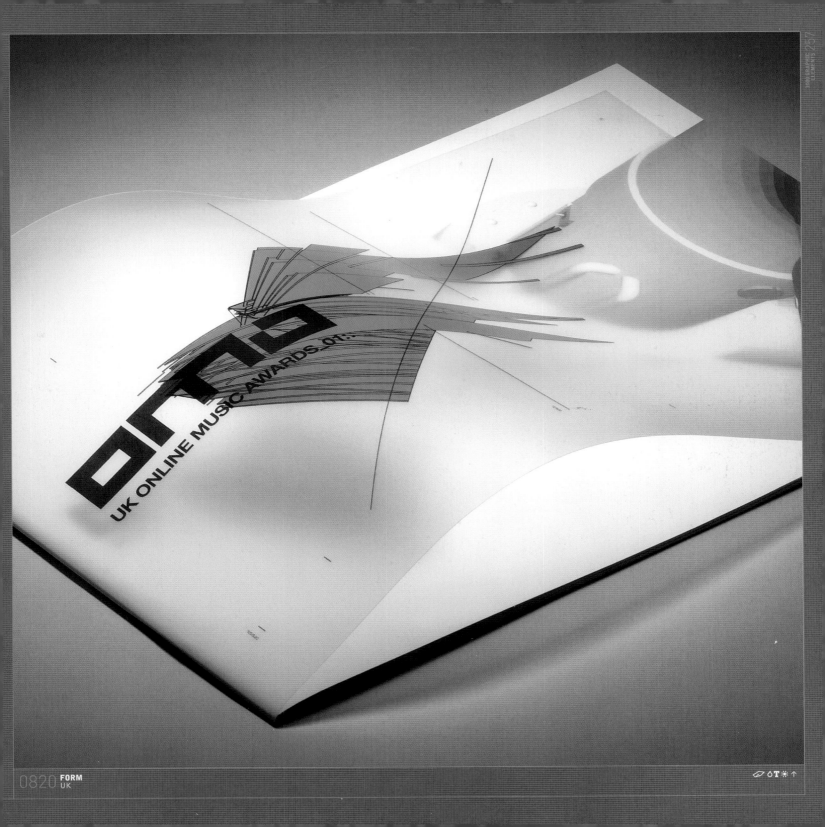

UK ONLINE MUSIC AWARDS_OT

0821

_06

GRAPHIC
DEVICES

TYPETREATMENT
GRAPHIC ELEMENTS
IMAGE MANIPULATION

1000

0821 **SCANDINAVIAN DESIGN GROUP**
DENMARK
T ↑

0822 **ZIP DESIGN**
UK
T ☀ ⊘ ✍ ↑

0823 **LCTS**
UK
T ☀ ◊ ↑

0824 **CAPSULE**
USA
T ☀ ◊ ↑

0827 MACHINE
THE NETHERLANDS

0828 MACHINE
THE NETHERLANDS

0829 MACHINE
THE NETHERLANDS

0830 CUCKOOLAND
UK

0831 MACHINE
THE NETHERLANDS

0832 AND PARTNERS
USA

0833 MACHINE
THE NETHERLANDS

0834 BASIA KNOBLOCH
THE NETHERLANDS

0835 KOEWEIDEN POSTMA
THE NETHERLANDS

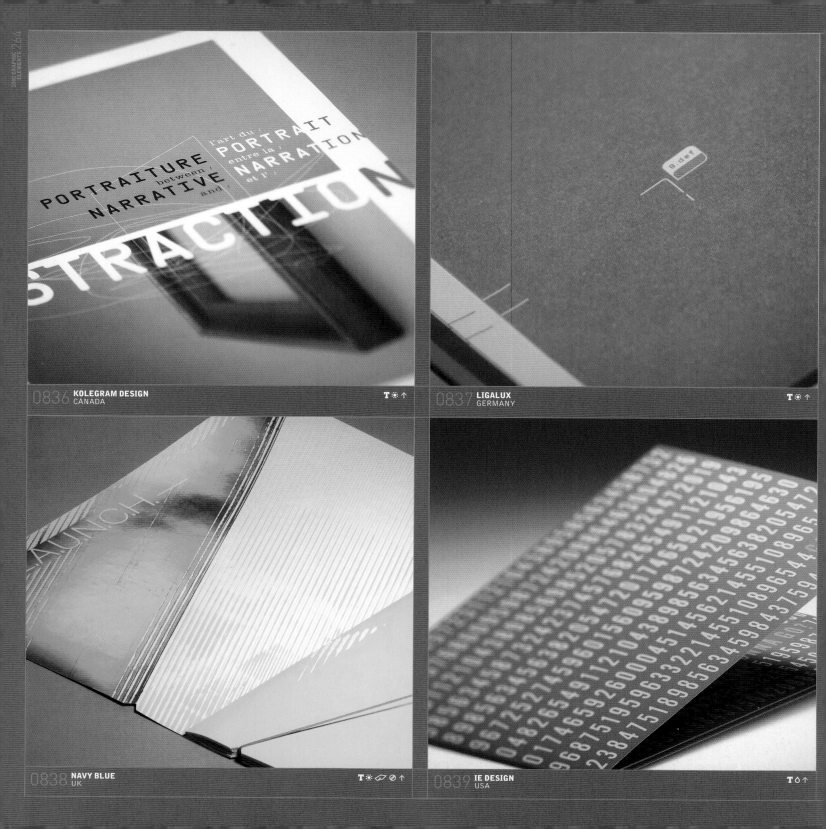

0836 **KOLEGRAM DESIGN**
CANADA
T ✳ ↑

0837 **LIGALUX**
GERMANY
T ✳ ↑

0838 **NAVY BLUE**
UK
T ✳ ⬮ ⊘ ↑

0839 **IE DESIGN**
USA
T ⬮ ↑

3XW
DOTCOM
NO DEAD ENDS
WAY STREETS

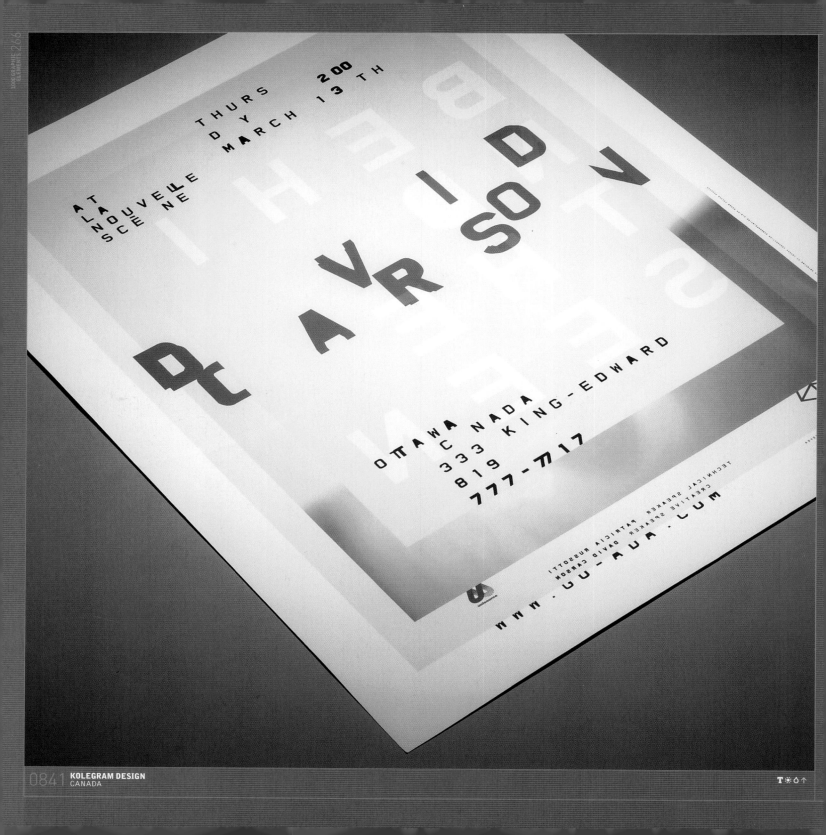

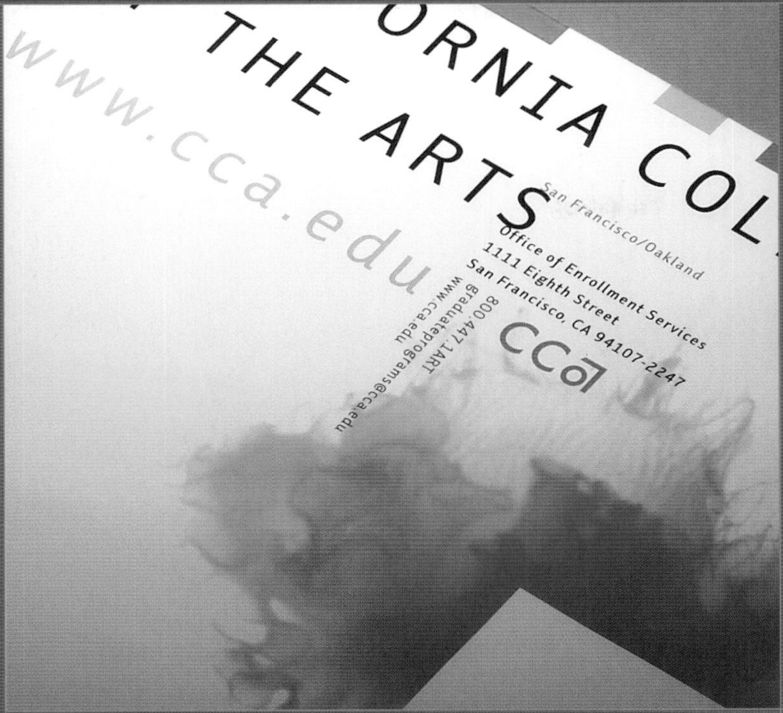

0842 **AUFULDISH & WARINNER**
USA

0843 **FIBRE**
UK

0844 **...,STAAT**
THE NETHERLANDS

0845 **TRACY DESIGN**
USA

0846 **BLOK DESIGN**
MEXICO

0847 **MARIUS FAHRNER DESIGN**
GERMANY

0848 **STARSHOT**
GERMANY

0849 **GROOTHUIS + MALSY**
UK

startalk

Warum
rasiert sich Simoni die Be

052

054

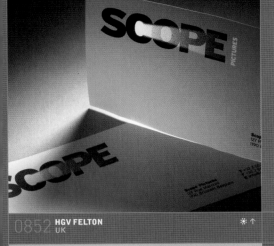

0852 HGV FELTON
UK

0853 CUCKOOLAND
UK

0854 CUCKOOLAND
UK

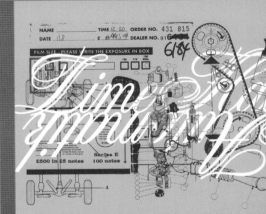

0855 LIPPA PEARCE DESIGN
UK

0856 SAS
UK

0857 CUCKOOLAND
UK

0858 CUCKOOLAND
UK

0859 CUCKOOLAND
UK

0860 AUFULDISH & WARINNER
USA

03 10/

MÄRZ / MARCH / MARS / MARZO //

heartbeat
MOMENT # 03 ≙ HEARTFACT, NR 3

AT THE HEART OF THE HEART

PUMPLEISTUNG (PRO STUNDE)
>>> durchschnittliche pumpleistung des herzens eines erwachsenen

normalzustand 300 l / h ·

during heartbeat moments 450 l / h **

PERFORMANCE (PER HOUR) >>> average performance of an adult's heart · normal state 300 l / h
CAPACITÉ DU CŒUR À POMPER (PAR HEURE) > capacité horaire d'un cœur adulte à pomper · état normal 300 l / h
PULSAZIONI (ALL'ORA) > pulsazioni medie del cuore di un adulto · situazione normale 300 l / h //

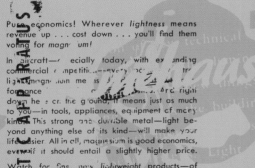

0862 ...,STAAT
THE NETHERLANDS
T ✳ ◊ ↑

0863 GILLESPIE DESIGN
USA
T ✳ ↑

0864 CUCKOOLAND
UK
T ✳ ◊ ⬳ ↑

0865 KOLEGRAM DESIGN
CANADA
T ⬡ ⬳ ✳ ◊ ↑

0866   **KOLEGRAM DESIGN**
CANADA   T ✳ ◊ ↑

0867   **CDT DESIGN**
UK   T ◊ ↑

0868   **VIVA DOLAN COMMUNICATIONS & DESIGN**
CANADA   ✳ ↑

0869   **CDT DESIGN**
UK   T ◊ ✑ ↑

0870   **MOTIVE DESIGN RESEARCH**
USA   T ◊ ✳ ✐ ✑ ↑

0871   **THOMPSON**
UK   T ✳ ✐ ↑

0872   **STOLTZE DESIGN**
USA   ✳ ◊ ↑

0873   **SCANDINAVIAN DESIGN GROUP**
DENMARK   T ✑ ↑

0874   **SCANDINANVIAN DESIGN GROUP**
DENMARK   T ✳ ✐ ↑

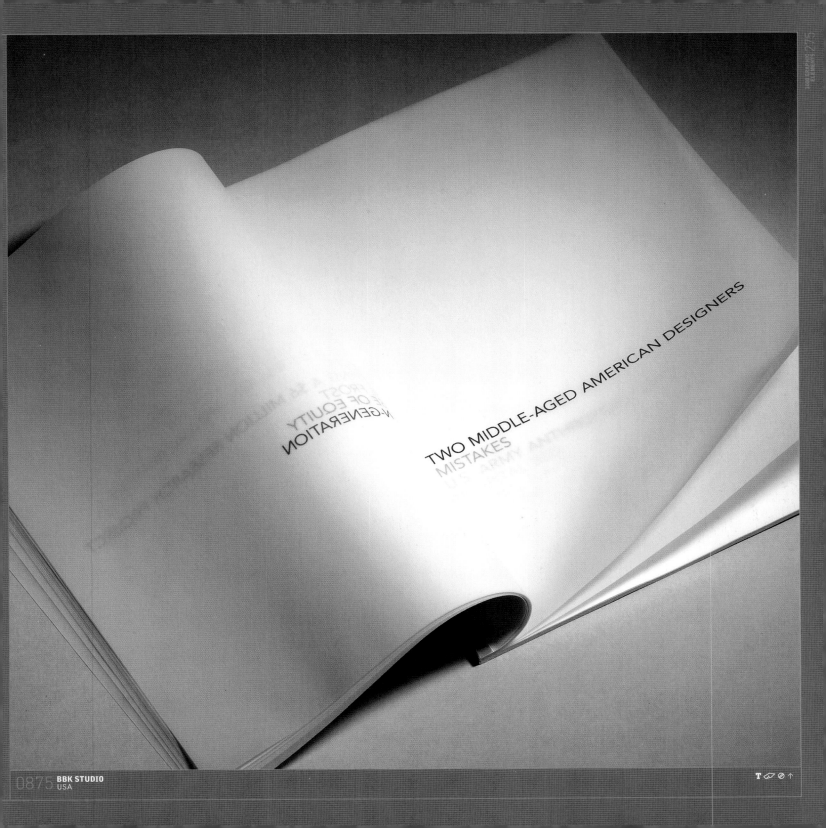

A COLLECTION OF
10 POSTCARDS

TEN POSTCARDS WITH UNIQUE VISUAL
NARRATIVES THAT PAY TRIBUTE TO THE MOST
POWERFUL METHOD OF COMMUNICATION —
THE HUMAN VOICE

0877 **RADLEY YELDAR**
UK

0878 **CHEN DESIGN ASSOCIATES**
USA

0879 **LIPPA PEARCE DESIGN**
UK

0880 **GREENZWEIG DESIGN**
USA

0881 **SALTERBAXTER**
UK

0882 **SCANDINAVIAN DESIGN GROUP**
DENMARK

0883 **SALTERBAXTER**
UK

0884 **WALLACE CHURCH**
USA

0885 **V06**
BRAZIL

0886 **CHEN DESIGN ASSOCIATES**
USA

T ✳ ❧ ↑

0887 **GOUTHIER DESIGN**
USA

T ✳ ☰ ↑

0888 **MIRIELLO GRAFICO**
USA

T ✳ ◊ ↑

0889 **CRUSH DESIGN**
UK

✳ ✐ ◯ ↑

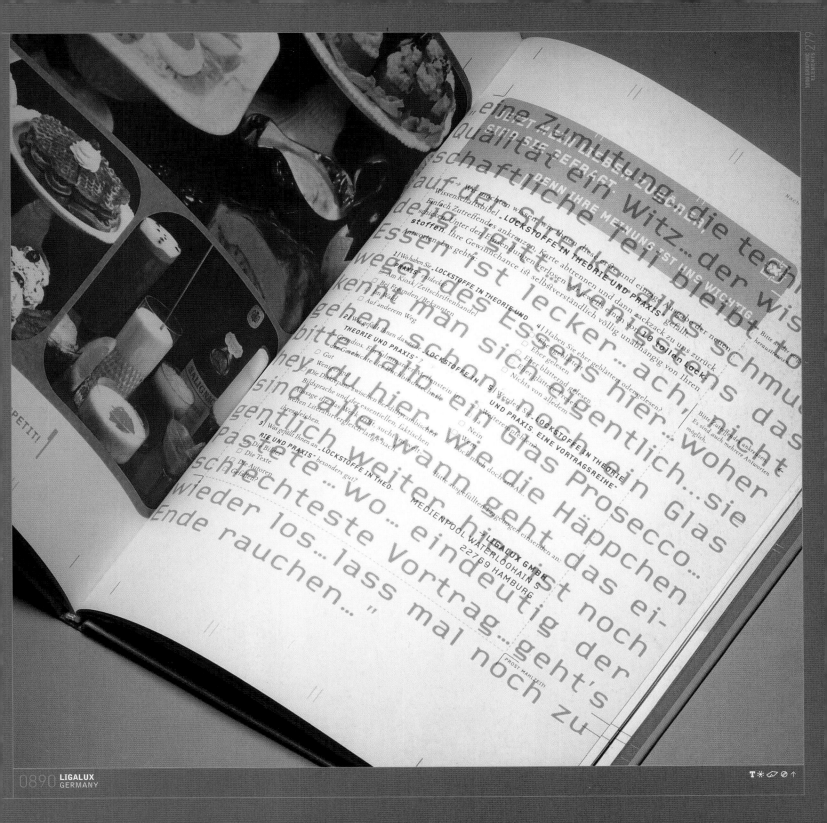

0891 **MADE THOUGHT**
UK
T ○ ◇ ↑

0892 **BLOK DESIGN**
MEXICO
T ☀ ◇ ↑

0893 **THE DESIGN DELL**
UK
T ↑

0894 **KOLEGRAM DESIGN**
CANADA
T ○ ◇ ⊘ ↑

0895 **SAS**
UK
T ↑

0896 **D-FUSE**
UK
T ☀ ↑

0897 **MIRIELLO GRAFICO**
USA
T ☀ ○ ◇ ✎ ↑

0898 **FAITH**
CANADA
T ☀ ◇ ↑

0899 **PLAN-B STUDIO**
UK
T ☀ ↑

Telefonseelsorge Jahresbericht 1999

f . i

raum

r e

ituation

m

elt

w

s e

0902 **KOLEGRAM DESIGN**
CANADA

0903 **JONES DESIGN GROUP**
UK

0904 **AUFULDISH & WARINNER**
USA

0905 **MACHINE**
THE NETHERLANDS

0906 **SAMPSONMAY**
UK

0907 **METAL**
USA

0908 **CUCKOOLAND**
UK

0909 **THE FAMILY**
UK

0910 **EGBG**
THE NETHERLANDS

T✳∅↑

0916 **PHYX DESIGN**
USA

0917 **MORLA DESIGN**
USA

0918 **MADE THOUGHT**
UK

0919 **LIGALUX**
GERMANY

0920 **ROYCROFT DESIGN**
USA

0921 **TAXI STUDIO**
UK

0922 **FOTOGRAFIE & GESTALTUNG
CHRISTIAN NIELINGER**
GERMANY

0923 **BBK STUDIO**
USA

0924 **PH.D**
USA

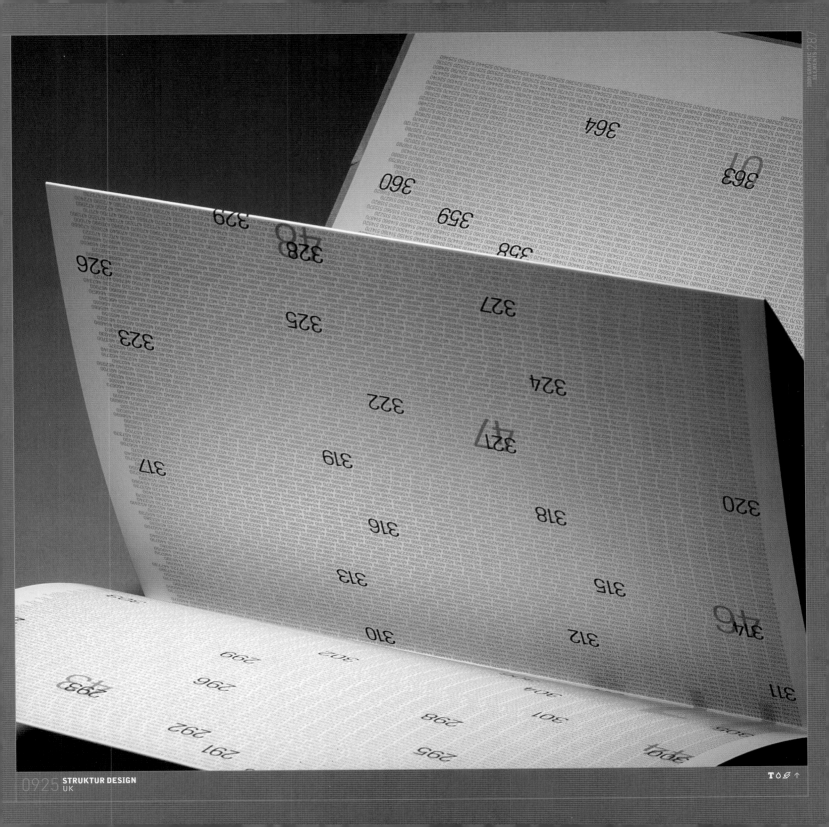

0927 **DESIGN DEPOT CREATIVE BUREAU**
RUSSIA

0928 **DESIGN DEPOT CREATIVE BUREAU**
RUSSIA

0929 **DESIGN DEPOT CREATIVE BUREAU**
RUSSIA

0930 **DESIGN DEPOT CREATIVE BUREAU**
RUSSIA

0931 **DESIGN DEPOT CREATIVE BUREAU**
RUSSIA

0932 **DESIGN DEPOT CREATIVE BUREAU**
RUSSIA

0933 **DESIGN DEPOT CREATIVE BUREAU**
RUSSIA

0934 **DESIGN DEPOT CREATIVE BUREAU**
RUSSIA

0935 **DESIGN DEPOT CREATIVE BUREAU**
RUSSIA

0937 D-FUSE
UK
T ✳ ⬚ ♢ ↑

0938 DESIGN HOCH DREI
GERMANY
T ✳ ⬚ ↑

0939 BWA DESIGN
UK
T ⬚ ♢ ♢ ↑

At the International Art Exhibi...

Introduction

AFTER YEARS OF MINIMALIST RULE, GRAPHI...
RETURN TO A MORE DECORATIVE, **MAXIMALIST** APPROACH...
ARCHITECTURE IS MORE CURVACEOUS, FASHION MORE GLA...
SILHOUETTE AND BOTANICAL MOTIFS ARE T...

CHAPTER ONE
Decoration
Ornament, handicraft, technolog...

0940 HARRIMANSTEEL
UK
T ⬚ ↑

0941 WILSON HARVEY
UK
T ♢ ↑

0942 WILSON HARVEY
UK
T ✳ ↑

Maxima
THE GRAPHIC DESIGN OF DI...

Contents *Introduction*
004

...OWLEDGMENTS FIRSTLY, I
...SAY THANK-YOU TO ALL THE
...NERS AND CREATIVES WHO
...TTED WORK FOR INCLUSION
...S BOOK. WE RECEIVED SOME
...Y FANTASTIC PROJECTS AND
...ATELY, WITHOUT THEM,
...OOK WOULD NOT HAVE BEEN

0943 WILSON HARVEY
UK
T ✳ ♢ ↑

0944 WILSON HARVEY
UK
T ✳ ♢ ↑

0945 WILSON HARVEY
UK
T ✳ ↑

AUDIO**GRAPHIC**

FUNDRAISER

20 **SF** 03

0947 **CAHAN & ASSOCIATES**
USA   T ↑

0948 **UNTITLED**
UK   T ✳ ↑

0949 **CHIMERA DESIGN**
USA   T ✳ ◊ ↑

0950 **ZIP DESIGN**
UK   T ✳ ◊ ↑

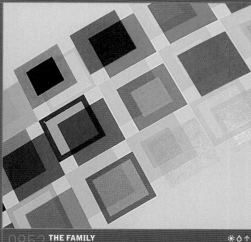

0951	**THE FAMILY** UK	T ☀ ↑
0952	**THE FAMILY** UK	☀ ◊ ↑
0953	**BAUMANN & BAUMANN** GERMANY	T ☀ ↑

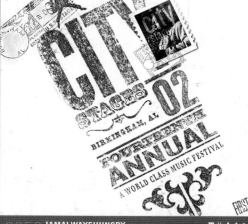

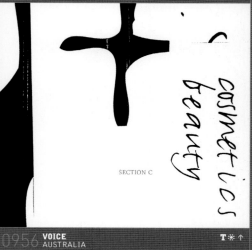

0954	**RADLEY YELDER** UK	T ↑
0955	**EMPIRE DESIGN STUDIO** USA	T ◊ ✍ ↑
0956	**VOICE** AUSTRALIA	T ☀ ↑

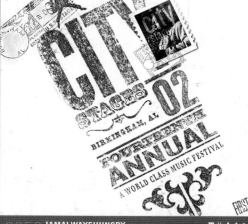

0957	**FROST DESIGN** UK	T ☀ ↑
0958	**IAMALWAYSHUNGRY** USA	T ☀ ✚ ◊ ↑
0959	**BAUMANN & BAUMANN** GERMANY	T ☀ ↑

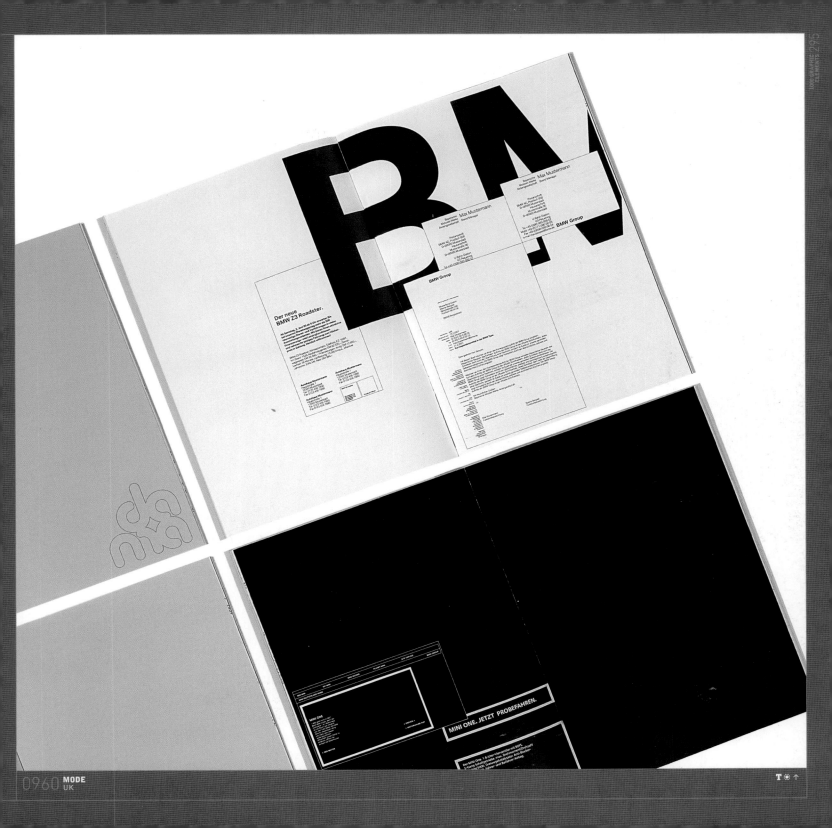

Michael Johnson

RUNNING:
99% MENTAL,
99% PHYSICAL.
AIR MAX

HAVE MERCY.
KILL QUICKLY.
Zoom Air
is speed

Jason Kidd

too FAST. too STRONG. too BAD.
Zoom Air
is speed
cushioning

Scottie Pippen

EVERYBODY GOTTA LAND sometime
AIR MAX
is maximum cushioning

FICTION TWO

UNDER THE WEATHER
BY JAMES HODKIN

proof.

vorlesungen zur filmprofessur. hochschule für gestaltung offenbach am main, schlossstraße 31, raum 101
01. 11. 02 freitag:: **stephan sachs** 09:00 uhr **dr. boris penth** 10:45 uhr **h. joachim hofmann** 13:00 uhr **reinhard franz** 14:45 uhr
04. 11. 02 montag:: **philine hofmann** 14:00 uhr **rotraut pape** 15:45 uhr **maike mia höhne** 17:30 uhr

0967 **MODE** UK T☀◊↑

0968 **MODE** UK T☀◊↑

0969 **MODE** UK T☀◊↑

0970 **MODE** UK T☀◊↑

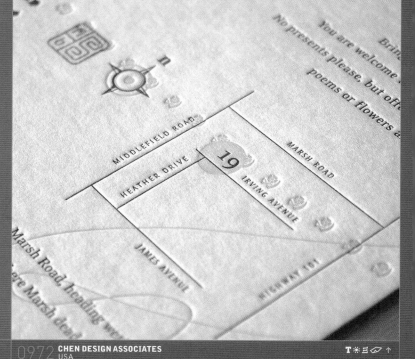

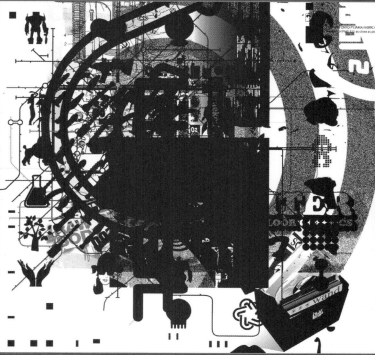

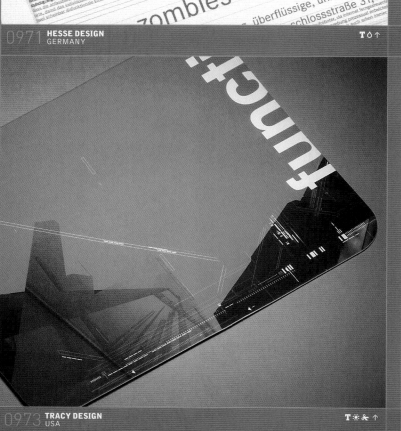

0971 **HESSE DESIGN**
GERMANY
T ○ ↑

0972 **CHEN DESIGN ASSOCIATES**
USA
T ✳ ☱ ◇ ↑

0973 **TRACY DESIGN**
USA
T ✳ ⚹ ↑

0974 **CRUSH DESIGN**
UK
T ✳ ↑

0976 **LIPPA PEARCE DESIGN**
UK

0977 **THIRTEEN**
UK

0978 **KOEWEIDEN POSTMA**
THE NETHERLANDS

0979 **TEMPLIN BRINK DESIGN**
USA

0980 **MORLA DESIGN**
USA

0981 **SAS**
UK

0982 **FELDER GRAFIKDESIGN**
AUSTRIA

0983 **GROOTHUIS + MALSY**
UK

0984 **IAMALWAYSHUNGRY**
USA

YOU R 3RD IN LINE>>>

0986 **FROST DESIGN**
UK   T ☀ ↑

0987 **MOTIVE DESIGN RESEARCH**
USA   T ⊘ ↑

0988 **DURSO DESIGN**
USA   T ☀ ◊ ↑

0989 **MODE**
UK   ☀ ↑

SANCHAKOU
BY MATTHEW KNEALE
Photograph by Nadav Kander

A PASSION
FOR PICTURES

YOU'VE ALREADY BEEN MOVED
BY ONE OF OUR IMAGES.

It made you laugh. Or made you think. Or made
You see images every day in magazines, on TV
surprised how many of them come from Getty

getty images

DURSODESIGN
communication/arts/design
address
1404 3rd Street Promenade, Suite 202
Santa Monica, CA 90401

start:-

to:-

DURSODESIGN
BOVANE DURSO

#090

D-FUSE

PRESENTS
PAOLA
MARANGOLO
/ALTER EGO
(ITALY)

TITLE LIGHTMOTIV

CONTACT
P.O.BOX 39943, LONDON EC1V 0YZ, UK.
T.+44 (0)20 7253 3462 F.+44 (0)20 7566 0181
E-MAIL 061@DFUSE.COM WEB WWW.DFUSE.COM

T✳↑

0992 **IRIDIUM, A DESIGN AGENCY**
CANADA T ◊ ↑

0993 **KINETIC SINGAPORE**
SINGAPORE T ↑

0994 **IAMALWAYSHUNGRY**
USA T ✳ ◊ ↑

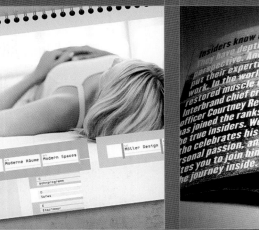

0995 **KEARNEY ROCHOLL**
GERMANY T ✳ ∅ ↑

0996 **MIRES**
USA T ⊘ ↑

0997 **KESSELS KRAMER**
THE NETHERLANDS T ✑ ↑

0998 **KOEWEIDEN POSTMA**
THE NETHERLANDS T ✳ ↑

0999 **SELTZER DESIGN**
USA T ✳ ✑ ↑

1000 **FROST DESIGN**
UK T ✳ ✳ ↑

0001 0002 0003 0004 0005 0006 0007 0008 0009 0010 0011 0012 0013 0014 0015 0016 0017 0018 0019 0020 0021 0022 0023 0024 0025
0026 0027 0028 0029 0030 0031 0032 0033 0034 0035 0036 0037 0038 0039 0040 0041 0042 0043 0044 0045 0046 0047 0048 0049 0050
0051 0052 0053 0054 0055 0056 0057 0058 0059 0060 0061 0062 0063 0064 0065 0066 0067 0068 0069 0070 0071 0072 0073 0074 0075
0076 0077 0078 0079 0080 0081 0082 0083 0084 0085 0086 0087 0088 0089 0090 0091 0092 0093 0094 0095 0096 0097 0098 0099 0100
0101 0102 0103 0104 0105 0106 0107 0108 0109 0110 0111 0112 0113 0114 0115 0116 0117 0118 0119 0120 0121 0122 0123 0124 0125
0126 0127 0128 0129 0130 0131 0132 0133 0134 0135 0136 0137 0138 0139 0140 0141 0142 0143 0144 0145 0146 0147 0148 0149 0150
0151 0152 0153 0154 0155 0156 0157 0158 0159 0160 0161 0162 0163 0164 0165 0166 0167 0168 0169 0170 0171 0172 0173 0174 0175
0176 0177 0178 0179 0180 0181 0182 0183 0184 0185 0186 0187 0188 0189 0190 0191 0192 0193 0194 0195 0196 0197 0198 0199 0200
0201 0202 0203 0204 0205 0206 0207 0208 0209 0210 0211 0212 0213 0214 0215 0216 0217 0218 0219 0220 0221 0222 0223 0224 0225
0226 0227 0228 0229 0230 0231 0232 0233 0234 0235 0236 0237 0238 0239 0240 0241 0242 0243 0244 0245 0246 0247 0248 0249 0250
0251 0252 0253 0254 0255 0256 0257 0258 0259 0260 0261 0262 0263 0264 0265 0266 0267 0268 0269 0270 0271 0272 0273 0274 0275
0276 0277 0278 0279 0280 0281 0282 0283 0284 0285 0286 0287 0288 0289 0290 0291 0292 0293 0294 0295 0296 0297 0298 0299 0300
0301 0302 0303 0304 0305 0306 0307 0308 0309 0310 0311 0312 0313 0314 0315 0316 0317 0318 0319 0320 0321 0322 0323 0324 0325
0326 0327 0328 0329 0330 0331 0332 0333 0334 0335 0336 0337 0338 0339 0340 0341 0342 0343 0344 0345 0346 0347 0348 0349 0350
0351 0352 0353 0354 0355 0356 0357 0358 0359 0360 0361 0362 0363 0364 0365 0366 0367 0368 0369 0370 0371 0372 0373 0374 0375
0376 0377 0378 0379 0380 0381 0382 0383 0384 0385 0386 0387 0388 0389 0390 0391 0392 0393 0394 0395 0396 0397 0398 0399 0400
0401 0402 0403 0404 0405 0406 0407 0408 0409 0410 0411 0412 0413 0414 0415 0416 0417 0418 0419 0420 0421 0422 0423 0424 0425
0426 0427 0428 0429 0430 0431 0432 0433 0434 0435 0436 0437 0438 0439 0440 0441 0442 0443 0444 0445 0446 0447 0448 0449 0450
0451 0452 0453 0454 0455 0456 0457 0458 0459 0460 0461 0462 0463 0464 0465 0466 0467 0468 0469 0470 0471 0472 0473 0474 0475
0476 0477 0478 0479 0480 0481 0482 0483 0484 0485 0486 0487 0488 0489 0490 0491 0492 0493 0494 0495 0496 0497 0498 0499 0500
0501 0502 0503 0504 0505 0506 0507 0508 0509 0510 0511 0512 0513 0514 0515 0516 0517 0518 0519 0520 0521 0522 0523 0524 0525
0526 0527 0528 0529 0530 0531 0532 0533 0534 0535 0536 0537 0538 0539 0540 0541 0542 0543 0544 0545 0546 0547 0548 0549 0550
0551 0552 0553 0554 0555 0556 0557 0558 0559 0560 0561 0562 0563 0564 0565 0566 0567 0568 0569 0570 0571 0572 0573 0574 0575
0576 0577 0578 0579 0580 0581 0582 0583 0584 0585 0586 0587 0588 0589 0590 0591 0592 0593 0594 0595 0596 0597 0598 0599 0600
0601 0602 0603 0604 0605 0606 0607 0608 0609 0610 0611 0612 0613 0614 0615 0616 0617 0618 0619 0620 0621 0622 0623 0624 0625
0626 0627 0628 0629 0630 0631 0632 0633 0634 0635 0636 0637 0638 0639 0640 0641 0642 0643 0644 0645 0646 0647 0648 0649 0650
0651 0652 0653 0654 0655 0656 0657 0658 0659 0660 0661 0662 0663 0664 0665 0666 0667 0668 0669 0670 0671 0672 0673 0674 0675
0676 0677 0678 0679 0680 0681 0682 0683 0684 0685 0686 0687 0688 0689 0690 0691 0692 0693 0694 0695 0696 0697 0698 0699 0700
0701 0702 0703 0704 0705 0706 0707 0708 0709 0710 0711 0712 0713 0714 0715 0716 0717 0718 0719 0720 0721 0722 0723 0724 0725
0726 0727 0728 0729 0730 0731 0732 0733 0734 0735 0736 0737 0738 0739 0740 0741 0742 0743 0744 0745 0746 0747 0748 0749 0750
0751 0752 0753 0754 0755 0756 0757 0758 0759 0760 0761 0762 0763 0764 0765 0766 0767 0768 0769 0770 0771 0772 0773 0774 0775
0776 0777 0778 0779 0780 0781 0782 0783 0784 0785 0786 0787 0788 0789 0790 0791 0792 0793 0794 0795 0796 0797 0798 0799 0800
0801 0802 0803 0804 0805 0806 0807 0808 0809 0810 0811 0812 0813 0814 0815 0816 0817 0818 0819 0820 0821 0822 0823 0824 0825
0826 0827 0828 0829 0830 0831 0832 0833 0834 0835 0836 0837 0838 0839 0840 0841 0842 0843 0844 0845 0846 0847 0848 0849 0850
0851 0852 0853 0854 0855 0856 0857 0858 0859 0860 0861 0862 0863 0864 0865 0866 0867 0868 0869 0870 0871 0872 0873 0874 0875
0876 0877 0878 0879 0880 0881 0882 0883 0884 0885 0886 0887 0888 0889 0890 0891 0892 0893 0894 0895 0896 0897 0898 0899 0900
0901 0902 0903 0904 0905 0906 0907 0908 0909 0910 0911 0912 0913 0914 0915 0916 0917 0918 0919 0920 0921 0922 0923 0924 0925
0926 0927 0928 0929 0930 0931 0932 0933 0934 0935 0936 0937 0938 0939 0940 0941 0942 0943 0944 0945 0946 0947 0948 0949 0950
0951 0952 0953 0954 0955 0956 0957 0958 0959 0960 0961 0962 0963 0964 0965 0966 0967 0968 0969 0970 0971 0972 0973 0974 0975
0976 0977 0978 0979 0980 0981 0982 0983 0984 0985 0986 0987 0988 0989 0990 0991 0992 0993 0994 0995 0996 0997 0998 0999 1000

9th

NOISE

UNIFORM, DRABNESS

DECAY

240v

ELEVATION

TRANSFORMER

WATTS

NEVER SEEN THE 9TH FLOOR / NO SENSE LOSS / NOISE / PARTICULATE / CONCRETE / BEST OFFICE IN THE BUILDING / COMES UP HERE / ELEVATION / 3 PHASE / NOISE AGGREGATES ONLY REALLY KNOW THIS BLOCK / GRANITE ALL WEATHERS / STAIRWELL / A FRIEND / 2 FLOORS UP / CAN RES WEATHER / HEAR THE TA'PIPE / CLEANING SERVICES / DUCTS / CORRESPONDING TO HEAR / ROOF SLAB / BASEMENT / ELECTRICAL / GREAT MEMORIES / FOR THE EXIT / WATCH OTHER BUILDINGS / THE LOST, LOOKING / SCHOOL OF ART, ARCHITECTURE AND DESIGN / SEEN EVERY FLOOR EXCEPT 6 / SMOKERS / STAND OUTSIDE / TOO HIGH FOR A FIRE ENGINE / LADDER

@RADICAL.MEDIA
0110
ART DIRECTOR: RAFAEL ESQUER DESIGNERS: RAFAEL ESQUER PRODUCER: GEOFF REINHARD CLIENT: @RADICAL.MEDIA TOOLS: ILLUSTRATOR, PHOTOSHOP, MAC MATERIALS: ANIMATED 3D LENTICULAR IMAGE

0739
ART DIRECTOR: RAFAEL ESQUER DESIGNERS: WENDY WEN, JONATHAN EVA CLIENT: OUTPOST DIGITAL TOOLS: ILLUSTRATOR, QUARK, MAC MATERIALS: TRANSILWRAP PLASTICS FROSTY CLEAR MATTE, CALENDARED VINYL

0806
ART DIRECTOR: RAFAEL ESQUER DESIGNERS: RAFAEL ESQUER, WENDY WEN PRODUCTION SUPERVISOR: WENDY WEN CLIENT: @RADI-CAL.MEDIA COPYWRITER: GREGORY GROSS PRODUCTION TEAM: HEIKE SPERBER, JAY MIOLLA, JÖRG SCHEUERPFLUG PRODUCTION INTERN: NADIA VERTLIB PRINTER: JOE PRESTINO TOOLS: ILLUSTRATOR, MAC MATERIALS: CANVAS, BLACK RIBBON

A2-GRAPHICS/SW/HK
0461
ART DIRECTORS: SCOTT WILLIAM, HENRIK KUBEL DESIGNERS: SCOTT WILLIAM, HENRIK KUBEL CLIENT: THE INTERNATIONAL SOCIETY OF TYPOGRAPHIC DESIGNERS TOOLS: MAC MATERIALS: CONSORT ROYAL

0463
ART DIRECTORS: SCOTT WILLIAM, HENRIK KUBEL DESIGNERS: SCOTT WILLIAM, HENRIK KUBEL CLIENT: 1508 MATERIALS: LUMI SILK

0499
ART DIRECTORS: SCOTT WILLIAM, HENRIK KUBEL DESIGNERS: SCOTT WILLIAM, HENRIK KUBEL CLIENT: ARNOLFINI TOOLS: MAC MATERIALS: MUNKEN LYNX, CONSORT ROYAL

0646
ART DIRECTORS: SCOTT WILLIAM, HENRIK KUBEL DESIGNERS: SCOTT WILLIAM, HENRIK KUBEL CLIENT: HAYWARD GALLERY/ARTS COUNCIL COLLECTION MATERIALS: COLOURPLAN, ARTIC SILK

ABOUD SADANO
0435
ART DIRECTOR: ALAN ABOUD DESIGNERS: ELLIE RIDSDALE, ALAN ABOUT CLIENT: PAUL SMITH

ADDUCI STUDIOS
0288
ART DIRECTOR: STEPHEN ADDUCI DESIGNER: STEPHEN ADDUCI CLIENT: ADDUCI STUDIOS TOOLS: ILLUSTRATOR, MAC

AFTERHOURS CREATIVE
0173
ART DIRECTOR: AFTERHOURS DESIGNER: AFTERHOURS CLIENT: CLEARDATA.NET TOOLS: ILLUSTRATOR

0390
ART DIRECTOR: AFTERHOURS DESIGNER: AFTERHOURS CLIENT: BLUESPACE TOOLS: ILLUSTRATOR

0644, 0793
ART DIRECTOR: AFTERHOURS DESIGNER: AFTERHOURS CLIENT: COTTON CENTER TOOLS: ILLUSTRATOR MATERIALS: COTTON

0645
ART DIRECTOR: AFTERHOURS DESIGNER: AFTERHOURS CLIENT: ROSIN + BOULÉ TOOLS: ILLUSTRATOR

0650
ART DIRECTOR: AFTERHOURS DESIGNER: AFTERHOURS CLIENT: AFTERHOURS TOOLS: ILLUSTRATOR MATERIALS: JIFFY POP

0789
ART DIRECTOR: AFTERHOURS DESIGNER: AFTERHOURS CLIENT: MAX + LUCY TOOLS: ILLUSTRATOR MATERIALS: CARDBOARD, RUBBER STAMPS

ALOOF DESIGN
0092
ART DIRECTOR: SAM ALOOF DESIGNER: CHRIS BARHAM CLIENT: GEORGINA GOODMAN MATERIALS: MACHINE-COATED, 1-SIDED TISSUE PAPER

0268
ART DIRECTOR: SAM ALOOF DESIGNER: SAM ALOOF CLIENT: GEORGINA GOODMAN MATERIALS: G.F. SMITH COLOURPLAN MIST MATT LAM

0275
ART DIRECTOR: SAM ALOOF DESIGNER: SAM ALOOF CLIENT: GEORGINA GOODMAN MATERIALS: CX22

AND PARTNERS
0311
ART DIRECTOR: DAVID SCHIMMEL DESIGNER: DAVID SCHIMMEL CLIENT: AND PARTNERS TOOLS: ILLUSTRATOR, MAC

0552
ART DIRECTOR: DAVID SCHIMMEL CLIENT: AMEX PUBLISHING TOOLS: QUARK, MAC MATERIALS: BIBLE PAPER, SUNDANCE BEET, CRANE'S

0595
ART DIRECTOR: DAVID SCHIMMEL DESIGNER: SARAH HOLLOWOOD CLIENT: AND PARTNERS TOOLS: PHOTOSHOP, QUARK, MAC

0600
ART DIRECTOR: DAVID SCHIMMEL CLIENT: AND PARTNERS TOOLS: ILLUSTRATOR, QUARK, MAC MATERIALS: MOHAWK SUPERFINE, GROMMETS

0722
ART DIRECTOR: DAVID SCHIMMEL CLIENT: BRINSILLITS/NYC TOOLS: QUARK MATERIALS: ZANDERS METALLIC AND SAPPI COATED

0832
ART DIRECTOR: DAVID SCHIMMEL DESIGNER: TYLER SMALL CLIENT: B-HIVE STUDIO TOOLS: ILLUSTRATOR, QUARK, MAC MATERIALS: MOHAWK OPTIONS SUPERFINE

ANDERSON THOMAS DESIGN
0096
ART DIRECTOR: JAY SMITH DESIGNER: JAY SMITH CLIENT: W PUBLISHING TOOLS: QUARK, PHOTOSHOP MATERIALS: FRENCH BUTCHER COVER AND TEXT

0269
ART DIRECTORS: JOEL ANDERSON, ROY ROPER DESIGNER: ROY ROPER CLIENT: ANDERSON THOMAS DESIGN TOOLS: PHOTOSHOP, QUARK

0486
ART DIRECTOR: JAY SMITH DESIGNER: JAY SMITH CLIENT: ROCKETOWN YOUTH SERVICES TOOLS: PHOTOSHOP, QUARK, MAC MATERIALS: GILBERT ESSE 80LB COVER

AUFULDISH & WARINNER
0842
DESIGNER: BOB AUDFULDISH CLIENT: CALIFORNIA COLLEGE OF ARTS AND CRAFTS TOOLS: ILLUSTRATOR, PHOTOSHOP, MAC MATERIALS: MOHAWK NAVAJO COVER

0860, 0904
DESIGNER: BOB AUDFULDISH CLIENT: CALIFORNIA COLLEGE OF ARTS AND CRAFTS TOOLS: ILLUSTRATOR, PHOTOSHOP, MAC MATERIALS: FINCH OPAQUE COVER

AVE DESIGN STUDIO
0114, 0744
ART DIRECTOR: MARY ANN AVE DESIGNER: JENNIFER AVE CLIENT: LUBRIZOL TOOLS: PHOTOSHOP, QUARK, MAC MATERIALS: STRATHMORE ELEMENTS, INFLATABLE PLASTIC BAG, REFLECTIVE MIRROR STOCK

BARCELONA
0204
ART DIRECTOR: MICHAEL LEONARDINI DESIGNER: ARIS BAJAR CLIENT: IMAX THEATRE TOOLS: ILLUSTRATOR, MAC MATERIALS: STARWHITE

0392
ART DIRECTOR: MICHAEL LEONARDINI DESIGNER: MICHAEL LEONARDINI CLIENT: BARCELONA TOOLS: FREEHAND, MAC MATERIALS: STARWHITE

BAUMANN & BAUMANN
0953, 0959
ART DIRECTORS: BARBARA BAUMANN, GERD BAUMANN DESIGNERS: BARBARA BAUMANN, GERD BAUMANN CLIENT: HATJE CANTZ TOOLS: PHOTOSHOP, FREEHAND MATERIALS: PHOENIXMOTION

BBK STUDIO
0216, 0415
ART DIRECTOR: YANG KIM DESIGNER: YANG KIM CLIENT: BBK STUDIO TOOLS: QUARK MATERIALS: MOHAWK, POLYPROPYLENE, TIN

0252
ART DIRECTOR: YANG KIM DESIGNER: YANG KIM CLIENT: BBK STUDIO TOOLS: ILLUSTRATOR MATERIALS: PARALUX, CRANES

0353, 0606
ART DIRECTOR: YANG KIM DESIGNER: MICHELE CHARTIER CLIENT: HAAC TOOLS: QUARK, PHOTOSHOP MATERIALS: FINCH

0432
ART DIRECTOR: SHARON OLENICZAK DESIGNER: SHARON OLENICZAK CLIENT: MANDIRA GAZAL TOOLS: QUARK

0488
ART DIRECTOR: YANG KIM DESIGNER: YANG KIM CLIENT: JACK RIDL TOOLS: QUARK MATERIALS: MONADNOCK ASTROLITE

0664
ART DIRECTOR: SHARON OLENICZAK DESIGNER: MICHELE CHARTIER CLIENT: DYER-IVES FOUNDATION TOOLS: QUARK MATERIALS: BENEFIT/ VIA

0808
ART DIRECTOR: KEVIN BUDELMANN DESIGNER: ALISON POPP CLIENT: HERMAN MILLER TOOLS: QUARK

0875, 0923
ART DIRECTOR: STEVE FRYKHOLM DESIGNERS: YANG KIM, MICHELE CHARTIER CLIENT: HERMAN MILLER TOOLS: QUARK MATERIALS: GLAMA BECKETT

BEAULIEU CONCEPTS GRAPHIQUES, INC.
0287
ART DIRECTOR: GILLES BEAULIEU DESIGNER: GILLES BEAULIEU CLIENT: STYLISMOPTION INC. TOOLS: ILLUSTRATOR, PHOTO-SHOP, MAC MATERIALS: DOMTAR PROTERRA: "GRÈS" AND "PAILLE"

BECKER DESIGN
0626
ART DIRECTOR: NEIL BECKER DESIGNER: NEIL BECKER CLIENT: LONDON BY DESIGN TOOLS: ILLUSTRATOR, PHOTO-SHOP, QUARK, MAC MATERIALS: DOMTAR SOLUTIONS SOFT WHITE SUPER SMOOTH 100LB COVER, GLAMA VELLUM, BLACK SATIN RIBBON

BELYEA
0244
ART DIRECTOR: PATRICIA BELYEA DESIGNER: NAOMI MURPHY CLIENT: FRASER PAPERS ILLUSTRATORS: STEPHANIE DALTON COWAN, MARGARET CHODOS-IRVINE, ANSON LIAW PHOTOGRAPHERS: TOM COLLICOT, DARRELL PETERSON TOOLS: ILLUSTRATOR, MATERIALS: FRASER PAPERS GENESIS AND PASSPORT—ALL COLORS, WEIGHTS, AND FIN-ISHES, FRASER PAPERS OUTBACK SYDNEY SURF (COR-RUGATED PAPER), ELASTIC CLOSURE BAND

0351
ART DIRECTOR: PATRICIA BELYEA DESIGNER: NAOMI MURPHY CLIENT: COLORGRAPHICS SEATTLE TOOLS: ILLUSTRATOR, MAC MATERIALS: SPECKLETONE STARCH VINE BOOK, 80LB CURIOUS GALVANIZED BOOK (ENVELOPES), 100LB SIGNATURE TRUE DULL (INVI-TATIONS), 100LB SIGNATURE GLOSS COVER (COVER), GROMETS

0444
ART DIRECTOR: PATRICIA BELYEA DESIGNER: RON LARS HANSEN CLIENT: COLORGRAPHICS SEATTLE TOOLS: ILLUSTRATOR, MAC MATERIALS: FREEFORM INVI-TATION: 80LB GILBERT OXFORD BLUE COVER, 80LB GILBERT OXFORD BLACK COVER, 100LB SIGNATURE SUEDE BOOK; LYRICAL AMBIGUITY INVITA-TION: 100LB CRUSHED LEAF LIME, 100LB CRUSHED LEAF COCOA, 100LB SIGNATURE SUEDE BOOK; DIVERGENT REALITIES INVITATION: 11;B HAVANA TIERRA COVER, 111LB HAVANA OSCURO COVER, 100LB SIGNATURE SUEDE BOOK

0755
ART DIRECTOR: PATRICIA BELYEA DESIGNER: NAOMI MURPHY CLIENT: FRASER PAPERS ILLUSTRATORS: STEPHANIE DALTON COWAN, MARGARET CHODOS-IRVINE, ANSON LIAW PHOTOGRAPHERS: TOM COLLICOT, DARRELL PETERSON TOOLS: ILLUSTRATOR, MATERIALS: FRASER PAPERS GENESIS AND PASSPORT—ALL COLORS, WEIGHTS, AND FIN-ISHES, FRASER PAPERS OUTBACK SYDNEY SURF (COR-RUGATED PAPER), ELASTIC CLOSURE BAND

0759
ART DIRECTOR: PATRICIA BELYEA DESIGNER: NAOMI MURPHY CLIENT: IMPERIAL LITHOGRAPH PHOTOGRAPHER: ROSANNE OLSON CALLIGRAPHER: NANCY STENTZ TOOLS: ILLUSTRATOR, MAC MATERIALS: WESTVACO STERLINE ULTRA DULL 100C FOR WRAP AND CALENDAR PAGES

BIG ACTIVE
0291
ART DIRECTORS: GERARD SAINT, MAT MAITLAND DESIGNER: MAT MAITLAND CLIENT: SONY MUSIC UK MATERIALS: BLACK NATURALLY EXPANDED FLEXIBLE PVC

0506
ART DIRECTORS: GERARD SAINT, MAT MAITLAND DESIGNER: MAT MAITLAND CLIENT: BMG RECORDS LOGO: JASPER GOODALL MATERIALS: HEAVYWEIGHT BLACK MOLDED, WELDED, AND FOIL-BLOCKED ACRYLIC (EXTERIOR), HIGH-DENSITY ROUTED FOAM TRAY (INTERIOR), POLISHED STAINLESS STEEL

0565
ART DIRECTOR: GERARD SAINT DESIGNER: GERARD SAINT CLIENT: UNIVERSAL MUSIC MATERIALS: NYLON ADHESIVE "SECURITY" STICKER

0616
ART DIRECTORS: GERARD SAINT, MAT MAITLAND DESIGNER: MAT MAITLAND CLIENT: BMG RECORDS MATERIALS: SILVER MELINEX BOARD, SILKSCREEN, ROLLED BANKNOTE MATERIAL

BISQIT DESIGN
0187
DESIGNER: DAPHNE DIAMANT CLIENT: HILL AND KNOWLTON TOOLS: FREEHAND, QUARK, MAC MATERIALS: 270GSM SUPERCOL BUFF

0253
ART DIRECTOR: DAPHNE DIAMANT DESIGNER: ADAM MITCHINSON CLIENT: HILL + KNOWLTON TOOLS: ILLUSTRATOR, MAC MATERIALS: CHROMOLUX 700 GSM AND 350GSM

0561
ART DIRECTOR: DAPHNE DIAMANT DESIGNER: NICOLA TATUM CLIENT: HILL & KNOWLTON TOOLS: QUARK, MAC MATERI-ALS: BLACK CHROMOLUX 300, BLACK SILKSCREEN

0663
DESIGNER: DAPHNE DIAMANT CLIENT: HILL AND KNOWLTON TOOLS: ILLUSTRATOR, PHOTO-SHOP, QUARK, MAC MATERIALS: NEPTUNE UNIQUE

0819
DESIGNER: DAPHNE DIAMANT CLIENT: WORLD SNOOKER TOOLS: FREEHAND, QUARK, MAC MATERIALS: MEDLEY PURE, SOFT PVC

BLACKCOFFEE
0222
ART DIRECTORS: MARK GALLAGHER, LAURA SAVARD DESIGNERS: MARK GALLAGHER, LAURA SAVARD CLIENT: ROCKPORT PUBLISHERS TOOLS: ILLUSTRATOR, QUARK, MAC

0427, 0601
ART DIRECTORS: MARK GALLAGHER DESIGNERS: MARK GALLAGHER, LAURA SAVARD CLIENT: BLACKCOFFEE TOOLS: ILLUSTRATOR, PHOTOSHOP, MAC MATERIALS: COATED WHITE COVER (CARD), PLASTIC ENVELOPE WITH HANG TAB (ENVELOPE)

0716
ART DIRECTORS: MARK GALLAGHER, LAURA SAVARD DESIGNERS: MARK GALLAGHER, LAURA SAVARD CLIENT: BLACKCOFFEE TOOLS: ILLUSTRATOR, MAC MATERIALS: BURLAP SACK, SILVER GROMMETS, TWINE

0723
ART DIRECTORS: MARK GALLAGHER, LAURA SAVARD DESIGNERS: MARK GALLAGHER, LAURA SAVARD CLIENT: CONVERSE TOOLS: ILLUSTRATOR MATERIALS: EMBOSSED AND 1-COLOR SILKSCREENED METAL

0724
ART DIRECTORS: MARK GALLAGHER, LAURA SAVARD DESIGNERS: MARK GALLAGHER, LAURA SAVARD CLIENT: CONVERSE TOOLS: ILLUSTRATOR, MAC MATERIALS: WOOD VENEER

BLOK DESIGN
0316
ART DIRECTOR: VANESSA ECKSTEIN DESIGNER: VANESSA ECKSTEIN CLIENT: EYE CANDY TV.COM TOOLS: ILLUSTRATOR MATERIALS: STRATHMORE, PLASTIC

0525
ART DIRECTOR: VANESSA ECKSTEIN DESIGNERS: VANESSA ECKSTEIN, FRANCES CHEN CLIENT: RGD/ONTARIO TOOLS: ILLUSTRATOR

0708
ART DIRECTOR: VANESSA ECKSTEIN DESIGNERS: VANESSA ECKSTEIN, FRANCES CHEN CLIENT: EL ZANJON TOOLS: ILLUSTRATOR MATERIALS: STRATHMORE ULTIMATE

0809
ART DIRECTOR: VANESSA ECKSTEIN DESIGNERS: VANESSA ECKSTEIN, MARIANA CONTEGNI CLIENT: NIKE TOOLS: ILLUSTRATOR MATERIALS: STRATHMORE, CURIOUS COLORS

0846, 0892
ART DIRECTOR: VANESSA ECKSTEIN DESIGNERS: VANESSA ECKSTEIN, FRANCES CHEN, STEPHANIE YOUNG CLIENT: THE PRODUCTION KITCHEN TOOLS: ILLUSTRATOR MATERIALS: BECKETT EXPRESSION

0850
ART DIRECTOR: VANESSA ECKSTEIN DESIGNERS: VANESSA ECKSTEIN, FRANCES CHEN, STEPHANIE YOUNG CLIENT: BLOK DESIGN TOOLS: ILLUSTRATOR

BNIM ARCITECTS
0232
ART DIRECTORS: ERIN GEHLE, ZACK SHUBKAGEL DESIGNER: ANGIELA MEYER CLIENT: BNIM ARCITECTS TOOLS: INDESIGN, MAC MATERIALS: CRANE'S 179LB COVER WHITE

0236
ART DIRECTOR: SHAWN GEHLE DESIGNERS: ZACK SHUBKAGEL, ERIN GEHLE CLIENT: BNIM ARCITECTS TOOLS: INDESIGN, NEEDLE MATERIALS: ART-BOARD, THREAD, PUNCH

0420
DESIGNERS: ZACK SHUBKAGEL, ERIN GEHLE CLIENT: BNIM ARCITECTS TOOLS: ILLUSTRATOR, INDESIGN, NEE-DLE MATERIALS: CANVAS, THREAD, GROMMETS

0602
DESIGNERS: ERIN GEHLE, ZACK SHUBKAGEL CLIENT: BNIM ARCITECTS TOOLS: INDESIGN, PHOTOSHOP, MAC MATERIALS: VELLUM, WIRE-O, GROMMETS

BRAD TERRES DESIGN
0327
ART DIRECTOR: BRAD TERRES DESIGNER: BRAD TERRES CLIENT: TAYLOR ROBERTS TOOLS: QUARK, MAC G4 MATERIALS: GMUND BIER PAPIER LUSTRO DULL

BRUKETA & ZINIC
0025, 0090, 0155, 0241, 0745, 0747
ART DIRECTORS: DAVOR BRUKETA, NIKOLA ZINIC DESIGNERS: DAVOR BRUKETA, NIKOLA ZINIC CLIENT: PRODRAVKA D.D TOOLS: PHOTOSHOP, FREEHAND, MAC MATERIALS: AGRIPINA

0085
ART DIRECTORS: DAVOR BRUKETA, NIKOLA ZINIC DESIGNERS: DAVOR BRUKETA, NIKOLA ZINIC CLIENT: BRUKETA & ZINIC TOOLS: PHOTOSHOP, FREEHAND, MAC MATERIALS: AGRIPINA

0581, 0686, 0731
ART DIRECTORS: DAVOR BRUKETA, NIKOLA ZINIC DESIGNERS: DAVOR BRUKETA, NIKOLA ZINIC CLIENT: PODRAVKA D.D. TOOLS: PHOTOSHOP, FREEHAND, MAC MATERIALS: AGRIPINA, SCENTED COLOR

BUREAU GRAS
0318
ART DIRECTOR: RUUD WINDER DESIGNER: RUUD WINDER CLIENT: METIS_NL TOOLS: ILLUSTRATOR MATERIALS: FEORIGONI

0545
ART DIRECTOR: RUUD WINDER DESIGNER: RUUD WINDER CLIENT: BK CORPORATE TOOLS: ILLUSTRATOR

BÜRO SCHELS FÜR GESTALTUNG
0729
ART DIRECTOR: CHRISTINA SCHELS DESIGNER: CHRISTINA SCHELS CLIENT: TOP-CITY-KUTSTEIN GMBH TOOLS: QUARK, MAC MATERIALS: KEAYKOLOUR/ARJOWIGGINS 300GSM

BWA DESIGN
0202, 0419
ART DIRECTORS: BWA DESIGN DESIGNER: BWA DESIGN CLIENT: RED CROSS TOOLS: PHOTOSHOP, QUARK

0211
ART DIRECTOR: BWA DESIGN DESIGNER: BWA DESIGN CLIENT: RED ROOSTER TOOLS: ILLUSTRATOR, QUARK MATERIALS: REVIVE SILK

0347
ART DIRECTOR: BWA DESIGN DESIGNER: BWA DESIGN CLIENT: GRAN BUTLER TOOLS: QUARK

0406
ART DIRECTOR: BWA DESIGN DESIGNER: BWA DESIGN CLIENT: BWA DESIGN TOOLS: ILLUSTRATOR, QUARK

0421, 0939
ART DIRECTOR: BWA DESIGN DESIGNER: BWA DESIGN CLIENT: THE BIG ISSUE FOUNDATION TOOLS: QUARK, PHOTOSHOP MATERIALS: CYCLUS OFFSET

0423
ART DIRECTOR: BWA DESIGN DESIGNER: BWA DESIGN CLIENT: STIRLING ACKROYD TOOLS: ILLUSTRATOR, QUARK MATERIALS: SILK LAMINATED

0534
ART DIRECTOR: BWA DESIGN DESIGNER: BWA DESIGN CLIENT: MARKS + SPENCER TOOLS: ILLUSTRATOR, QUARK MATERIALS: SILK

CAHAN & ASSOCIATES
0361
ART DIRECTOR: BILL CAHAN DESIGNER: TODD SIMMONS CLIENT: LINEAR TECHNOLOGY CORP. TOOLS: ILLUSTRATOR, QUARK MATERIALS: KROMEKOTE, UTOPIA 2 DULL

0501
ART DIRECTOR: BILL CAHAN DESIGNER: CRAIG BAILEY CLIENT: NETOBJECTS TOOLS: ILLUSTRATOR, QUARK MATERIALS: KROMEKOTE, CONCORD MATTE

0515
ART DIRECTORS: BILL CAHAN, BOB DINETZ DESIGNER: BOB DINETZ CLIENT: GARTNER TOOLS: ILLUSTRATOR, PHOTO-SHOP, QUARK MATERIALS: ACCENT OPAQUE

0516
ART DIRECTORS: BILL CAHAN, KEVIN ROBERSON DESIGNER: KEVIN ROBERSON CLIENT: COLLATERAL THERAPEUTICS TOOLS: ILLUSTRATOR, PHOTO-SHOP, QUARK MATERIALS: MEAD SIGNATURE, CHAMPION CARNIVAL

0517
ART DIRECTORS: BILL CAHAN, KEVIN ROBERSON, BOB DINETZ DESIGNERS: BOB DINETZ, MARK GIGLIO, KEVIN ROBERSON CLIENT: STORAENSO/CONSOLI-DATED PAPERS TOOLS: QUARK, ILLUSTRATOR MATERIALS: REFLECTIONS SILK

0947
ART DIRECTORS: BILL CAHAN, BOB DINETZ DESIGNER: BOB DINETZ CLIENT: BRE PROPERTIES TOOLS: ILLUSTRATOR, PHOTO-SHOP, QUARK MATERIALS: UTOPIA 2 MATTE 80LB

CAPSULE
0144, 0494, 0824
ART DIRECTOR: BRIAN ADDUCCI DESIGNER: BRIAN ADDUCCI CLIENT: COMPASS MARKETING TOOLS: ILLUSTRATOR, PHOTO-SHOP, QUARK, MAC MATERIALS: FIBERMARK TOUCHE, GALVA-NIZED STEEL

0277, 0339, 0490
ART DIRECTOR: BRIAN ADDUCCI DESIGNERS: DAN BAGGENSTOSS, GREG BROSE CLIENT: CAPSULE TOOLS: ILLUSTRATOR, PHOTO-SHOP, QUARK, MAC MATERIALS: STAINLESS STEEL, FRENCH BUTCHER, CURIOUS METALLICS, FOUND OBJECTS

CARTER WONG TOMLIN
0762
ART DIRECTOR: PHIL CARTER DESIGNER: NEIL HEDGER CLIENT: HOWIES TOOLS: RUBBER STAMP MATERIALS: RECYCLED KRAFT PAPER

CASERTA DESIGN COMPANY
0213
ART DIRECTOR: FRED CASERTA DESIGNER: FRED CASERTA CLIENT: CASERTA DESIGN COMPANY TOOLS: ILLUSTRA-TOR, PHOTOSHOP, QUARK, MAC G4 MATERIALS: 100LB PRODUCTOLITH

CDT DESIGN
0105, 0867, 0869
ART DIRECTOR: CHRISTIAN ALTMANN DESIGNER: ALISTAIR HALL CLIENT: THE ROYAL COLLEGE OF ART TOOLS: QUARK MATERIALS: STOCK: IMAGINE, CHROMOLUX

CHEN DESIGN ASSOCIATES
0084, 0972
ART DIRECTOR: JOSHUA C. CHEN DESIGNER: MAX SPECTOR CLIENT: BARRY AND MAYA SPECTOR TOOLS: ILLUSTRATOR, QUARK, MAC MATERIALS: BLOT-TER PAPER, JAPANESE PAPER

0300
ART DIRECTOR: JOSHUA C. CHEN DESIGNERS: MAX SPECTOR, JENNIFER TOLO CLIENT: ADAMO LONDON TOOLS: ILLUSTRATOR, QUARK, MAC MATERIALS: CRANE

0515
ART DIRECTOR: JOSHUA C. CHEN DESIGNERS: MAX SPECTOR, JENNIFER TOLO CLIENT: AIGA WRITER: JENNIFER TOLO TOOLS: QUARK, ILLUSTRATOR, PHOTOSHOP, MAC MATERIALS: FOX RIVER CORONADO, BRIGHT WHITE VELLUM, GILBERT CLEARFOLD WHITE LIGHT

0886
ART DIRECTOR: JOSHUA C. CHEN DESIGNERS: MAX SPECTOR, JOSH CHEN CLIENT: SEQUOIA HOSPITAL TOOLS: ILLUSTRATOR, QUARK, MAC MATERIALS: MOHAWK SUPERFINE

CHENG DESIGN
0633
DESIGNER: JENNIFER CHENG CLIENT: SEATTLE ARTS & LECTURES TOOLS: PHOTOSHOP, QUARK, MAC MATERIALS: DOMTAR TITANIUM

CHIMERA DESIGN
0383
ART DIRECTORS: JOHN MARGART DESIGNER: KEELIE TEASDALE CLIENT: MOMAC HAIRDRESSING STITCHING: KEELIE TEASDALE TOOLS: ILLUSTRATOR, PHOTOSHOP MATERIALS: K.W. DOGGETT, CONQUEROR CONCEPT

0411
ART DIRECTORS: JOHN MARGART DESIGNER: NAOMI MACE CLIENT: TENNIS VICTORIA TOOLS: PHOTOSHOP, QUARK MATERIALS: RALEIGH PAPER, BOTANY DUPLEX, GRANGE, RECYCLED TENNIS BALL TUBES

0949
ART DIRECTORS: JOHN MARGART DESIGNER: KEELIE TEASDALE CLIENT: FALLS CREEK FILM FESTIVAL 3D MODELING: ANDREW MARGART TOOLS: 3DS MAX, ILLUSTRATOR, PHOTOSHOP MATERIALS: K.W. DOGGETT, HANNO ART SILK

CHRONICLE BOOKS
0014
ART DIRECTOR: HENRY QUIROGA DESIGNERS: TOM LEE AND ROB REGER OF COSMIC DEBRIS CLIENT: CHRONICLE BOOKS TOOLS: ILLUSTRATOR, MAC MATERIALS: 350GSM MATTE CIS CARDSTOCK WITH MATTE LAMINATION (CASE), PET-G LENTICULAR, 120GSM WHITE WOODFREE (TEXT), 125GSM WHITE ARLIN OVER 10PT CIS ARTBOARD WITH MATTE VARNISH (SPINE), 120GSM WHITE WOODFREE (END SHEETS)

0206
ART DIRECTOR: SHAWN HAZEN DESIGNER: SHAWN HAZEN CLIENT: CHRONICLE BOOKS TOOLS: QUARK MATERIALS: 157GSM MATTE ART

0214
ART DIRECTOR: AMY ENNIS DESIGNER: NOEL TORENTINO OF COSMIC DEBRIS CLIENT: CHRONICLE BOOKS TOOLS: ILLUSTRATOR, MAC MATERIALS: 1-PIECE CASE COVERED WITH CONCEALED WIRE-O, 128GSM COATED ART PAPER (COVER), 130GSM WHITE TCF WOODFREE (TEXT), 320GSM COATED TWO-SIDED ARTBOARD WITH MYLAR (TABS)

0217, 0429
ART DIRECTOR: AZI RAD DESIGNER: HENRIK DRESCHER CLIENT: CHRONICLE BOOKS TOOLS: QUARK MATERIALS: 157GSM MATTE ART

0617, 0658
ART DIRECTOR: ALETHEA MORRISON DESIGNERS: VINNIE D'ANGELO, ALTHEA MORRISON CLIENT: CHRONICLE BOOKS TOOLS: PHOTOSHOP, QUARK MATERIALS: 157GSM MATTE ART

CINCODEMAYO DESIGN
0324
ART DIRECTOR: MAURICIO ALANIS DESIGNER: MAURICIO ALANIS CLIENT: CINCODEMAYO TOOLS: FREEHAND, MAC MATERIALS: FIRENZE OPALINA

CIRCLE K STUDIO
0340
ART DIRECTOR: JULIE KEENAN DESIGNER: JULIE KEENAN CLIENT: CIRCLE K STUDIO TOOLS: ILLUSTRATOR, MAC MATERIALS: RIVES BFK

0682
ART DIRECTOR: JULIE KEENAN DESIGNER: JULIE KEENAN CLIENT: CIRCLE K STUDIO TOOLS: ILLUSTRATOR, MAC MATERIALS: CRESCENT RAG

CIRCULO SOCIAL
0588
ART DIRECTOR: MAURICIO ALANIS DESIGNER: SONIA SALINAS CLIENT: AIXA & EDUARDO TOOLS: FREEHAND

COLLEGE DESIGN
0465
ART DIRECTOR: TONY KNIGHT DESIGNER: MAK LEVERTON CLIENT: TENON GROUP PLC. TOOLS: PHOTOSHOP, QUARK MATERIALS: POLYPROPYLENE, TAFFETA IVORY PRINTING: 2-COLOR SCREEN, 4-COLOR PROCESS PLUS 1 SPECIAL

0734
ART DIRECTOR: GUY LANE DESIGNER: MARCUS BENNETT CLIENT: DELANCEY ESTATES PLC. TOOLS: PHOTOSHOP, QUARK MATERIALS: STARDREAM, CANSON SATIN PRINTING: 4-COLOR PLUS 2 SPECIALS

CRANHAM ADVERTISING
0130
ART DIRECTOR: MARC CRADDOCK DESIGNER: EMMA ROBINSON CLIENT: ZEON LIMITED TOOLS: PHOTOSHOP, QUARK, MAC MATERIALS: SILK ART, PLASTIC

CRUSH DESIGN
0004
ART DIRECTOR: CARL RUSH DESIGNER: CARL RUSH CLIENT: FULL ON FILMS MATERIALS: GLOSS CORE 130GSM

0039, 0799
ART DIRECTOR: CARL RUSH DESIGNER: SIMON SLATER CLIENT: CRUSH TOOLS: HANDS MATERIALS: FOUND WOOD, NAILS, HARDBOARD, RECYCLED BAG, RECYCLED TISSUE PAPER, POSTCARDS PRINTED ON FLORA ANTIQUE

0158
ART DIRECTOR: CARL RUSH DESIGNER: CARL RUSH CLIENT: PALM PICTURES MATERIALS: BOARD, STICKER

0359, 0788
ART DIRECTOR: CARL RUSH DESIGNER: TIM DIACON CLIENT: SIMULTANE TOOLS: ILLUSTRA-TOR, PHOTOSHOP, QUARK MATERIALS: STORA FINE 115GSM, PATTERNED CUTTING BOARD COVER, RUBBER BAND

0783
ART DIRECTOR: CARL RUSH DESIGNER: CARL RUSH CLIENT: PALM PICTURES TOOLS: ILLUSTRATOR MATERIALS: CD PACK, POLYSHIELD STATIC SHIELDING BAG, BURIED METAL TYPE, STICKER

0889
ART DIRECTOR: CARL RUSH DESIGNER: CARL RUSH CLIENT: URBAN THEORY TOOLS: ILLUSTRATOR, QUARK MATERIALS: FOLD-OUT DIGIPACK

0974
ART DIRECTOR: CARL RUSH DESIGNER: CARL RUSH CLIENT: CRUSH MATERIALS: T-SHIRTS, WEB

CUCKOOLAND
0637
ART DIRECTOR: ADE WOOD DESIGNER: ADE WOOD CLIENT: SONNETI TOOLS: FREEHAND

0830, 0864
ART DIRECTOR: ADE WOOD DESIGNER: DAN LOWE CLIENT: LIMEHAUS TOOLS: PHOTOSHOP, FREEHAND, MAC MATERIALS: JERSEY

0853
ART DIRECTOR: ADE WOOD DESIGNER: DAN LOWE CLIENT: LIMEHAUS TOOLS: PHOTOSHOP, FREEHAND, MAC MATERIALS: JERSEY

0854
ART DIRECTOR: ADE WOOD DESIGNER: ADE WOOD CLIENT: LIMEHAUS TOOLS: PHOTOSHOP, FREEHAND, MAC MATERIALS: DENIM, LEATHER

0857, 0859
ART DIRECTOR: ADE WOOD DESIGNER: ADE WOOD CLIENT: LIMEHAUS TOOLS: PHOTOSHOP, FREEHAND, MAC MATERIALS: JERSEY

0858
ART DIRECTOR: ADE WOOD DESIGNER: ADE WOOD CLIENT: FULL CIRCLE TOOLS: PHOTOSHOP, FREEHAND, MAC MATERIALS: JERSEY, CANVAS

0908
ART DIRECTOR: ADE WOOD DESIGNER: ADE WOOD CLIENT: LIMEHAUS TOOLS: PHOTOSHOP, FREEHAND, MAC MATERIALS: CANVAS

BETH CURTIS
0219
DESIGNER: BETH CURTIS CLIENT: OXFORD CONVERSIS MATERIALS: NEPTUNE

DAVID CARTER DESIGN
0535
ART DIRECTOR: DONNA ALDRIDGE DESIGNER: DONNA ALDRIGE CLIENT: DAVID CARTER DESIGN TOOLS: ILLUSTRATOR, QUARK

0677
ART DIRECTOR: DONNA ALDRIDGE DESIGNER: DONNA ALDRIGE CLIENT: LAJITAS: THE ULTIMATE HIDEOUT TOOLS: ILLUSTRATOR MATERIALS: FIBERMARK SUEDE TEXT

0735
ART DIRECTOR: DONNA ALDRIDGE DESIGNER: DONNA ALDRIGE CLIENT: LAJITAS: THE ULTIMATE HIDEOUT TOOLS: ILLUSTRATOR MATERIALS: SUEDETEX PAPER, LEATHER

DESIGN 5
0298
ART DIRECTOR: RON NIKKEL DESIGNER: DESIGN 5 CLIENT: TIGE BOATS TOOLS: ILLUSTRA-TOR, PHOTOSHOP, MAC G4

0304
ART DIRECTOR: RON NIKKEL DESIGNER: RON NIKKEL CLIENT: FRESNO REGIONAL FOUNDATION TOOLS: ILLUSTRATOR, MAC G4

0305
ART DIRECTOR: RON NIKKEL DESIGNER: CHRIS DUBURG CLIENT: UNITED WAY TOOLS: ILLUSTRATOR, MAC G4 MATERIALS: M REAL

DESIGN HOCH DREI GMBH & CO. KG
0377
ART DIRECTOR: SONJA MARTENS CLIENT: DESIGN HOCH DREI GMBH & CO. KG MATERIALS: SEWN PAPER

0938
ART DIRECTOR: TOBIAS KOLLMANN CLIENT: DAIMLER CHRYSLER AG MATERIALS: SILKSCREEN PRINTING ON GLASS

THE DESIGN DELL
0623, 0893
ART DIRECTOR: DAN DONOVAN DESIGNER: DAN DONOVAN CLIENT: THE DESIGN DELL TOOLS: QUARK MATERIALS: CYCLUS OFFSET

DESIGN DEPOT CREATIVE BUREAU
0078
ART DIRECTORS: PETR BANKOV, KATERINA KOJOUKHOVA DESIGNER: PETR BANKOV CLIENT: NORILSKY NICKEL TOOLS: MAC MATERIALS: KRAFT PAPER, WOODEN STICK

0927, 0928, 0929, 0930, 0931, 0932, 0933, 0934, 0935
ART DIRECTORS: PETR BANKOV, KATERINA KOJOUKHOVA DESIGNERS: KATERINA KOKOUKHOVA, MIKHAIL LOSKOV CLIENT: DESIGN DEPOT TOOLS: MAC MATERIALS: GALLERY ART

DEW GIBBONS
0542
ART DIRECTOR: SHAUN DEW DESIGNER: CHRISTIAN EVES CLIENT: MAQUIS MATERIALS: EPISODE 4 (COVER), MUNKEN PURE (TEXT)

D-FUSE
0896, 0937, 0991
ART DIRECTOR: MIKE FAULKNER DESIGNER: MIKE FAULKNER CLIENT: D-FUSE TOOLS: PHOTOSHOP, FREEHAND

DINNICK & HOWELLS
0054, 0787
ART DIRECTOR: JONATHAN HOWELLS DESIGNER: JONATHAN HOWELLS CLIENT: DAVID DREBIN TOOLS: PHOTOSHOP, QUARK

0191
ART DIRECTORS: JONATHAN HOWELLS, PAUL GARBETT DESIGNER: JONATHAN HOWELLS CLIENT: IRON DESIGN TOOLS: ILLUSTRATOR, QUARK MATERIALS: MOHAWK VELLUM

DOSSIERCREATIVE INC.
0184
ART DIRECTOR: DON CHISHOLM DESIGNER: PATRICK SMITH CLIENT: VINCOR INTERNATIONAL TOOLS: ILLUSTRATOR MATERIALS: FASSON

0194
ART DIRECTOR: DON CHISHOLM CLIENT: STEVEN BOLIGER

DURSO DESIGN
0988
ART DIRECTOR: ROUANE DURSO DESIGNER: ROUANE DURSON

DYNAMO A&D
0691
ART DIRECTOR: NINA WISHNOK DESIGNER: NINA WISHNOK CLIENT: V PLIANT TOOLS: PHOTOSHOP, QUARK, MAC, RUBBER STAMP MATERIALS: OLD POSTCARDS, VELLUM, OLD BOOKS, CLOTH, CHAMPION BENEFIT PAPER

EGBG
0027
ART DIRECTOR: MARTIJN ENGELBREGT DESIGNER: MARTIJN ENGELBREGT CLIENT: 7X11 TOOLS: QUARK MATERIALS: HVO PRINTING: OFFSET, 2 PMS COLORS

0134
ART DIRECTOR: MARTIJN ENGELBREGT DESIGNER: MARTIJN ENGELBREGT CLIENT: BOTH ENDS TOOLS: ILLUSTRATOR, QUARK MATERIALS: 70GSM

0758
ART DIRECTOR: MARTIJN ENGELBREGT DESIGNER: MARTIJN ENGELBREGT CLIENT: HOOGSTRAATMAKERS TOOLS: ILLUSTRATOR MATERIALS: GARBAGE BAG, STICK UP LOGO

0910
ART DIRECTOR: MARTIJN ENGELBREGT DESIGNER: MARTIJN ENGELBREGT CLIENT: 7X11 TOOLS: ILLUSTRATOR, MICROSOFT EXCEL MATERIALS: HTS 160GSM

EGGERS & DIAPER
0072
ART DIRECTOR: MARK DIAPER DESIGNER: MARK DIAPER CLIENT: ARTANGEL TOOLS: QUARK

0748
ART DIRECTOR: MARK DIAPER DESIGNER: MARK DIAPER CLIENT: PHAIDON TOOLS: QUARK MATERIALS: PROMICA PRISTINE STEEL

11D—ELEVEN DESIGN
0151, 0522, 0695
ART DIRECTORS: OLE LUND, JAN NIELSEN DESIGNERS: OLE LUND, JAN NIELSEN CLIENT: 2GD—2 GRAPHIC DESIGN TOOLS: ILLUSTRATOR, PHOTOSHOP

0507, 0513
ART DIRECTORS: OLE LUND, JAN NIELSEN DESIGNERS: OLE LUND, JAN NIELSEN CLIENT: BRUUNS BAZAAR TOOLS: ILLUSTRATOR, PHOTOSHOP MATERIALS: LUMIART SILK 300GSM

0508, 0509
ART DIRECTORS: OLE LUND, JAN NIELSEN DESIGNERS: OLE LUND, JAN NIELSEN CLIENT: KØNRÖG TOOLS: ILLUSTRATOR, PHOTOSHOP

0521
ART DIRECTORS: OLE LUND, JAN NIELSEN DESIGNERS: OLE LUND, JAN NIELSEN CLIENT: BLACKBOX MAGAZINE TOOLS: ILLUSTRATOR, PHOTOSHOP

ELFEN
0818
CLIENT: ELFEN TOOLS: ILLUSTRATOR MATERIALS: PULPBOARD, 2,000 MICRONS

ELMWOOD
0150
ART DIRECTOR: ALAN AINSLEY DESIGNERS: ALAN AINSLEY, STEVE SHAW, JAYNE WORKHAM CLIENT: SCHEUFELEN PREMIUM PAPERS TOOLS: PHOTOSHOP, ILLUSTRATOR, MAC MATERIALS: LENTICULAR LENS, 464 MICRON, 75 LPI

0784
ART DIRECTOR: RICHARD SCHOLEY DESIGNER: KEVIN BLACKBURN CLIENT: BBC MATERIALS: CARPET

0790
ART DIRECTOR: JON STUBLEY DESIGNERS: JON STUBLEY, BEN GREENGRASS CLIENT: MICROBAN TOOLS: PHOTOSHOP, QUARK, MAC MATERIALS: SILK ART 400GSM, THERMOCHROMIC INK

0791
ART DIRECTOR: RICHARD SCHOLEY DESIGNERS: GRAHAM STURZAKER, PAUL SUDRON CLIENT: REBECCA HOPKINSON AND MICHAEL KITCHING MATERIALS: ROBERT HORNE STARDREAM SILVER, ACETATE

0798
ART DIRECTOR: RICHARD SCHOLEY DESIGNERS: RICHARD SCHOLEY, STEVE SHAW, MIKE OWEN CLIENT: ELMWOOD MATERIALS: FENNER PAPER COMPANY FLOCKAGE

0802
DESIGNERS: PAUL SUNDRON, GRAHAM STURZAKER CLIENT: HOT TIN ROOF PR

EMERY VINCENT DESIGN
0076
ART DIRECTOR: EMERY VINCENT DESIGN DESIGNER: EMERY VINCENT DESIGN CLIENT: MULTIPLEX TOOLS: QUARK, MAC

0207
ART DIRECTOR: EMERY VINCENT DESIGN DESIGNER: EMERY VINCENT DESIGN CLIENT: MULTIPLEX TOOLS: QUARK, MAC MATERIALS: SILVER INTERSCREWS

0215
ART DIRECTOR: EMERY VINCENT DESIGN DESIGNER: EMERY VINCENT DESIGN CLIENT: CSR TOOLS: QUARK, MAC MATERIALS: ALUMINUM CASE, LEATHER

0408
ART DIRECTOR: EMERY VINCENT DESIGN DESIGNER: EMERY VINCENT DESIGN CLIENT: CSR TOOLS: QUARK, MAC

EMPIRE DESIGN STUDIO
0198
ART DIRECTOR: GARY TOOTH CLIENT: SAKS FIFTH AVENUE TOOLS: QUARK MATERIALS: FRENCH PAPER CO.

0212
ART DIRECTOR: GARY TOOTH CLIENT: FIT TOOLS: ILLUSTRATOR MATERIALS: STRATHMORE

0407, 0571
ART DIRECTOR: GARY TOOTH CLIENT: CHRONICLE BOOKS TOOLS: QUARK MATERIALS: SUEDE CLOTH

0955
ART DIRECTOR: GARY TOOTH DESIGNER: CARRIE HAMILTON CLIENT: ABRAMS TOOLS: ILLUSTRATOR, QUARK

EMSPACE DESIGN GROUP
0647
ART DIRECTOR: GAIL SNODGRASS DESIGNER: GAIL SNODGRASS CLIENT: FIRST NATIONAL MERCHANT SOLUTIONS TOOLS: QUARK MATERIALS: SYNERGY RED, CLASSIC COTTON CREAM

ERBE DESIGN
0167, 0467
ART DIRECTOR: MAUREEN ERBE DESIGNERS: MAUREEN ERBE, RITA SOWINS PHOTOGRAPHER: HENRY BLACKHAM CLIENT: MOTOROLA LIFE SCIENCES TOOLS: QUARK, MAC G3 MATERIALS: APPLETON CURIOUS PAPERS

ERIC HESEN GRAPHIC DESIGN
0125
ART DIRECTOR: ERIC HESEN DESIGNERS: ERIC HESEN, JORIS HULSBOSCH CLIENT: SINTLUCAS SCHOOL FOR COMMUNICATION AND DESIGN TOOLS: ILLUSTRATOR, PHOTOSHOP, QUARK, MAC MATERIALS: TOLLIUS, IVERCOTE

FAITH
0201
ART DIRECTOR: PAUL SYCH DESIGNER: PAUL SYCH CLIENT: FAITH TOOLS: ILLUSTRATOR, MAC MATERIALS: CURIOUS PAPERS

0777
ART DIRECTOR: PAUL SYCH DESIGNER: PAUL SYCH CLIENT: FAITH TOOLS: ILLUSTRATOR, MAC MATERIALS: ZANDERS (CARDS), MIRRI STOCK

0898
ART DIRECTOR: PAUL SYCH DESIGNER: PAUL SYCH CLIENT: FAITH GALLERY TOOLS: PHOTOSHOP MATERIALS: CANVAS

THE FAMILY
0122
ART DIRECTOR: ANDREW ROBINSON DESIGNERS: GRAHAM NUTTALL, ANDREW KING CLIENT: LAUREUS WORLD SPORTS AWARDS TOOLS: ILLUSTRATOR, MAC MATERIALS: CHELSEA CLOTH LAMINATED TO BOARD AND FOILED

0248
ART DIRECTOR: ANDREW ROBINSON DESIGNER: ANDREW KING CLIENT: AKEBONO TOOLS: ILLUSTRATOR, PHOTOSHOP, QUARK MATERIALS: SKY SILK

0274
ART DIRECTOR: ANDREW ROBINSON DESIGNERS: ANDREW KING, DOUGLAS MAIN CLIENT: ALFRED DUNHILL CALLIGRAPHY: SATWINDER TOOLS: ILLUSTRATOR, QUARK, MAC MATERIALS: ZERKALL BÜTTEN WITH DECAL EDGE

0579
ART DIRECTOR: ANDREW ROBINSON DESIGNERS: GRAHAM NUTTALL, ANDREW KING CLIENT: LAUREUS WORLD SPORTS AWARDS TOOLS: ILLUSTRATOR, MAC MATERIALS: LEATHER LAMINATED TO BOARD

0592
ART DIRECTOR: ANDREW ROBINSON DESIGNERS: ANDREW KING, DOUGLAS MAIN CLIENT: GRANADA MEDIA TOOLS: ILLUSTRATOR, PHOTOSHOP, QUARK, MAC MATERIALS: FAULKNERS HANDMADE PAPER, FOIL RUBDOWNS, FEATHER

0909, 0951, 0952
ART DIRECTOR: ANDREW ROBINSON CLIENT: DONSIDE PAPER TOOLS: ILLUSTRATOR, QUARK, MAC MATERIALS: DONSIDE LABEL PAPER, 10 COLOR PLUS FOILS

0912
ART DIRECTOR: ANDREW ROBINSON CLIENT: DONSIDE PAPER TOOLS: ILLUSTRATOR, QUARK, MAC MATERIALS: DONSIDE LABEL PAPER, 10 COLOR AND FOILS

FAUXPAS
0265
ART DIRECTOR: MARTIN STILLHART DESIGNER: MARTIN STILLHART ILLUSTRATOR: MARTIN STILLHART CLIENT: SEVERAL ART GALLERIES TOOLS: ILLUSTRATOR, MAC MATERIALS: BEER COASTER PRINTING: OFFSET

FELDER GRAFIKDESIGN
0030, 0042, 0091
ART DIRECTOR: PETER FELDER CLIENT: FELDER GRAFIKDESIGN TOOLS: QUARK, MAC MATERIALS: WASTERPAPER, SPOILAGE

0132
ART DIRECTOR: PETER FELDER DESIGNERS: PETER FELDER, SIGI RAMOSER CLIENT: NEXT PAGE TOOLS: QUARK, MAC MATERIALS: IKONO SILK 170GSM, FOIL, PLASTIC FILM

0278
ART DIRECTOR: PETER FELDER CLIENT: FELDER GRAFIKDESIGN TOOLS: QUARK, MAC MATERIALS: ISKANDAR 115GSM AND 250GSM

0325
ART DIRECTORS: RENÉ DALPRA, PETER FELDER DESIGNER: PETER FELDER CLIENT: OTTO MÜLLER VERLAG/VERLAG DIE QUELLE TOOLS: QUARK, MAC MATERIALS: GMUND COLOR 300GSM, WERKDRUCK 100GSM

0376, 0381, 0636, 0639, 0651, 0679
ART DIRECTORS: PETER FELDER, JOHANNES RAUCH DESIGNER: PETER FELDER CLIENT: FELDER GRAFIKDESIGN TOOLS: QUARK, MAC MATERIALS: GMUND COLOR 49, 200GSM AND 135GSM

0693
ART DIRECTOR: PETER FELDER DESIGNER: PETER FELDER CLIENT: GEBHARD MATHIS TOOLS: QUARK, MAC MATERIALS: TRANSPARENT PAPER 115GSM

0901
ART DIRECTOR: PETER FELDER DESIGNERS: RENÉ DALPRA, PETER FELDER CLIENT: TELEFONSEELSORGE VORARLBERG TOOLS: QUARK, MAC MATERIALS: ELK MUNKEN OFFSET 150GSM

0982
ART DIRECTOR: PETER FELDER DESIGNERS: RENÉ DALPRA, PETER FELDER CLIENT: TELEFONSEELSORGE VORARLBERG TOOLS: QUARK, MAC MATERIALS: ELK MUNKEN OFFSET 150GSM

FELTON COMMUNICATION
0464
ART DIRECTOR: BRION FURNELL CLIENT: TERRENCE HIGGINS TRUST TOOLS: PHOTOSHOP, QUARK MATERIALS: CHALLENGER OFFSET, VINYL

FIBRE
0183
ART DIRECTOR: DAVID RAINBIRD CLIENT: MOTOROLA MATERIALS: DIE-CUT CARTON BOARD

0382
ART DIRECTOR: NATHAN LANDER DESIGNER: GARY BUTCHER CLIENT: NIKE MATERIALS: POLYPROPYLENE, HIGH-DENSITY FOAM, TRIPLE SILK, CD

0391
ART DIRECTOR: NATHAN LANDER DESIGNER: NATHAN LANDER CLIENT: NIKE

0393, 0794
ART DIRECTOR: NATHAN LANDER DESIGNERS: NATHAN LANDER, TOMMY MILLER CLIENT: NIKE MATERIALS: FILM TIN, FRISBEE, HIGH-DENSITY FOAM, TRIPLE SILK, CD

0640, 0795
ART DIRECTOR: NATHAN LANDER DESIGNER: NATHAN LANDER CLIENT: NIKE MATERIALS: NCR PAPER, FILE MASTER, X-RAY FILM, LUSTRELUX, TREASURY TAGS

0655
ART DIRECTOR: NATHAN LANDER DESIGNER: TOMMY MILLER CLIENT: NIKE MATERIALS: BOX BOARD, TISSUE PAPER, TRIPLE SILK

0843
ART DIRECTOR: DAVID RAINBIRD DESIGNER: TOMMY MILLER CLIENT: MOTOROLA MATERIALS: SCREWPACK, PLASTIC TUBE, CHROMOLUX SILVER AND RED

FIELD DESIGN CONSULTANTS
0035
ART DIRECTOR: SARAH PATERSON DESIGNER: SARAH PATERON CLIENT: GROUNDWORK EAST LONDON TOOLS: PHOTOSHOP, QUARK MATERIALS: EVOLUTION SATIN, GREYBACK 100

0653
ART DIRECTOR: NIGEL ROBERTS DESIGNER: NIGEL ROBERTS CLIENT: FIELD TOOLS: PHOTOSHOP, QUARK

FLIGHT CREATIVE
0012, 0182, 0388
ART DIRECTOR: LISA NANKERVIS DESIGNER: LISA NANKERVIS CLIENT: FLIGHT CREATIVE TOOLS: ILLUSTRATOR MATERIALS: SUMO 200GSM, 250GSM, 300GSM; CYBERSTAR 90GSM, 110GSM

FORM
0108
ART DIRECTOR: PAULA BENSON DESIGNER: PAULA BENSON CLIENT: INDOOR GARDEN DESIGN TOOLS: PHOTOSHOP, FREEHAND, MAC MATERIALS: CONSORT ROYAL SILK

0174
ART DIRECTORS: PAULA BENSON, PAUL WEST DESIGNERS: PAULA BENSON, PAUL WEST, NICK HARD CLIENT: FORM TOOLS: FREEHAND, MAC MATERIALS: COURIER SUPER WOVE, HARD-ROLLED STAINLESS STEEL

0409
ART DIRECTORS: PAUL WEST, PAULA BENSON DESIGNER: PAUL WEST CLIENT: THE MOVING PICTURE COMPANY TOOLS: FREEHAND, MAC MATERIALS: CHROMALUX

0414
ART DIRECTOR: PAUL WEST
DESIGNER: NICK HARD CLIENT:
DAZED AND CONFUSED/TOP
SHOP TOOLS: PHOTOSHOP,
FREEHAND, MAC

0491
ART DIRECTOR: PAUL WEST
DESIGNER: PAUL WEST CLIENT:
VISION ON TOOLS: QUARK, MAC
MATERIALS: BALACRON BOOK-
BINDING FABRIC, PAPER BELLY
BAND

0493
ART DIRECTOR: PAULA BENSON
DESIGNERS: PAULA BENSON,
CRAIG ROBINSON, CLAIRE
WARNER CLIENT: DESIGN
COUNCIL TOOLS: FREEHAND
MATERIALS: MUNKEN LYNX

0609
ART DIRECTORS: PAULA
BENSON, PAUL WEST
DESIGNER: NICK HARD CLIENT:
UNIFORM TOOLS: FREEHAND,
MAC CLIENT: SELF-ADHE-
SIVE STICKER SHEET, COURIER
BLANK SHEET

0697
ART DIRECTORS: PAULA
BENSON, PAUL WEST
DESIGNERS: PAULA BENSON,
PAUL WEST, NICK HARD CLIENT:
FORM TOOLS: FREEHAND, MAC
MATERIALS: BEER MAT, TRAC-
ING PAPER ENVELOPES

0704
ART DIRECTORS: PAULA
BENSON, PAUL WEST
DESIGNER: NICK HARD CLIENT:
UNIFORM TOOLS: FREEHAND,
MAC MATERIALS: GREEN
GLOW-EDGE POLYCARBONATE

0743
ART DIRECTORS: PAULA
BENSON, PAUL WEST
DESIGNER: CLAIRE WARNER
CLIENT: UNIFORM TOOLS:
FREEHAND, MAC MATERIALS:
PLASTIC AIR BAG

0749
ART DIRECTOR: PAUL WEST
DESIGNER: PAUL WEST CLIENT:
VISION ON TOOLS: QUARK, MAC
MATERIALS: DEBOSSED LOGO
ON VELVET

0820
ART DIRECTOR: PAUL WEST
DESIGNERS: PAUL WEST, CHRIS
HILTON CLIENT: MUSIC
WEEK/CMP TOOLS: PHOTOSHOP,
FREEHAND, QUARK, MAC
MATERIALS: SCREEN-PRINTED
FROMACONE COVER

FORM FÜNF
0566
ART DIRECTORS: ECKHARD
JUNG, DANIEL BASTIAN
DESIGNERS: DAVID
LINEDEMANN, RASMUS GIESEL,
ISABELL ZIRBECK CLIENT:
GOHRSHUHLE BANKPOST
TOOLS: FREEHAND MATERIALS:
STÜRKEN DRUCK

0990
ART DIRECTORS: DANIEL
BASTIAN, ULYSSES VOE TOOLS:
QUARK MATERIALS: GOHRS
MÜHLE

THE FORMATION
0387
ART DIRECTOR: ADRIAN KILBY
DESIGNERS: ADRIAN KILBY,
AIMÉE MARTEN CLIENT: THE
FORMATION MATERIALS: G.F.
SMITH COLOURPLAN, CURTISS
SUPERWOVE

FORTYFOUR DESIGN
0049, 0066, 0200, 0234, 0773
ART DIRECTORS: LISA
MINICHIELLO, DEAN GORISSEN
DESIGNER: LISA MINICHIELLO
CLIENT: CRC FOR FCS
ILLUSTRATOR: DEAN GORISSEN
PHOTOGRAPHER: JAMES
BRAUND TOOLS: ILLUSTRATOR,
PHOTOSHOP, QUARK, MAC
MATERIALS: SPICERS IMPRESS
SATIN, CURIOUS

FOTOGRAFIE & GESTALTUNG CHRISTIAN NIELINGER
0922
ART DIRECTOR: CHRISTIAN
NIELINGER DESIGNER:
CHRISTIAN NIELINGER CLIENT:
CHRISTIAN NIELINGER TOOLS:
PHOTOSHOP, QUARK, MAC
MATERIALS: ARJOWIGGINS
CURIOUS METALLICS OXYGEN
WHITE 240GSM

FOUR-LETTER WORD
0239
ART DIRECTOR: PETER WARD
DESIGNER: NEIL QUIDDINGTON
CLIENT: YI-BAN RESTAURANT
TOOLS: ILLUSTRATOR, PHOTO-
SHOP, QUARK, MAC

FOXINABOX
0431, 0727
TOOLS: ILLUSTRATOR,
PHOTOSHOP, QUARK

FROST DESIGN, LONDON
0957, 0965, 0986, 1000
ART DIRECTOR: VINCE FROST
DESIGNERS: VINCE FROST,
MATT WILLEY CLIENT: SIMON
FINCH RARE BOOKS
MATERIALS: WOODFREE GLOSS
PAPER 250GSM, OPP MATT LAM-
INATE PAGES (COVER), GALERIE
FINE PAPER 90GSM (TEXT)

GEE & CHUNG DESIGN
0229
ART DIRECTOR: EARL GEE
DESIGNERS: EARL GEE, FANI
CHUNG CLIENT: COMVENTURES
PHOTOGRAPHER: HENRIK KAM
TOOLS: PHOTOSHOP, QUARK,
MAC G4 MATERIALS: POTLATCH
MCCOY SILK COVER 80LB AND
120LB

0260, 0264
ART DIRECTOR: EARL GEE
DESIGNERS: EARL GEE, FANI
CHUNG PHOTOGRAPHER: KEVIN
IRBY CLIENT: XINET, INC.
TOOLS: ILLUSTRATOR, PHOTO-
SHOP, QUARK MATERIALS:
POTLATCH MCCOY UNCOATED
80LB COVER, MOHAWK
SUPERFINE SMOOTH 65LB
COVER PRINTING: OFFSET
LITHOGRAPHY

GILLESPIE DESIGN
0389
ART DIRECTOR: MAUREEN
GILLESPIE DESIGNER: LIZ
SCHENKEL CLIENT: WENDY
AND AMY TOOLS: ILLUSTRATOR,
QUARK, MAC MATERIALS:
NEENAH ENVIRONMENT

0489
ART DIRECTOR: MAUREEN
GILLESPIE DESIGNER: LIZ
SCHENKEL CLIENT: GILLESPIE
DESIGN TOOLS: PHOTOSHOP,
QUARK, MAC

0497, 0863
ART DIRECTOR: MAUREEN
GILLESPIE DESIGNER: LIZ
SCHENKEL CLIENT: GILLESPIE
DESIGN TOOLS: PHOTOSHOP,
QUARK, MAC MATERIALS:
CHAMPION BENEFIT

0701
ART DIRECTOR: MAUREEN
GILLESPIE DESIGNER:
MAUREEN GILLESPIE CLIENT:
AMERICA ONLINE TOOLS:
ILLUSTRATOR, QUARK, MAC
MATERIALS: HONEYCOMB
ORANGE VINYL

GIORGIO DAVANZO DESIGN
0162
DESIGNER: GIORGIO DAVANZO
CLIENT: LOOPWORX TOOLS:
PHOTOSHOP, QUARK, MAC
MATERIALS: CRANE'S CREST
100% COTTON

0175
DESIGNER: GIORGIO DAVANZO
CLIENT: SENOK TEA TOOLS:
PHOTOSHOP, QUARK, MAC
MATERIALS: STRATHMORE
CLASSIC

0176
DESIGNER: GIORGIO DAVANZO
CLIENT: GIORGIO DAVANZO
TOOLS: PHOTOSHOP, QUARK,
MAC MATERIALS: METAL

0649
DESIGNER: GIORGIO DAVANZO
CLIENT: GIORGIO DAVANZO
TOOLS: ILLUSTRATOR, PHOTO-
SHOP, QUARK, MAC MATERIALS:
STRATHMORE SCRIPT

0801
DESIGNER: GIORGIO DAVANZO
CLIENT: GIORGIO DAVANZO
TOOLS: ILLUSTRATOR, MAC
MATERIALS: LEXAN

GOUTHIER DESIGN INC.
0044
ART DIRECTOR: JONATHAN
GOUTHIER DESIGNER:
JONATHAN GOUTHIER CLIENT:
AIGA MIAMI, XPEDX, MOHAWK
TOOLS: ILLUSTRATOR, PHOTO-
SHOP, QUARK, MAC MATERIALS:
MOHAWK SUPERFINE

0484
ART DIRECTOR: JONATHAN
GOUTHIER DESIGNERS:
JONATHAN GOUTHIER, KILEY
DEL VALLE CLIENT: GOUTHIER
DESIGN INC. TOOLS: ILLUSTRA-
TOR, PHOTOSHOP, QUARK, MAC
MATERIALS: FRENCH
CONSTRUCTION, STORA ENZO
CENTRALE

0610
ART DIRECTOR: JONATHAN
GOUTHIER DESIGNERS:
JONATHAN GOUTHIER, KILEY
DEL VALLE CLIENT:
ADVERTISING FEDERATION OF
GREATER FORT LAUDERDALE
TOOLS: ILLUSTRATOR, QUARK,
MAC MATERIALS: EPSON HIGH
QUALITY INKJET, FRENCH
CONSTRUCTION

0611
ART DIRECTOR: JONATHAN
GOUTHIER DESIGNERS:
JONATHAN GOUTHIER, KILEY
DEL VALLE CLIENT: SAMANTHA
SCOTT PHOTOGRAPHY TOOLS:
ILLUSTRATOR, PHOTOSHOP,
QUARK, MAC MATERIALS:
FRENCH PAPER SMART WHITE

0634
ART DIRECTOR: JONATHAN
GOUTHIER DESIGNER:
JONATHAN GOUTHIER CLIENT:
GOUTHIER DESIGN INC. TOOLS:
ILLUSTRATOR, PHOTOSHOP,
QUARK, MAC MATERIALS:
PORCELAIN, GLASS

0887
ART DIRECTOR: JONATHAN
GOUTHIER DESIGNERS:
JONATHAN GOUTHIER, KILEY
DEL VALLE CLIENT: GOUTHIER
DESIGN INC. TOOLS:
ILLUSTRATOR, QUARK, MAC
MATERIALS: MOHAWK
SUPERFINE

GRAPEFRUIT DESIGN
0209
ART DIRECTOR: MARIUS
URSACHE DESIGNER: MARIUS
URSACHE CLIENT: GRAPEFRUIT
DESIGN TOOLS: ILLUSTRATOR,
PHOTOSHOP MATERIALS:
GARDA MATT

GRAPHISCHE FORMGEBUNG
0060
ART DIRECTOR: HERBERT
ROHSIEPE DESIGNER:
HERBERT ROHSIEPE CLIENT:
GRAPHISCHE FORMGEBUNG
HERBERT ROHSIEPE
PHOTOGRAPHER: HERBERT
ROHSIEPE TOOLS: PHOTOSHOP,
FREEHAND, MAC MATERIALS:
ARJOWIGGINS IMPRESSIONS
RIVES ARTIST SENSATION
NATUR 250GSM

0101
ART DIRECTOR: HERBERT
ROHSIEPE DESIGNER:
HERBERT ROHSIEPE CLIENT:
SORADIOSO/CYRUS KARGAR
TOOLS: PHOTOSHOP, FREEHAND,
MAC

0551
ART DIRECTOR: HERBERT
ROHSIEPE DESIGNER:
HERBERT ROHSIEPE CLIENT:
WP.DATA, RAINER
SCHUMACHER & JÜRGEN
SEIFERT TOOLS: PHOTOSHOP,
FREEHAND, MAC MATERIALS:
SCHNEIDERSOEHNE,
LUXOSAMTOFFSET

GREENFIELD/BELSER
0462
ART DIRECTOR: BURKEY
BELSER DESIGNERS: BURKEY
BELSER, LIZA CORBETT CLIENT:
WEIL GOTSHAL AND MANGES
TOOLS: PHOTOSHOP, QUARK
MATERIALS: MCCOY 120LB SILK
COVER, MCCOY 100LB SILK TEXT
PRINTING: 2 PMS, SGV, SDV
(COVER), 4-COLOR, SGV, SDV
(TEXT)

GREENEWEIG DESIGN
0880
ART DIRECTOR: TIM
GREENEWEIG DESIGNER: TIM
GREENEWEIG CLIENT:
GREENEWEIG DESIGN TOOLS:
PHOTOSHOP, QUARK, MAC
MATERIALS: 120LB REPLY

GRETEMAN GROUP
0694
ART DIRECTOR: SONIA
GRETEMAN DESIGNERS:
JAMES STRANGE, CRAIG
TOMSON CLIENT: GRETEMAN
GROUP TOOLS: FREEHAND

GROOTHUIS + MALSY
0849, 0983
ART DIRECTORS: RAINER
GROOTHUIS, GILMAR WENDT
DESIGNERS: RAINER GROOTHUIS,
GILMAR WENDT CLIENT:
VERLAG KLAUS WAGENBACH
TOOLS: QUARK, MAC

HAND MADE GROUP
0018
ART DIRECTOR: ALESSANDRO
ESTERI DESIGNER: GIOMA
MAIARECCI CLIENT: LANIFICIO
F. LLI CERROTII TOOLS: QUARK
MATERIALS: PLIKE
CORDEMONS

0068, 0258, 0642, 0670, 0728
ART DIRECTOR: ALESSANDRO
ESTERI DESIGNER: GIOMA
MAIARECCI CLIENT: LANIFICIO
F. LLI CERROTII TOOLS:
PHOTOSHOP, QUARK
MATERIALS: ZANDERS

0550
ART DIRECTOR: ALESSANDRO
ESTERI DESIGNER: GIOMA
MAIARECCI CLIENT: LANIFICIO
F. LLI CERROTII TOOLS: QUARK
MATERIALS: GSK ZANDERS

0593, 0678
ART DIRECTOR: ALESSANDRO
ESTERI DESIGNER:
ALESSANDRO ESTERI CLIENT:
OSO TOOLS: QUARK

HANS DESIGN
0332
ART DIRECTORS: BILL HANS, T.
MARTI DESIGNER: KRISTIN
MIASO CLIENT: SALON GIA
TOOLS: ILLUSTRATOR, QUARK
MATERIALS: FRASER

HARRIMANSTEEL
0558
ART DIRECTOR:
HARRIMANSTEEL DESIGNER:
HARRIMANSTEEL CLIENT: NIKE
MATERIALS: RETREEVE

0643
ART DIRECTOR:
HARRIMANSTEEL DESIGNER:
HARRIMANSTEEL CLIENT:
HARRIMANSTEEL MATERIALS:
KRAFT PAPER

0763
ART DIRECTOR:
HARRIMANSTEEL DESIGNER:
HARRIMANSTEEL CLIENT:
HARRIMANSTEEL MATERIALS:
BOOKLET PAPER VERUSION
120GSM

0765
ART DIRECTOR:
HARRIMANSTEEL DESIGNER:
HARRIMANSTEEL CLIENT: NIKE
MATERIALS: TESLIN 305
MICRONS (WATERPROOF
PAPER), PVC POUCH, MUD,
CLEAR GEL (TO LOOK LIKE
WATER)

0771, 0812
ART DIRECTOR:
HARRIMANSTEEL DESIGNER:
HARRIMANSTEEL CLIENT: NIKE
MATERIALS: POLYPROPYLENE

0940
ART DIRECTOR:
HARRIMANSTEEL DESIGNER:
HARRIMANSTEEL CLIENT:
HARRIMANSTEEL MATERIALS:
FEDRIGONI SPLENDOURLUX

AMANDA HAVEL
0100
DESIGNER: AMANDA HAVEL
CLIENT: BREEANNA REILLY
TOOLS: ILLUSTRATOR, MAC
MATERIALS: COLORED WAX,
BRASS STAMP

HEATHER BIANCHI DESIGN
0367
DESIGNER: HEATHER BIANCHI
CLIENT: HEATHER BIANCHI
TOOLS: PHOTOSHOP, QUARK
MATERIALS: RIBBON, CLEAR
PHOTOCORNERS

HESSE DESIGN
0023, 0138, 0966, 0971
ART DIRECTOR: KLAUS HESSE
DESIGNER: KLAUS HESSE
CLIENT: ACADEMY OF ART AND
DESIGN OFFENBACH/MAIN

HGV FELTON
0019
ART DIRECTOR: PIERRE
VERMEIR DESIGNER: PIERRE
VERMEIR CLIENT: HGV
MATERIALS: 300GSM
MODIGLIANNI NOTTURNO
(COVER), CHROMOLUX GLOSS
ART (TEXT)

0156
ART DIRECTOR: PIERRE
VERMEIR DESIGNER: PIERRE
VERMEIR CLIENT: ROYAL MAIL
MATERIALS: THERMOCHROMIC
INK, EMBOSSING, HOLO-
GRAPHIC FOIL, INTAGLIO

0218
ART DIRECTOR: PIERRE
VERMEIR DESIGNER: FARRAH
GUDGEON CLIENT: HGV
MATERIALS: 1,000 MICRONS
GREYBOARD

0257
ART DIRECTOR: PIERRE
VERMEIR DESIGNER: TOMMY
TAYLOR CLIENT: VANILLA

0405, 0424
ART DIRECTOR: PIERRE
VERMEIR DESIGNER: DAMIAN
NOWELL CLIENT: BAILHACHE
LABESSE MATERIALS:
CONSORT ROYAL

0430
ART DIRECTOR: PIERRE
VERMEIR DESIGNER: PIERRE
VERMEIR CLIENT: BAILACHE
LABESSE MATERIALS:
CONSORT ROYAL

0766, 0816
ART DIRECTOR: PIERRE
VERMEIR DESIGNER: DAMIAN
NOWELL CLIENT: HGV FELTON
MATERIALS: LIVE EDGE

0852
ART DIRECTOR: PIERRE
VERMEIR DESIGNER: TOMMY
TAYLOR, DAMIAN NOWELL
CLIENT: SCOPE TOOLS:
PHOTOSHOP MATERIALS:
70GSM PRINTSPEED

HORNALL ANDERSON DESIGN WORKS
0225
ART DIRECTOR: JACK ANICKER
DESIGNERS: KATHY SAITO,
HENRY YIU, SONJA MAX
CLIENT: INSITE WORKS
ARCHITECTS

0449
ART DIRECTOR: JACK
ANDERSON DESIGNERS: JACK
ANDERSON, HENRY YIU CLIENT:
BOEING

0455
ART DIRECTORS: JACK
ANDERSON, KATHA DALTON
DESIGNERS: KATHA DALTON,
GRETCHEN COOK, SONJA MAX,
HENRY YIU CLIENT: LINCOLN
SQUARE

0466
ART DIRECTORS: JACK
ANDERSON, JOHN ANICKER
DESIGNERS: JACK ANDERSON,
JOHN ANICKER, ANDREW
SMITH, ANDREW WICKLUND,
MARY HERMES, JOHN ANDERLE
PHOTOGRAPHER: SHARON
GREEN CLIENT: ONEWORLD
CHALLENGE TOOLS: FREEHAND
MATERIALS: 80LB GOLD ESSE
TEXTURE (COVER), 70LB
RECYCLED WHITE MOHAWK
SUPERFINE TEXT SMOOTH (TEXT)

0712
ART DIRECTOR: JACK ANDERSON DESIGNERS: JULIE LOCK, JANA WILSON ESSER CLIENT: OKAMOTO CORPORATION

DAWN HOSKINSON
0398, 0673
ART DIRECTOR: DAWN HOSKINSON DESIGNERS: SEAN CULLEN, SIMON HIGBY CLIENT: DAWN HOSKINSON TOOLS: QUARK MATERIALS: TIN CAN, PAPER

MINGZHAN HUANG
0433, 0572
DESIGNER: MINGZHAN HUANG CLIENT: VISUAL WORK FOR MASTER'S IN VISUAL COMMUNICATION TOOLS: ILLUSTRATOR, PHOTOSHOP, MAC, PC MATERIALS: CONQUEROR PAPER, MISCELLANEOUS MATERIALS

IAMALWAYSHUNGRY
0053
ART DIRECTOR: NESSIM HIGSON DESIGNER: NESSIM HIGSON TOOLS: ILLUSTRATOR, QUARK MATERIALS: HANDMADE MULBERRY PAPER

0104
ART DIRECTOR: NESSIM HIGSON DESIGNER: NESSIM HIGSON CLIENT: IAMALWAYSHUNGRY TOOLS: PHOTOSHOP, TRANSFERS MATERIALS: HANDMADE PAPER

0385
ART DIRECTOR: NESSIM HIGSON DESIGNER: NESSIM HIGSON CLIENT: IAMALWAYSHUNGRY TOOLS: PHOTOSHOP, PHOTOCOPY MACHINE MATERIALS: ACETATE, PLEXIGLAS

0958
ART DIRECTOR: NESSIM HIGSON DESIGNER: NESSIM HIGSON CLIENT: CITY STYLES TOOLS: ILLUSTRATOR, TRANSFERS MATERIALS: T-SHIRT

0984
ART DIRECTOR: NESSIM HIGSON DESIGNER: NESSIM HIGSON CLIENT: VULCAN CORP. TOOLS: PHOTOSHOP MATERIALS: STORA ENSO 100LB

0994
ART DIRECTOR: NESSIM HIGSON DESIGNER: NESSIM HIGSON CLIENT: SHIFT TOOLS: PHOTOSHOP

IE DESIGN
0319
ART DIRECTOR: MARCIE CARSON CLIENT: IE DESIGN

0322
ART DIRECTOR: MARCIE CARSON CLIENT: EL CAMINO RESOURCES INTERNATIONAL TOOLS: PHOTOSHOP, QUARK

0326
ART DIRECTOR: MARCIE CARSON DESIGNER: RICHARD HAYNIE CLIENT: CREATIVE DESIGN GROUP TOOLS: ILLUSTRATOR

0395
ART DIRECTOR: MARCIE CARSON CLIENT: GOOD GRACIOUS! CATERING

0564
ART DIRECTOR: MARCIE CARSON CLIENT: JENNIFER NICHOLSON TOOLS: ILLUSTRATOR

0625
ART DIRECTOR: CAROL KUMMER CLIENT: USCF COMPREHENSIVE CANCER CENTER

0839
ART DIRECTOR: MARCIE CARSON CLIENT: USC SCHOOL OF ENGINEERING

IMAGINATION (GIC)
0400
ART DIRECTOR: CHRIS HAMMOND DESIGNER: STEPHANE HARRISON CLIENT: E.A. SHAW

0532
ART DIRECTOR: CHRIS HAMMOND DESIGNER: STEPHANE HARRISON CLIENT: E.A. SHAW MATERIALS: CONSORT

IRBE DESIGN
0711
ART DIRECTOR: IGORS IRBE CLIENT: IRBE DESIGN TOOLS: PHOTOSHOP, QUARK, MAC MATERIALS: GILBERT CLEAR VELLUM

IRIDIUM, A DESIGN AGENCY
0048
ART DIRECTORS: JEAN-LUC DENAT, GAÉTAN ALBERT DESIGNER: GAÉTAN ALBERT CLIENT: OTTAWA KNIGHTS TOOLS: ILLUSTRATOR, QUARK, MAC MATERIALS: DOMTAR FUSION (5 COLORS)

0123
ART DIRECTORS: JEAN-LUC DENAT, MARIO L'ÉCUYER DESIGNER: MARIO L'ÉCUYER CLIENT: MITEL CORPORATION TOOLS: PHOTOSHOP, QUARK, MAC MATERIALS: GRAPHIKA LINEAL, POTLATCH MCCOY GLOSS, FRENCH PAPERS CONSTRUCTION

0223
ART DIRECTOR: MARIO L'ÉCUYER DESIGNER: MARIO L'ÉCUYER CLIENT: NYGEM CORPORATION TOOLS: ILLUSTRATOR, PHOTOSHOP, QUARK, MAC MATERIALS: MOHAWK SUPERFINE

0224
ART DIRECTORS: MARIO L'ÉCUYER, JEAN-LUC DENAT DESIGNER: MARIO L'ÉCUYER CLIENT: SCHOELER + HEATON ARCHITECTS TOOLS: ILLUSTRATOR, PHOTOSHOP, QUARK, MAC MATERIALS: FOX RIVER STARWHITE

0226
ART DIRECTORS: JEAN-LUC DENAT, ETIENNE BESSETTE DESIGNER: ETIENNE BESSETTE CLIENT: SERVICE PLUS TOOLS: ILLUSTRATOR, QUARK, MAC MATERIALS: CONDAT SUPREME GLOSS

0281
ART DIRECTORS: MARIO L'ÉCUYER, JEAN-LUC DENAT DESIGNER: MARIO L'ÉCUYER CLIENT: TETHER CAM SYSTEMS TOOLS: ILLUSTRATOR, PHOTOSHOP, QUARK, MAC MATERIALS: MOHAWK SUPERFINE, FRENCH PAPERS CONSTRUCTION

0314
ART DIRECTORS: JEAN-LUC DENAT, MARIO L'ÉCUYER DESIGNERS: MARIO L'ÉCUYER, DAVID DAIGLE CLIENT: SSHRC TOOLS: ILLUSTRATOR, PHOTOSHOP, QUARK, MAC MATERIALS: SAPPI LUSTRO DULL, DOMTAR CORNWALL PINWEAVE CIS, ROLLAND OPAQUE

0315
ART DIRECTOR: JEAN-LUC DENAT DESIGNERS: MARIO L'ÉCUYER, MARY KOCH CLIENT: MITEL CORPORATION TOOLS: ILLUSTRATOR, PHOTOSHOP, QUARK, MAC MATERIALS: BECKETT CAMBRIC, SAPPI HORIZON SILK

0323
ART DIRECTOR: MARIO L'ÉCUYER DESIGNER: MARIO L'ÉCUYER CLIENT: NEXWARE CORPORATION TOOLS: QUARK, ILLUSTRATOR, PHOTOSHOP, MAC MATERIALS: BECKETT EXPRESSION, GILBERT GILCLEAR

0355, 0684
ART DIRECTORS: MARIO L'ÉCUYER, JEAN-LUC DENAT DESIGNER: MARIO L'ÉCUYER ILLUSTRATOR: MARIO L'ÉCUYER CLIENT: COCREATIONS LIGHTING DESIGN TOOLS: PHOTOSHOP, QUARK, MAC G3 MATERIALS: GEORGIA-PACIFIC PROTERRA, FOX RIVER CONFETTI

0384
ART DIRECTORS: JEAN-LUC DENAT, MARIO L'ÉCUYER, DAVID DAIGLE DESIGNER: MARIO L'ÉCUYER CLIENT: GENOME CANADA TOOLS: ILLUSTRATOR, PHOTOSHOP, QUARK, MAC MATERIALS: DOMTAR PLAINFIELD HOMESPUN, DOMTAR SKYTONE, GLAMA NATURAL

0510
ART DIRECTOR: MARIO L'ÉCUYER DESIGNER: MARIO L'ÉCUYER CLIENT: CANADA DANCE FESTIVAL TOOLS: PHOTOSHOP, QUARK, MAC MATERIALS: CURTIS TUSCAN ANTIQUE, FOX RIVER CONFETTI AND CIRCA

0514
ART DIRECTORS: JEAN-LUC DENAT, MARIO L'ÉCUYER DESIGNER: MARIO L'ÉCUYER CLIENT: COCREATIONS LIGHTING DESIGN TOOLS: ILLUSTRATOR, PHOTOSHOP, QUARK, MAC MATERIALS: GEORGIA-PACIFIC PROTERRA, FOX RIVER CIRCA, CHICAGO SCREWS

0556
ART DIRECTORS: MARIO L'ÉCUYER, JEAN-LUC DENAT DESIGNER: MARIO L'ÉCUYER CLIENT: CANADIAN INSTITUTES OF HEALTH RESEARCH TOOLS: ILLUSTRATOR, PHOTOSHOP, QUARK, MAC MATERIALS: MOHAWK SUPERFINE EGGSHELL, GLAMA NATURAL, RIVETS

0576
ART DIRECTORS: JEAN-LUC DENAT, MARIO L'ÉCUYER, DAVID DAIGLE DESIGNER: MARIO L'ÉCUYER CLIENT: GENOME CANADA TOOLS: ILLUSTRATOR, PHOTOSHOP, QUARK, MAC MATERIALS: DOMTAR PLAINFIELD HOMESPUN, DOMTAR SKYTONE, GLAMA NATURAL

0629
ART DIRECTOR: JEAN-LUC DENAT DESIGNER: MARIO L'ÉCUYER CLIENT: CANADIAN INDEPENDENT FILM AND VIDEO FUND TOOLS: PHOTOSHOP, QUARK, MAC MATERIALS: STRATHMORE ELEMENTS, SHREDDED PAPER, FILM CAN

0992
ART DIRECTOR: ETIENNE BESSETTE DESIGNER: ETIENNE BESSETTE CLIENT: EPSILON TOOLS: ILLUSTRATOR, PHOTOSHOP, QUARK MATERIALS: SAPPI HORIZON SILK

JADE DESIGN
0330
ART DIRECTOR: JAMES ALEXANDER DESIGNER: JAMES ALEXANDER CLIENT: TYPOGRAPHIC CIRCLE TOOLS: ILLUSTRATOR, QUARK, MAC MATERIALS: COLORPLAN

0710
ART DIRECTOR: JAMES ALEXANDER DESIGNER: JAMES ALEXANDER CLIENT: TYPOGRAPHIC CIRCLE TOOLS: ILLUSTRATOR, QUARK, MAC MATERIALS: PLASMA POLYCOAT (CLEAR)

0810
ART DIRECTOR: JAMES ALEXANDER CLIENT: RGL TOOLS: ILLUSTRATOR, QUARK, MAC MATERIALS: ENCAPSULATED OILS

JASON & JASON
0058
ART DIRECTOR: JONATHAN JASON DESIGNER: DALIA INBAR CLIENT: ESRA TOOLS: PHOTOSHOP, FREEHAND MATERIALS: 300GSM CHROME PAPER

0168
ART DIRECTOR: JONATHAN JASON DESIGNER: DALIA INBAR CLIENT: TELRAD TOOLS: PHOTOSHOP, FREEHAND MATERIALS: 300GSM CHROME PAPER

0227
ART DIRECTOR: JONATHAN JASON DESIGNER: TAMAR LOURIE CLIENT: NUR MACROPRINTERS TOOLS: PHOTOSHOP, FREEHAND MATERIALS: 300GSM CHROME

0254, 0441
ART DIRECTOR: JONATHAN JASON DESIGNER: DALIA INBAR CLIENT: KERYX BIOPHARMACEUTICALS INC. COPYWRITER: AUDREY GERBER PHOTOGRAPHER: YORUM ASHAIM TOOLS: PHOTOSHOP, FREEHAND MATERIALS: 300GSM CHROME (COVER), 250GSM CHROME (INTERIOR)

0273
ART DIRECTOR: JONATHAN JASON DESIGNER: TAMAR LOURIE CLIENT: RR DONNELLY TOOLS: PHOTOSHOP, FREEHAND MATERIALS: 300GSM CHROME

0299
ART DIRECTOR: JONATHAN JASON DESIGNER: DALIA INBAR CLIENT: GILON TOOLS: PHOTOSHOP, FREEHAND MATERIALS: 300GSM CHROME PAPER

0309
ART DIRECTOR: JONATHAN JASON DESIGNER: DALIA INBAR CLIENT: ACTIMIZE TOOLS: PHOTOSHOP, FREEHAND MATERIALS: 300GSM CHROME PAPER

0364
ART DIRECTOR: JONATHAN JASON DESIGNERS: DALIA INBAR, TAMAR LOURIE CLIENT: RR DONNELLY TOOLS: PHOTOSHOP, FREEHAND MATERIALS: 300GSM CHROME PAPER (COVER), 225GSM CHROMO (INTERIOR)

0445
ART DIRECTOR: JONATHAN JASON DESIGNER: TAMAR LOURIE CLIENT: NUR MACROPRINTERS COPYWRITER: AUDREY GERBER TOOLS: PHOTOSHOP, FREEHAND MATERIALS: 300GSM CHROME

JOHNSON BANKS
0306
ART DIRECTOR: MICHAEL JOHNSON DESIGNER: MICHAEL JOHNSON CLIENT: CAMPAIGN FOR CLIMATE CHANGE TOOLS: FREEHAND MATERIALS: MAP PAPER

0539
ART DIRECTOR: MICHAEL JOHNSON DESIGNER: SARAH FULLERTON CLIENT: DESIGN COUNCIL TOOLS: QUARK MATERIALS: NEPTUNE UNIQUE

0540, 0549
ART DIRECTOR: MICHAEL JOHNSON DESIGNER: SARAH FULLERTON CLIENT: JOHNSON BANKS TOOLS: QUARK MATERIALS: THIN UNCOATED

0726
ART DIRECTOR: MICHAEL JOHNSON DESIGNERS: JULIA WOOLAMS, KRAN OCTOPUS CLIENT: CONRAN OCTOPUS TOOLS: QUARK MATERIALS: CLOTH, MACHINE EMBROIDERY

JONES DESIGN GROUP
0111
ART DIRECTOR: VICKY JONES DESIGNER: BETSY PEREZ CLIENT: COCA-COLA TOOLS: QUARK MATERIALS: DOMTAR FELTWEAVE 100LB COVER

0344
ART DIRECTOR: VICKY JONES DESIGNER: HOLLEY SILIRIE CLIENT: DEVIN PROPERTIES TOOLS: PHOTOSHOP, QUARK MATERIALS: 100LB COUGAR OPAQUE NATURAL COVER

0618, 0630
ART DIRECTOR: VICKY JONES DESIGNER: BRODY BOYER CLIENT: JONES DESIGN GROUP TOOLS: ILLUSTRATOR, QUARK MATERIALS: AIR FRESHENER

0761
ART DIRECTOR: VICKY JONES DESIGNER: HOLLEY SILIRIE CLIENT: COCA-COLA TOOLS: ILLUSTRATOR, QUARK MATERIALS: CARDBOARD, MYLAR

0903
ART DIRECTOR: VICKY JONES DESIGNERS: KATHERINE STAGGS, BRODY BOYE CLIENT: JONES DESIGN GROUP TOOLS: ILLUSTRATOR, QUARK MATERIALS: TATTOOS

JULIA TAM DESIGN
0210
ART DIRECTOR: JULIA CHONG TAM DESIGNER: JULIA CHONG TAM CLIENT: JULIA TAM DESIGN TOOLS: ILLUSTRATOR, QUARK, MAC

KBDA
0093
ART DIRECTOR: KIM BAER DESIGNER: KATE RIVINUS CLIENT: JEWISH COMMUNITY FOUNDATION TOOLS: MAC

0303, 0627
ART DIRECTOR: KIM BAER DESIGNER: JAMIE DIERSING CLIENT: KBDA TOOLS: QUARK, MAC

0529
ART DIRECTOR: KIM BAER DESIGNER: BARBARA COOPER CLIENT: LEE BURKHART LIU TOOLS: MAC

0536, 0732
ART DIRECTOR: KIM BAER DESIGNER: MAGGIE VAN OPPEN CLIENT: ARMORY CENTER FOR THE ARTS TOOLS: MAC

KEARNEY ROCHOLL
0374
ART DIRECTOR: FRANK ROCHOLL DESIGNER: DMITRI LAVROW CLIENT: MÖLLER DESIGN TOOLS: QUARK, MAC MATERIALS: ZANDERS GALAXY KERA

0782
ART DIRECTOR: FRANK ROCHOLL CLIENT: KEARNEY ROCHOLL TOOLS: QUARK MATERIALS: ZANDERS GALAXY 250GSM, PLEXIGLAS

0995
ART DIRECTOR: FRANK ROCHOLL DESIGNER: DMITRI LAVROW CLIENT: MÖLLER DESIGN TOOLS: QUARK, MAC MATERIALS: ZANDERS GALAXY KERA

KESSELS KRAMER
0251
ART DIRECTOR: ERIK KESSELS COPYWRITER: JOHAN KRAMER

0436
ART DIRECTORS: ERIK KESSELS, KAREN HEUTER CLIENT: DO FUTURE COPYWRITER: DAVE BELL

0443
ART DIRECTORS: ERIK KESSELS, KRISTA ROZEMA CREATIVE DIRECTOR: DAVE BELL CLIENT: 55 DSL—CHRISTINA CLERICI, ANDREA ROSSO, JEAN-LUC BATTAGLIA COPYWRITER: PATRICK VAN DER GRONDE PHOTOGRAPHER: ROD MORATA PRODUCTION: PIETER LEENDERTSE

0446
ART DIRECTOR: ERIK KESSELS COPYWRITER: CHAD RHEA PHOTOGRAPHER: ROY TZIDON

0450
ART DIRECTOR: ERIK KESSELS COPYWRITER: LORENZO DE RITA

0454
ART DIRECTORS: ERIK KESSELS, PIM VAN NUENEN COPYWRITER: LORENZO DE RITA

0456, 0457
ART DIRECTOR: ERIK KESSELS

0459
ART DIRECTOR: ERIK KESSELS CLIENT: DIESEL SPA COPYWRITER: TYLER WHISNAND PHOTOGRAPHER: FINLAY MACKAY @ MARCO SANTUCCI STRATEGY: MATTHIJS DE JONGH PRODUCTION: PIETER LEENDERTSE VISUALIZATION: ARNO PETERS

0657
ART DIRECTORS: ERIK KESSELS, PIM VAN NUENEN CLIENT: ONVZ

0665
ART DIRECTORS: ERIK KESSELS COPYWRITER: JUYITOKUDA

0786
ART DIRECTORS: ERIK KESSELS, KRISTA ROZEMA COPYWRITER: TYLER WHISNAND

0796
ART DIRECTOR: ERIK KESSELS CLIENT: DIESEL SPA COPYWRITER: JOHAN KRAMER PHOTOGRAPHER: CARL DE KEYZER STRATEGY: MATTHIJS DE JONGH TYPOGRAPHER: ANTHONY BURRILL PRODUCER: LUCIE TENNEY FROM DIESEL: STEFANO CAPUTO, GIORGIO PRESCA, WILBERT DAS

0997
ART DIRECTORS: ERIK KESSELS, KRISTA ROZEMA CLIENT: HANS BRINKER COPYWRITER: DAVE BELL

KINETIC SINGAPORE
0157, 0331
ART DIRECTORS: PANN LIM, LENG SOH, ROY POH DESIGNERS: PANN LIM, LENG SOH, ROY POH CLIENT: KINETIC SINGAPORE TOOLS: FREEHAND MATERIALS: WOODFREE PAPER

0242, 0246, 0250
ART DIRECTORS: ROY POH, PANN LIM DESIGNERS: ROY POH, PANN LIM CLIENT: SINGLETREK CYCLE TOOLS: PHOTOSHOP, FREEHAND MATERIALS: ART PAPER

0279, 0993
ART DIRECTORS: PANN LIM, LENG SOH, ROY POH DESIGNERS: PANN LIM, LENG SOH, ROY POH CLIENT: AMARA HOLDINGS LTD. TOOLS: PHOTOSHOP, FREEHAND MATERIALS: ART CARD, ART PAPER

BASIA KNOBLOCH
0834
ART DIRECTOR: BASIA KNOBLOCH DESIGNER: BASIA KNOBLOCH CLIENT: ART ACADEMY FINAL PROJECT TOOLS: ILLUSTRATOR, MAC MATERIALS: PAPER, SILKSCREEN PRINT

KOEWEIDEN POSTMA
0562
ART DIRECTORS: JACQUES KOEWEIDEN, PAUL POSTMA DESIGNER: JACQUES KOEWEIDEN CLIENT: BOOK INDUSTRY PUBLISHERS

0580
ART DIRECTORS: JACQUES KOEWEIDEN, PAUL POSTMA DESIGNERS: JACQUES KOEWEIDEN, PAUL POSTMA CLIENT: PHOTOGRAPHY ASSOCIATION OF THE NETHERLANDS

0835
ART DIRECTORS: JACQUES KOEWEIDEN, PAUL POSTMA, ALVIN CHAN DESIGNERS: JACQUES KOEWEIDEN, PAUL POSTMA, ALVIN CHAN CLIENT: MIND THE GAP

0961, 0962, 0963, 0964
ART DIRECTORS: JACQUES KOEWEIDEN, PAUL POSTMA DESIGNERS: JACQUES KOEWEIDEN, PAUL POSTMA CLIENT: NIKE EUROPE

0975
ART DIRECTORS: JACQUES KOEWEIDEN DESIGNER: JACQUES KOEWEIDEN CLIENT: MEULENHOFF

0978
ART DIRECTORS: JACQUES KOEWEIDEN, PAUL POSTMA, ALVIN CHAN DESIGNERS: JACQUES KOEWEIDEN, PAUL POSTMA, ALVIN CHAN CLIENT: MINISTRY OF EDUCATION, CULTURE & SCIENCE

0998
ART DIRECTOR: ALVIN CHAN DESIGNER: ALVIN CHAN CLIENT: LEINE & ROEBANA

KOLEGRAM DESIGN
0077
ART DIRECTOR: JEAN-FRANÇOIS PLANTE DESIGNER: JEAN-FRANÇOIS PLANTE CLIENT: ISFI CANADA TOOLS: ILLUSTRATOR, QUARK

0276
ART DIRECTOR: MIKE TEIXEIRA DESIGNER: ANNIE TANGUAY CLIENT: BAYSHORE SHOPPING CENTRE TOOLS: ILLUSTRATOR, QUARK, MAC

0284
ART DIRECTOR: GOWTRAN BLAIS DESIGNER: GOWTRAN BLAIS CLIENT: LE GARAGE TOOLS: ILLUSTRATOR, QUARK, MAC

0285
ART DIRECTOR: GOWTRAN BLAIS DESIGNER: GOWTRAN BLAIS CLIENT: DU PROGRES TOOLS: ILLUSTRATOR, QUARK, MAC

0286, 0668
ART DIRECTOR: MIKE TEIXEIRA DESIGNER: MIKE TEIXEIRA CLIENT: KOLEGRAM DESIGN TOOLS: ILLUSTRATOR, QUARK, MAC

0337
ART DIRECTOR: GOWTRAN BLAIS DESIGNER: GOWTRAN BLAIS CLIENT: CANADIAN COMMISSION FOR UNESCO TOOLS: ILLUSTRATOR, QUARK MATERIALS: TEXTURED PAPER

0363
ART DIRECTOR: MIKE TEIXEIRA DESIGNER: MIKE TEIXEIRA CLIENT: UNISOURCE TOOLS: ILLUSTRATOR, PHOTOSHOP, QUARK

0474, 0737
ART DIRECTOR: MIKE TEIXEIRA DESIGNER: MIKE TEIXEIRA CLIENT: KOLEGRAM AND HEADLIGHT IMAGERY TOOLS: ILLUSTRATOR, PHOTOSHOP, QUARK MATERIALS: PAPER AND CO CUPS, BUBBLE BAG

0482, 0596, 0865
ART DIRECTOR: MIKE TEIXEIRA DESIGNER: MIKE TEIXEIRA CLIENT: CENTRE D'ARTISTES AXENÉ07 TOOLS: ILLUSTRATOR, QUARK MATERIALS: PAPER, STICKER, PLASTIC BAG

0533
ART DIRECTOR: MIKE TEIXEIRA DESIGNER: ANDRÉ MITCHELL CLIENT: KOLEGRAM TOOLS: ILLUSTRATOR, QUARK MATERIALS: PAPER, PLASTIC BAG

0548
ART DIRECTOR: JEAN-FRANÇOIS PLANTE DESIGNER: JEAN-FRANÇOIS PLANTE CLIENT: PORTRAIT GALLERY OF CANADA TOOLS: ILLUSTRATOR, QUARK

0836
ART DIRECTOR: JEAN-FRANÇOIS PLANTE DESIGNER: JEAN-FRANÇOIS PLANTE CLIENT: PORTRAIT GALLERY OF CANADA TOOLS: ILLUSTRATOR, QUARK

0841
ART DIRECTOR: MIKE TEIXEIRA DESIGNER: MIKE TEIXEIRA CLIENT: ADVERTISING AND DESIGN ASSOCIATION OF OTTAWA TOOLS: ILLUSTRATOR, PHOTOSHOP, QUARK

0866
ART DIRECTOR: MIKE TEIXEIRA DESIGNER: MIKE TEIXEIRA CLIENT: KOLEGRAM DESIGN TOOLS: QUARK, MAC

0894
ART DIRECTOR: FRANÇOIS BOUCHER DESIGNER: FRANÇOIS BOUCHER CLIENT: CANADIAN HERITAGE TOOLS: PHOTOSHOP, QUARK, MAC

0902
ART DIRECTOR: MIKE TEIXEIRA DESIGNER: MIKE TEIXEIRA CLIENT: CENTRE D'ARTISTES AXENÉ07 TOOLS: PHOTOSHOP, QUARK MATERIALS: NEWSPA-PER, SEWING IMPLEMENTS

KONTRAPUNKT
0172
ART DIRECTOR: EDUARD CEHOVIN DESIGNER: EDUARD CEHOVIN CLIENT: IVANA WINGHAM MATERIALS: PAPER

0725
ART DIRECTOR: EDUARD CEHOVIN DESIGNER: EDUARD CEHOVIN CLIENT: KONTRAPUNKT MATERIALS: RUBBER BAND

LAVA
0052
CLIENT: STUDIO STALLINGA

0221, 0569
CLIENT: IBM NEDERLAND/VSLP

0240
CLIENT: AALSMEER FLOWER AUCTION

0410
CLIENT: ART DIRECTORS CLUB NEW YORK

0781
CLIENT: VAN HOEKEN/THOES ARCHITECTS TOOLS: PHOTOSHOP, PHOTOCOPY MACHINE

LAYFIELD
0064
ART DIRECTOR: STEPHEN LAYFIELD DESIGNER: STEPHEN LAYFIELD CLIENT: STEVEN AND JULIE SWIRES TOOLS: ILLUSTRATOR MATERIALS: RALEIGH SUPERFINE ULTRA WHITE SMOOTH 352GSM

0169
ART DIRECTOR: STEPHEN LAYFIELD DESIGNER: STEPHEN LAYFIELD CLIENT: THE CATS' HOME TOOLS: ILLUSTRATOR MATERIALS: RALEIGH SUPERFINE ULTRA WHITE SMOOTH 352GSM

0177
ART DIRECTOR: STEPHEN LAYFIELD DESIGNER: STEPHEN LAYFIELD CLIENT: THE SHIRT COMPANY TOOLS: ILLUSTRATOR MATERIALS: RALEIGH SUPERFINE ULTRA WHITE SMOOTH 118GSM

LCTS
0041, 0823
DESIGNER: STEPHANE HARRISON CLIENT: LCTS

LEWIS COMMUNICATIONS
0357
ART DIRECTOR: ROBERT FROEDGE WRITER: CINDY SARGENT CLIENT: LEWIS COMMUNICATIONS TOOLS: PHOTOSHOP, QUARK

0502
ART DIRECTOR: ROBERT FROEDGE WRITER: CINDY SARGENT CLIENT: NASHVILLE SOUNDS BASEBALL TOOLS: PHOTOSHOP, QUARK

0527, 0531
ART DIRECTOR: ROBERT FROEDGE WRITER: CINDY SARGENT CLIENT: NEXTLINK TOOLS: PHOTOSHOP, QUARK MATERIALS: CLASSIC CREST

LIGALUX GMBH
0001, 0837, 0890, 0900, 0919
ART DIRECTOR: CLAUDIA FISCHER-APPELT DESIGNERS: CLAUDIA FISCHER-APPELT, LARS NIEBUHR CLIENT: LIGALUX GMBH TOOLS: FREEHAND, MAC MATERIALS: MUNKEN LUXOMAG

0047
ART DIRECTOR: CLAUDIA FISCHER-APPELT DESIGNER: FLORIAN SCHOFFRO CLIENT: LIGALUX GMBH TOOLS: FREEHAND MATERIALS: 100GSM ATTRACTION

0050
ART DIRECTOR: CLAUDIA FISCHER-APPELT DESIGNER: FLORIAN SCHOFFRO CLIENT: LIGALUX GMBH TOOLS: FREEHAND MATERIALS: 410GSM INVERCOTE DUO

0307
ART DIRECTOR: CLAUDIA FISCHER-APPELT DESIGNERS: ISABELLA HAENDLER, LARS NIEBUHR CLIENT: LIGALUX GMBH

0587
ART DIRECTORS: PETRA MATOUSCHEK, MARTINA MASSONG DESIGNER: ISABELLA MAENOLER CLIENT: FISCHER-APPELT KOMMUNIKATION AND LIGALUX TOOLS: FREEHAND MATERIALS: 135GSM MUNKENPRINT

0608
ART DIRECTORS: PETRA MATOUSCHEK, MARTINA MASSONG DESIGNER: ISABELLA MAENOLER CLIENT: FISCHER-APPELT KOMMUNIKATION AND LIGALUX TOOLS: FREEHAND MATERIALS: 135GSM MUNKENPRINT

0659
ART DIRECTOR: CLAUDIA FISCHER-APPELT DESIGNER: LARS NIEBUHR CLIENT: FISCHER-APPELT KOMMUNIKATION AND LIGALUX TOOLS: FREEHAND, MAC MATERIALS: 135GSM PROFI SILK

0671
ART DIRECTOR: CLAUDIA FISCHER-APPELT DESIGNER: FLORIAN SCHOFFRO CLIENT: LIGALUX GMBH TOOLS: FREEHAND MATERIALS: 300GSM TAURO

LIPPA PEARCE DESIGN
0070, 0403
ART DIRECTOR: HARRY PEARCE DESIGNERS: DOMENIC LIPPA, JEREMY ROO CLIENT: BEN KELLY DESIGN

0135, 0145
ART DIRECTOR: HARRY PEARCE DESIGNER: HARRY PEARCE CLIENT: "26"

0181, 0189
ART DIRECTOR: HARRY PEARCE DESIGNER: HARRY PEARCE CLIENT: LIPPA PEARCE

0192
ART DIRECTOR: DOMENIC LIPPA DESIGNERS: DOMENIC LIPPA, MARK DIAPER CLIENT: CULTURAL INDUSTRIES

0193, 0879
ART DIRECTOR: DOMENIC LIPPA DESIGNER: DOMENIC LIPPA CLIENT: D+AD

0203, 0597
ART DIRECTOR: DOMENIC LIPPA DESIGNER: RACHAEL DINNIS CLIENT: SOUP OPERA

0308
ART DIRECTOR: DOMENIC LIPPA DESIGNERS: DOMENIC LIPPA, MUKESH PALMER CLIENT: ARTHUR ANDERSEN

0338
ART DIRECTOR: HARRY PEARCE DESIGNER: HARRY PEARCE CLIENT: LIPPA PEARCE DESIGN

0378
ART DIRECTOR: HARRY PEARCE DESIGNER: HARRY PEARCE CLIENT: KENNETH GRANGE

0604
ART DIRECTOR: DOMENIC LIPPA DESIGNER: MARK DIAPER CLIENT: TERRENCE HIGGINS TRUST

0615
ART DIRECTOR: DOMENIC LIPPA DESIGNER: DOMENIC LIPPA CLIENT: TORZO MACARONIA

0699
ART DIRECTOR: DOMENIC LIPPA DESIGNERS: DOMENIC LIPPA, MARK DIAPER CLIENT: CULTURAL INDUSTRIES

0855
ART DIRECTOR: HARRY PEARCE DESIGNER: HARRY PEARCE CLIENT: LIPPA PEARCE DESIGN

0976
ART DIRECTOR: DOMENIC LIPPA DESIGNERS: DOMENIC LIPPA, MUKESH PALMER CLIENT: THE TYPOGRAPHIC CIRCLE

LISKA + ASSOCIATES
0495
ART DIRECTOR: STEVE LISKA DESIGNER: KIM FRY CLIENT: LISKA + ASSOCIATES, INC. TOOLS: PHOTOSHOP, QUARK, MAC MATERIALS: SAPPI STROBE GLOSS PRINTING: 4-COLOR PROCESS

LIQUID AGENCY, INC.
0080
ART DIRECTOR: JOSHUA SWANBECK DESIGNER: JOSHUA SWANBECK CLIENT: ICA TOOLS: MAC MATERIALS: STRATHMORE GRANDEE

0290
ART DIRECTOR: JOSHUA SWANBECK DESIGNER: JOSHUA SWANBECK CLIENT: LIQUID AGENCY, INC. TOOLS: MAC MATERIALS: CHROME KOTE

0365
ART DIRECTOR: JOSHUA SWANBECK DESIGNER: JOSHUA SWANBECK CLIENT: BUSINESS OBJECTS TOOLS: MAC MATERIALS: RUBBER BAND BINDING

LLOYDS GRAPHIC DESIGN AND COMMUNICATION
0013
ART DIRECTOR: ALEXANDER LLOYD DESIGNER: ALEXANDER LLOYD CLIENT: PRENZEL DISTILLING COMPANY TOOLS: FREEHAND, MAC MATERIALS: MATT ARTBOARD 300GSM, GRANDEE BLACK 216GSM

0417
ART DIRECTOR: ALEXANDER LLOYD DESIGNER: ALEXANDER LLOYD CLIENT: LLOYDS GRAPHIC DESIGN AND COMMUNICATION TOOLS: FREEHAND, MAC MATERIALS: VIA PURE WHITE ULTRA SMOOTH 216GSM

0178
ART DIRECTOR: ALEXANDER LLOYD DESIGNER: ALEXANDER LLOYD CLIENT: CPR DISTRIBUTORS LTD. (COFFEE PREMIUM ROAST) TOOLS: FREEHAND, MAC MATERIALS: MATT ARTBOARD 300GSM

0199
ART DIRECTOR: ALEXANDER LLOYD DESIGNER: ALEXANDER LLOYD CLIENT: JASON TRIPE CONTRACTING LTD. TOOLS: FREEHAND, MAC MATERIALS: MATT ARTBOARD 300GSM

HENRI LUCAS/MARTIJN ENGELBREGT
0496
ART DIRECTORS: HENRI LUCAS, MARTIJN ENGELBREGT DESIGNERS: HENRI LUCAS, MARTIJN ENGELBREGT CLIENT: CENTRAAL MUSEUM TOOLS: QUARK MATERIALS: CHROMOLUX PRINTING, CMYK PLUS 2 PMS

MACHINE
0827, 0828, 0829
ART DIRECTOR: MACHINE DESIGNER: MACHINE CLIENT: RUSHHOUR TOOLS: ILLUSTRA-TOR, PHOTOSHOP, MAC MATERIALS: HVO 300GSM

0831, 0905
ART DIRECTOR: MACHINE DESIGNER: MACHINE CLIENT: CLUB PARADISO TOOLS: ILLUSTRATOR MATERIALS: HVO 300GSM

0833
ART DIRECTOR: MACHINE DESIGNER: MACHINE CLIENT: MACHINE TOOLS: ILLUSTRATOR, MAC MATERIALS: SILKSCREEN ON COTTON

MADE THOUGHT
0010, 0082, 0095
ART DIRECTORS: BEN PARKER, PAUL AUSTIN CLIENT: THE MILL

0011, 0918
ART DIRECTORS: BEN PARKER, PAUL AUSTIN CLIENT: VIADUCT

0029
ART DIRECTORS: BEN PARKER, PAUL AUSTIN CLIENT: SUZY HOODLESS

0160
ART DIRECTORS: BEN PARKER, PAUL AUSTIN CLIENT: JUMP

0233
ART DIRECTORS: BEN PARKER, PAUL AUSTIN CLIENT: ESTHER FRANKLIN

0891
ART DIRECTORS: BEN PARKER, PAUL AUSTIN CLIENT: SCULPTURE AT GOODWOOD/PEGGY GUGGENHEIM COLLECTION

MAGMA
0685
ART DIRECTOR: LARS HARMSEN DESIGNER: CHRIS STEURER CLIENT: PT AG TOOLS: PHOTOSHOP, QUARK, MAC

0776
ART DIRECTOR: LARS HARMSEN CLIENT: MAGMA TOOLS: FREEHAND, QUARK, MAC MATERIALS: METAL BOX

MAIOW CREATIVE BRANDING
0148
ART DIRECTOR: PAUL RAPACIOLI DESIGNERS: PAUL RAPACIOLI, DAVE WORTHINGTON CLIENT: WOODHOUSE HUGHES TOOLS: FREEHAND MATERIALS: 350GSM NEPTUNE UNIQUE

0153
ART DIRECTORS: PAUL RAPACIOLI, MAI IKUZANA DESIGNER: PAUL RAPACIOLI CLIENT: MAIOW CREATIVE BRANDING TOOLS: QUARK, FREEHAND DESIGN MATERIALS: 118GSM AND 325GSM MONADNOCK ASTRALITE SMOOTH

0523
ART DIRECTOR: MAI IKUZANA DESIGNER: MAI IKUZANA CLIENT: MAIOW CREATIVE BRANDING TOOLS: ILLUSTRATOR, QUARK MATERIALS: TOGSM CRUSADE OFFSET (BIBLE PAPER)

0702
ART DIRECTOR: PAUL RAPACIOLI DESIGNER: PAUL RAPACIOLI CLIENT: MAIOW CREATIVE BRANDING TOOLS: FREEHAND, QUARK MATERIALS: TOGSM CRUSADE OFFSET

MARIUS FAHRNER DESIGN
0067
ART DIRECTOR: MARIUS FAHRNER DESIGNER: MARIUS FAHRNER CLIENT: RESET PRINTERY TOOLS: FREEHAND MATERIALS: IVERCOTE, IGEPA 300GSM

0143
ART DIRECTOR: MARIUS FAHRNER DESIGNER: MARIUS FAHRNER CLIENT: LIA STAEHLIN JEWELERS TOOLS: FREEHAND MATERIALS: ROEMERTURM CURTIS ESPARTO

0170
ART DIRECTOR: MARIUS FAHRNER DESIGNER: MARIUS FAHRNER CLIENT: DERMATOLOGIUUM FOUNDATION TOOLS: FREEHAND MATERIALS: IGEPA EXTRA 120–250GSM

0296, 0594
ART DIRECTOR: MARIUS FAHRNER DESIGNER: MARIUS FAHRNER CLIENT: SBC, PROFESSOR STENKRAUS TOOLS: FREEHAND MATERIALS: ROEMERTURM PRECIOSO

0321
ART DIRECTOR: MARIUS FAHRNER DESIGNER: MARIUS FAHRNER CLIENT: FRITZEN MOETTER TOOLS: FREEHAND

0442
ART DIRECTOR: MARIUS FAHRNER DESIGNER: MARIUS FAHRNER CLIENT: DAHLER + COMPANY REAL ESTATE TOOLS: FREEHAND MATERIALS: IGEPA AGRIPINA 170–250GSM

0619
ART DIRECTOR: MARIUS FAHRNER DESIGNER: MARIUS FAHRNER CLIENT: RESET PRINTER TOOLS: FREEHAND MATERIALS: MUNKEN PURE 240GSM

0847
ART DIRECTOR: MARIUS FAHRNER DESIGNER: MARIUS FAHRNER CLIENT: ASIA AROUND TOOLS: FREEHAND

METAL
0297
ART DIRECTOR: PEAT JARIYA DESIGNERS: PEAT JARIYA, GABE SCHREIBER CLIENT: CAMDEN TOOLS: ILLUSTRATOR, PAGEMAKER, PHOTOSHOP, MAC G4 MATERIALS: POLYPROPY-LENE COVER .8 POINT

0475
ART DIRECTOR: PEAT JARIYA DESIGNERS: PEAT JARIYA, SHAD LINDO CLIENT: BIRDVIEW TOOLS: ILLUSTRATOR, PAGEMAKER, PHOTOSHOP, MAC G4 MATERIALS: POTLATCH MCCOY

0478
ART DIRECTOR: PEAT JARIYA DESIGNER: SHAD LINDO CLIENT: CAMDEN TOOLS: ILLUSTRATOR, PAGEMAKER, PHOTOSHOP, MAC G4 MATERIALS: CURIOUS

0792
ART DIRECTOR: PEAT JARIYA DESIGNERS: SHAD LINDO, PEAT JARIYA CLIENT: GCA TOOLS: ILLUSTRATOR, PAGEMAKER, PHOTOSHOP MATERIALS: CURIOUS TRANSLUCENT

0907
ART DIRECTOR: PEAT JARIYA DESIGNER: PEAT JARIYA CLIENT: RELIANCE

MIASO DESIGN
0119
ART DIRECTOR: KRISTIN MIASO DESIGNER: KRISTIN MIASO CLIENT: MIASO DESIGN TOOLS: ILLUSTRATOR MATERIALS: FRENCH CONSTRUCTION SLATE BLUE

MIRKO ILIC
0087
ART DIRECTOR: MIRKO ILIC DESIGNERS: MIRKO ILIC, HEATH HINEGARDNER CLIENT: VICTOR CALDERONE TOOLS: MAYA, QUARK

0317
ART DIRECTOR: MIRKO ILIC DESIGNER: MIRKO ILIC CLIENT: SARI LEVI, LEVI CREATIVE TOOLS: QUARK

0328
ART DIRECTOR: MIRKO ILIC DESIGNER: MIRKO ILIC CLIENT: 5K MEDIA TOOLS: PHOTOSHOP, QUARK

0375
ART DIRECTOR: MIRKO ILIC DESIGNER: MIRKO ILIC CLIENT: SLM TOOLS: PHOTOSHOP, QUARK

0524
ART DIRECTOR: MIRKO ILIC DESIGNER: MIRKO ILIC CLIENT: AMERICAN FRIENDS OF TEL AVIV MUSEUM OF ART AND MARNIE AND ADAM D. TIHANY TOOLS: ILLUSTRATOR, QUARK

MIRES
0270
ART DIRECTOR: JOSÉ SERRANO DESIGNERS: MIGUEL PEREZ, GALE SPITZLEY, JOY PRICE CLIENT: QUALCOMM

0272
ART DIRECTOR: JOSÉ SERRANO DESIGNER: GALE SPITZLEY CLIENT: J.F. SHEA COMPANY COPYWRITER: ERIC LABRECQUE PHOTOGRAPHERS: STEVE SIMPSON, KELLI RIPPEE MATERIALS: SUNDANCE FELT (COVER), GILBERT RELM (INSIDE)

0282
ART DIRECTOR: JOHN BALL DESIGNER: TAVO GALINDO CLIENT: J.F. LUX ART INSTITUTE COPYWRITER: JOHN BALL ILLUSTRATOR: TAVO GALINDO MATERIALS: MCCOY KARMA NATURAL 100% TEXT

0487
ART DIRECTOR: JOHN BALL DESIGNER: PAM MEIERDING CLIENT: MIRES COPYWRITER: ERIC LABRECQUE ILLUSTRATOR: VARIOUS PHOTOGRAPHER: VARIOUS

0996
ART DIRECTOR: SCOTT MIRES DESIGNER: JEN CADAM CLIENT: WOODS LITHOGRAPHICS COPYWRITER: ERIC LABRECQUE PHOTOGRAPHER: MARSHALL HARRINGTON MATERIALS: 600-LINE ULTRA DOT PRINTING WITH SPECIAL QUETONE COLOR INTEGRATION

MIRIELLO GRAFICO, INC.
0312, 0897, 0915
ART DIRECTOR: RON MIRIELLO DESIGNER: CHRIS KEENEY CLIENT: FOX RIVER PAPER TOOLS: ILLUSTRATOR, PHOTO-SHOP MATERIALS: STARWHITE VICKSBURG

0537, 0876, 0888
ART DIRECTOR: DENNIS GARCIA DESIGNER: DENNIS GARCIA CLIENT: MIRIELLO GRAFICO, INC. TOOLS: ILLUSTRATOR, PHO-TOSHOP MATERIALS: STARWHITE

0667
ART DIRECTOR: RON MIRIELLO DESIGNER: TRACEY MEINERS CLIENT: ISIS PHARMACEUTICALS TOOLS: ILLUSTRATOR MATERIALS: MCCOY SILK COVER AND BOOK

MODE
0008, 0231, 0989
ART DIRECTORS: PHIL COSTINI, IAN STYLES DESIGNER: DARRELL GIBBONS CLIENT: LOST ROBOT TOOLS: ILLUSTRA-TOR, PHOTOSHOP, EMAIL EFFECT, FONTOGRAPHER, QUARK, MATERIALS: 3M RADIANT LIGHT FILM

0097, 0960
ART DIRECTORS: PHIL COSTINI, IAN STYLES DESIGNERS: PHIL COSTINI, IAN STYLES CLIENT: DALTON MAAG TOOLS: ILLUS-TRATOR, PHOTOSHOP, QUARK

0137
ART DIRECTORS: PHIL COSTINI, IAN STYLES DESIGNER: DARRELL GIBBONS CLIENT: MODE TOOLS: ILLUSTRATOR, QUARK MATERIALS: IKONO GLOSS

0967, 0968, 0969, 0970
ART DIRECTORS: PHIL COSTINI, IAN STYLES DESIGNER: DARRELL GIBBONS CLIENT: DALTON MAAG TOOLS: ILLUSTRATOR, QUARK MATERIALS: CHALLENGER OFFSET

MONA MCDONALD DESIGN
0149
DESIGNER: MONA MCDONALD CLIENT: MARK BOLSTER TOOLS: QUARK, MAC MATERIALS: WHITE FOIL STAMP WITH HALF-TONE

MONDERER DESIGN
0511
ART DIRECTOR: STEWART MONDERER DESIGNER: JASON CK MILLER CLIENT: MONDERER DESIGN TOOLS: QUARK, MAC MATERIALS: ASTROLITE 120LB COVER

0807
ART DIRECTOR: JASON C.K. MILLER DESIGNER: JASON C.K. MILLER CLIENT: UNIVERSITY OF MASSACHUSETTS MEDICAL SCHOOL TOOLS: QUARK, MAC MATERIALS: UTOPIA, GILCLEAR, FRENCH

MONSTER DESIGN
0301
ART DIRECTORS: HANNAH WYGAL, THERESA MONICA DESIGNER: DENISE SAKAKI CLIENT: XTENSIVE MEDIA SOLUTIONS TOOLS: PHOTOSHOP, FREEHAND, MAC

0635
DESIGNERS: HANNAH WYGAL, THERESA MONICA CLIENT: MONSTER DESIGN TOOLS: FREEHAND, MAC

MORLA DESIGN
0917
ART DIRECTOR: JENNIFER MORLA DESIGNERS: JENNIFER MORLA, BRIAN SINGER CLIENT: MERVYN'S CALIFORNIA TOOLS: ILLUSTRATOR

0980
ART DIRECTOR: JENNIFER MORLA DESIGNERS: JENNIFER MORLA, HIZAM HARON CLIENT: AGI TOOLS: ILLUSTRATOR, PHO-TOSHOP MATERIALS: ROLLAND OPAQUE BRIGHT WHITE 80LB TEXT

MORTENSEN DESIGN, INC.
0292
ART DIRECTOR: GORDON MORTENSEN DESIGNER: ANN JORDAN CLIENT: CPP, INC. TOOLS: ILLUSTRATOR MATERIALS: STARWHITE STRIUS SMOOTH 130LB DOUBLE THICK COVER

0295
ART DIRECTOR: GORDON MORTENSEN DESIGNER: HELENA SEA CLIENT: MORTENSEN DESIGN, INC. TOOLS: ILLUSTRATOR MATERIALS: CRANE'S FLUORESCENT WHITE, KID FINISH 134LB (COVER), IMAGING FINISH 70LB TEXT (LETTERHEAD, AND ENVELOPE)

MOTIVE DESIGN RESEARCH
0074
ART DIRECTORS: KARI STRAND, MICHAEL CONNORS DESIGNER: PETER ANDERSON CLIENT: SUPREME TOOLS: PHOTOSHOP, QUARK, MAC MATERIALS: MOHAWK NAVAJO, THERMOGRAPHY

0256
ART DIRECTORS: KARI STRAND, MICHAEL CONNORS DESIGNER: KARI STRAND CLIENT: MOTIVE DESIGN RESEARCH TOOLS: FREEHAND, QUARK, MAC MATERIALS: MOHAWK SUPERFINE, BLOTTER PAPER (BUSINESS CARDS)

0266
ART DIRECTORS: MICHAEL CONNORS, KARI STRAND DESIGNER: HEATHER HEFLIN CLIENT: GETTY IMAGES TOOLS: ILLUSTRATOR, PHOTOSHOP, QUARK, MAC MATERIALS: SAPPI MCCOY SILK

0546
ART DIRECTORS: MICHAEL CONNORS, KARI STRAND DESIGNER: PETER ANDERSON CLIENT: N21+2 TOOLS: PHOTOSHOP, QUARK, MAC MATERIALS: FOX RIVER STARWHITE VICKSBURG, BUB-BLE WRAP, CUSTOM-PRINTED MASKING TAPE

0652
ART DIRECTORS: MICHAEL CONNORS, KARI STRAND DESIGNER: DAVID COX CLIENT: GETTY IMAGES TOOLS: ILLUS-TRATOR, PHOTOSHOP, QUARK, MAC MATERIALS: SAPPI MCCOY SILK

0660
ART DIRECTORS: MICHAEL CONNORS, KARI STRAND DESIGNER: PETER ANDERSON CLIENT: MOTIVE DESIGN RESEARCH TOOLS: ILLUSTRA-TOR, PHOTOSHOP, QUARK, MAC MATERIALS: FRENCH CONSTRUCTION CLASSIC CREST LABEL, GLASSINE BAG, WILD-FLOWERS

0870, 0987
ART DIRECTORS: MICHAEL CONNORS, KARI STRAND DESIGNER: KRIS DELANEY CLIENT: GETTY IMAGES TOOLS: PHOTOSHOP, FREEHAND, QUARK, MAC MATERIALS: STARWHITE VICKSBURG, GILCLEAR

NASSER DESIGN
0195
ART DIRECTOR: NELIDA NASSER DESIGNERS: NELIDA NASSER, MARGARITA ENCOMIENDA CLIENT: LOUISE WEGMANN SCHOOL TOOLS: ILLUSTRATOR, QUARK MATERIALS: SPENDORGEL 300LB, FABRIANO COLORE PERLA 200LB (FOR POP-OUTS)

0437
ART DIRECTOR: NELIDA NASSER DESIGNERS: MARGARITA ENCOMIENDA, NELIDA NASSER CLIENT: WEIDLINGER ASSOCIATES, INC., CONSULTING ENGINEERS TOOLS: ILLUSTRATOR, PHOTO-SHOP, QUARK MATERIALS: ZANDERS IKONO GLOSS 80LB COVER

0573
ART DIRECTOR: NELIDA NASSER DESIGNERS: MARGARITA ENCOMIENDA, NELIDA NASSER CLIENT: NASSER DESIGN TOOLS: QUARK MATERIALS: CHARTHAM TRANSLUCENTS PLATINUM 30LB, THIBIERGE ET COMAR CROMATICA (INSERT AND ENVELOPES)

NAVY BLUE
0185, 0386
ART DIRECTOR: CLARE LUNDY DESIGNER: CLARE LUNDY CLIENT: ZANDERS TOOLS: QUARK MATERIALS: ZANDERS ZETA SMOOTH BRILLIANT 850GSM

0624, 0838
DESIGNER: CLARE LUNDY CLIENT: ROBERT HORNE TOOLS: QUARK MATERIALS: PARILUX GLOSS 170GSM, IMAGINE 150GSM, HOLOPRISM BOARD 717GSM

NB:STUDIO
0116
ART DIRECTORS: BEN STOTT, ALAN DYE, NICK FINNEY DESIGNER: NICK VINCENT CLIENT: D&AD TOOLS: QUARK

0329
ART DIRECTORS: ALAN DYE, BEN STOTT, NICK FINNEY DESIGNERS: NICK VINCENT, CHARLIE SMITH CLIENT: NB:STUDIO TOOLS: ILLUSTRATOR, QUARK

0372
ART DIRECTORS: ALAN DYE, NICK FINNEY, BEN STOTT DESIGNER: NICK FINNEY CLIENT: MERCHANT TOOLS: QUARK

0526
ART DIRECTORS: ALAN DYE, NICK FINNEY, BEN STOTT, DESIGNER: CHARLIE SMITH CLIENT: CRAFTS COUNCIL MATERIALS: DUTCH GREYBOARD

0541
ART DIRECTORS: ALAN DYE, NICK FINNEY, BEN STOTT DESIGNERS: NICK VINCENT, CHARLIE SMITH CLIENT: MERCHANT MATERIALS: FENMER PAPER 7X STOCKS

0543
ART DIRECTORS: BEN STOTT, NICK FINNEY, ALAN DYE DESIGNER: NICK VINCENT CLIENT: SPEEDY HIRE TOOLS: ILLUSTRATOR, QUARK, PEN MATERIALS: MANILLA ENVELOPES

0544
ART DIRECTORS: ALAN DYE, BEN STOTT, NICK FINNEY DESIGNER: NICK VINCENT CLIENT: ROYAL SOCIETY OF ARTS TOOLS: QUARK

0690
ART DIRECTORS: NICK FINNEY, BEN STOTT, ALAN DYE DESIGNER: IAN PIERCE CLIENT: CRAFTS COUNCIL TOOLS: QUARK MATERIALS: FLY WEIGHT

0718
ART DIRECTORS: ALAN DYE, BEN STOTT, NICK FINNEY DESIGNER: JODIE WIGHTMAN CLIENT: THE HUB TOOLS: ILLUSTRATOR, QUARK MATERIALS: MEED CUSTOM NOTE

0805
ART DIRECTORS: ALAN DYE, NICK FINNEY, BEN STOTT DESIGNER: NICK VINCENT CLIENT: D&AD TOOLS: ILLUSTRATOR, QUARK MATERIALS: DUFEX

NBBJ GRAPHIC DESIGN
0554
ART DIRECTORS: LEO RAYMUNDO DESIGNER: LEO RAYMUNDO CLIENT: FOUR SEASONS RESIDENTIAL PROPERTIES TOOLS: FREEHAND, MAC G4 MATERIALS: CLASSIC CREST COVER, 110LB AVON BRILLIANT WHITE (ENVELOPE); 100LB CENTURA GLOSS (POSTCARDS); 60LB CENTURA DULL (BROCHURE)

NET#WORK BBDO
0228
ART DIRECTOR: GLENDA VENN DESIGNER: RENATO SABBIONI CLIENT: THE MIN INSTITUTE OF ART AND MATERIAL CULTURE TOOLS: FREEHAND, MAC MATERIALS: CONQUEROR WOVE

0570
ART DIRECTOR: GLENDA VENN DESIGNER: CHRIS GOUGH PALMER CLIENT: THE INDEPENDENT NEWSPAPER GROUP COPYWRITER: MICHELE PITHEY TOOLS: FREEHAND

0574
ART DIRECTOR: GLENDA VENN DESIGNER: CHRIS GOUGH PALMER CLIENT: THE INDEPENDENT NEWSPAPER GROUP COPYWRITER: MICHELE PITHEY TOOLS: FREEHAND

0585
ART DIRECTOR: CHRIS GOUGH PALMER DESIGNER: CHRIS GOUGH PALMER CLIENT: SAS INSTITUTE COPYWRITER: MICHELE PITHEY TOOLS: FREEHAND, MAC G4 MATERIALS: CUSTOM-MADE STEEL CAPSULE, BUBBLEWRAP, MAGNOMAT, WING NUT

NETSUCCESS
0302
ART DIRECTOR: ANNIS LEUNG DESIGNER: ANNIS LEUNG CLIENT: THOMPSON ADVISORY GROUP TOOLS: ILLUSTRATOR, MAC MATERIALS: NEENAH CLASSIC CREST

NYC COLLEGE OF TECHNOLOGY
0205
ART DIRECTOR: DOMINICK SARICA DESIGNER: JAMIE SNOW MARKOWITZ CLIENT: BROOKLYN BOROUGH PRESIDENT TOOLS: ILLUSTRATOR, PHOTOSHOP, MAC MATERIALS: BECKETT DUPLEX BLUE AND WHITE (COVER)

0698
ART DIRECTOR: DOMINICK SARICA DESIGNER: DOMINICK SARICA CLIENT: NEW YORK CITY COLLEGE OF TECHNOLOGY TOOLS: QUARK, MAC MATERIALS: BASEBALL, ASTROTURF, CORRUGATED BOX

NIELINGER & ROHSIEPE
0538
ART DIRECTORS: CHRISTIAN NIELINGER, HERBERT ROHSIEPE DESIGNER: HERBERT ROHSIEPE CLIENT: NIELINGER & ROHSIEPE PHOTOGRAPHER: CHRISTIAN NIELINGER TOOLS: PHOTOSHOP, FREEHAND, MAC MATERIALS: ARJOWIGGINS SENSATION 270GSM

NIKLAUS TROXLER DESIGN
0051
ART DIRECTOR: NIKLAUS TROXLER DESIGNER: NIKLAUS TROXLER CLIENT: JAZZ IN WILLISAU TOOLS: HANDMADE STAMP LETTER MATERIALS: POSTER PAPER, WRAP PAPER

0057
ART DIRECTORS: NIKLAUS TROXLER DESIGNER: NIKLAUS TROXLER CLIENT: JAZZ IN WILLISAU TOOLS: HANDMADE STAMP LETTER MATERIALS: POSTER PAPER

NO.PARKING
0083
ART DIRECTOR: SABINE LERCHER DESIGNER: ELISA DELL'ANGELO CLIENT: BURGDENTAL TOOLS: ILLUSTRATOR, QUARK MATERIALS: MAGNOMATT PAPER 120GSM, TRANSPARENT SHEETS, PLASTIC PAPER CLIP

0422
ART DIRECTOR: CATERINA ROMIO DESIGNER: CATERINA ROMIO CLIENT: NO.PARKING TOOLS: ILLUSTRATOR MATERIALS: PLASTIC CLIP

0730
ART DIRECTORS: CATERINA ROMIO, SABINE LERCHER DESIGNERS: CATERINA ROMIO, SABINE LERCHER CLIENT: J. MISHRA TOOLS: ILLUSTRATOR, PHOTOSHOP MATERIALS: HOLOGRAPHIC PAPER, NATURAL PAPER

OCTAVO DESIGN
0397
ART DIRECTOR: GARY DOMENY CLIENT: OCTAVO DESIGN TOOLS: ILLUSTRATOR, MAC MATERIALS: TWINE, HANDMADE PAPER

ONE O'CLOCK GUN DESIGN CONSULTANTS
0003
ART DIRECTOR: MARK HOSKER DESIGNER: MICHAEL DUNLOP CLIENT: ONE O'CLOCK GUN DESIGN CONSULTANTS TOOLS: ILLUSTRATOR MATERIALS: FLUORESCENT INK

ORANGESEED DESIGN
0136
ART DIRECTOR: DAMIEN WOLF DESIGNER: DAMIEN WOLF CLIENT: WILD MEADOWS TOOLS: PHOTOSHOP, QUARK, G4 MATERIALS: 80LB BRIGHT WHITE CORONADO VELLUM COVER

ORIGIN
0458
DESIGN DIRECTOR: MARK BOTTOMLEY CLIENT: MAT WRIGHT PHOTOGRAPHY MATERIALS: CURTIS MALTS PRINTING: 6-COLOR LITHO (INNER), 2-COLOR SILK SCREENED (OUTER)

PH.D
0043, 0188, 0197, 0334, 0401, 0638, 0654
ART DIRECTORS: CLIVE PIERCY, MICHAEL HODGSON DESIGNER: CAROL CONO-NOBLE CLIENT: DICKSON'S TOOLS: ILLUSTRATOR, PHOTOSHOP, QUARK MATERIALS: NEENAH CLASSIC CREST

0179
ART DIRECTOR: CLIVE PIERCY DESIGNER: CLIVE PIERCY CLIENT: THE FAD GALLERY TOOLS: ILLUSTRATOR, QUARK MATERIALS: MOHAWK NAVAJO COVER BRILLIANT WHITE 160LB (BUSINESS CARDS), MOHAWK NAVAJO WRITING, BRILLIANT WHITE 28LB (LETTERHEAD), MOHAWK NAVAJO WRITING BRILLIANT WHITE 24LB (ENVELOPE), ULTRABAK MATTE LITHO LABEL (LABEL), MOHAWK SUPERFINE SMOOTH COVER ULTRAWHITE 160LB (FOLDER)

0196, 0621
ART DIRECTOR: CLIVE PIERCY DESIGNER: CLIVE PIERCY CLIENT: QUIKSILVER TOOLS: PHOTOSHOP, QUARK, MAC

0402
ART DIRECTOR: CLIVE PIERCY DESIGNER: CLIVE PIERCY CLIENT: AIGA TOOLS: QUARK, ILLUSTRATOR MATERIALS: NEW LEAF 70LB REINCARNATION (POSTER), NEW LEAF 80LB REINCARNATION (BROCHURE)

0770
CLIENT: DEVELOPMENTOR

0814
CLIENT: DEVELOPMENTOR

0924
CLIENT: FOUNDATION PRESS MATERIALS: RELIANCE 140LB WHITE HALFTONE PRINTABLE BLOTTER (BUSINESS CARDS), CONVERTED DUR-O-TONE TEXT 60LB BUTCHER (ENVELOPES), MACTAC STARLINER NOVELTY UNCOATED 60LB WHITE (LABELS), CONSTRUCTION WRITING 70LB WHITEWASH (LETTERHEAD, SECOND SHEETS, NOTEPAD), DUR-O-TONE TEXT 60LB BUTCHER (FORMS), 15PT GENUINE ORANGE PRESSBOARD (PRESS KIT)

PHILLIPS
0166
ART DIRECTOR: PETER PHILLIPS CLIENT: BERG

0259
ART DIRECTOR: PETER PHILLIPS CLIENT: BEBOP

0262
ART DIRECTOR: PETER PHILLIPS CLIENT: REDIDOSE

0263
ART DIRECTOR: PETER PHILLIPS CLIENT: TSL

0452
ART DIRECTOR: PETER PHILLIPS CLIENT: PHILLIPS

0715
ART DIRECTOR: PETER PHILLIPS CLIENT: B+H
0741
ART DIRECTOR: PETER PHILLIPS

0757
ART DIRECTOR: PETER PHILLIPS CLIENT: VIRTUALL

0767
ART DIRECTOR: PETER PHILLIPS CLIENT: SONY

THE PHOENIX STUDIO
0036
ART DIRECTOR: KIM FRANCISCO DESIGNER: KIM FRANCISCO CLIENT: THE PHOENIX STUDIO TOOLS: FREEHAND MATERIALS: STARDREAM TEXT AND COVER, CURIOUS TEXT AND COVER

PHYX DESIGN
0916
ART DIRECTOR: MASAKI KOIKE DESIGNER: MASAKI KOIKE CLIENT: PHYX DESIGN TOOLS: MAC, SCREEN PRINT, HANDS MATERIALS: FRENCH PAPER COMPANY CONSTRUCTION

PLAN-B STUDIO
0899
ART DIRECTOR: STEVE PRICE DESIGNER: STEVE PRICE CLIENT: ROTOVISION TOOLS: PHOTOGRAPHIC DARKROOM, SCAPEL MATERIALS: 150GSM UNCOATED, ACETATE

0926
ART DIRECTOR: STEVE PRICE CLIENT: WALL OF SOUND RECORDINGS MATERIALS: DOUBLE WHITE BOARD

PLUS DESIGN INC.
0243
ART DIRECTOR: ANITA MEYER DESIGNER: ANITA MEYER CLIENT: THE EDMOND-HOWARD NETWORK TOOLS: QUARK, MAC MATERIALS: FRENCH CONSTRUCTION WHITEWASH 24LB TEXT (LETTERHEAD, SECOND SHEET, AND ENVELOPE), FRENCH CONSTRUCTION WHITEWASH 100LB COVER (BUSINESS CARDS)

0320
ART DIRECTOR: ANITA MEYER DESIGNER: ANITA MEYER CLIENT: THE INSTITUTE OF CONTEMPORARY ART TOOLS: PHOTOSHOP, QUARK MATERIALS: PLATINUM TRANSLUCENT (ENVELOPE), BECKETT EXPRESSION RADIANCE 100LB COVER (SLEEVE), CONSORT ROYAL SILK 80LB COVER (BROCHURE)

0662
ART DIRECTORS: ANITA MEYER, KARIN FICKETT DESIGNERS: ANITA MEYER, KARIN FICKETT, DINA ZACCAGNINI, MATT, NICOLE JUEN, CAROLINA SENIOR, VERONICA MAJIL CLIENT: PLUS DESIGN INC. MATERIALS: FRENCH BUTCHER WHITE 60LB TEXT (MEMO SHEET), FRENCH NEWSPRINT 70LB TEXT (LETTERHEAD), FRENCH PRIMER GOLD 60LB TEXT (ENVELOPE), CHIPBOARD (BUSINESS CARD AND FOLDER)

POINT BLANK DESIGN
0020
DESIGNER: PETER OWEN CLIENT: UNIVERSAL TOOLS: ILLUSTRATOR, PHOTOSHOP, QUARK

0350, 0368
ART DIRECTORS: STEVE WALLINGTON, NICK FOLEY DESIGNERS: STEVE WALLINGTON, NICK FOLEY CLIENT: DOCKERS TOOLS: QUARK

0373
DESIGNER: JAMES KELLEY CLIENT: UNIVERSAL TOOLS: FREEHAND, QUARK

0742
DESIGNER: PETER OWEN CLIENT: BBC TOOLS: ILLUSTRATOR, QUARK MATERIALS: FOIL RECOVERY BLANKET

0764
DESIGNER: POINT BLANK DESIGN CLIENT: AS WORN BY TOOLS: ILLUSTRATOR, QUARK MATERIALS: T-SHIRT, BOX

POPCORN INITIATIVE
0362
ART DIRECTOR: CHRIS JONES DESIGNER: CHRIS JONES CLIENT: KISSIMMEE UTILITY AUTHORITY TOOLS: ILLUSTRATOR, PHOTOSHOP, QUARK, MAC MATERIALS: MOHAWK NAVAJO, CHIPBOARD

0598
ART DIRECTOR: CHRIS JONES DESIGNERS: CHRIS JONES, ROGER WOOD CLIENT: POPCORN INITIATIVE TOOLS: ILLUSTRATOR, PHOTOSHOP, MAC MATERIALS: MOHAWK NAVAJO 120LB COVER

PRECURSOR
0007, 0124, 0687
ART DIRECTOR: PRECURSOR DESIGNER: PRECURSOR CLIENT: WOODHEAD CALLIVA TOOLS: ILLUSTRATOR, MAC MATERIALS: CURIOUS TOUCH, FAULKNERS FINE PAPERS (BOOKCLOTH)

0009, 0746
DESIGNER: PRECURSOR CLIENT: WOODHEAD CALLIVA TOOLS: ILLUSTRATOR, MAC MATERIALS: FLOCKAGE, PERSPEX

0040, 0139
DESIGNER: PRECURSOR CLIENT: PRECURSOR TOOLS: ILLUSTRATOR, MAC MATERIALS: CURIOUS TOUCH, FAULKNERS FINE PAPERS (BOOKCLOTH)

0294
ART DIRECTOR: PRECURSOR DESIGNER: PRECURSOR CLIENT: WOODHEAD CALLIVA TOOLS: ILLUSTRATOR, MAC MATERIALS: FLOCKAGE, COLORPLAN COLTSKIN, STAINLESS STEEL

0498
ART DIRECTOR: PRECURSOR DESIGNER: PRECURSOR CLIENT: WOODHEAD CALLIVA TOOLS: ILLUSTRATOR, MAC MATERIALS: COLORPLAN, TYVEK

PROGRESS
0106
CLIENT: CREATIVE REVIEW

0118
CLIENT: THIRTEEN (BRISTOL)

0245
DESIGNER: MILLER SEALE CLIENT: PRO-DG MATERIALS: METAL TIN

0247
CLIENT: UNICHEM MATERIALS: PAPER, BOARD

0469
CLIENT: REFLECTIVE TECHNOLOGIES MATERIALS: RIGID POLYPROPYLENE

0483
DESIGNER: BDW CLIENT: ALFA ROMEO MATERIALS: PVC

0567
CLIENT: TEQUILA

0688
DESIGNER: MCCANN ERICKSON CLIENT: MCCANN ERICKSON MATERIALS: PVC, THEATRICAL BLOOD

0689
CLIENT: MOLTEN TV

0709
CLIENT: THE PAINT FACTORY

0717
CLIENT: LIFFE

0752
CLIENT: ETNIES

0754
CLIENT: MOON ESTATES MATERIALS: ANTISTATIC FILM

0756
CLIENT: PDP MOMENTUM MATERIALS: TOUCH PVC, ALUMINUM

PROJECT88
0046, 0062, 0779
ART DIRECTORS: OLIVER HALL, GRAHAM SPILLER, ALED WILLIAMS DESIGNERS: OLIVER HALL, GRAHAM SPILLER, ALED WILLIAMS CLIENT: FIERCE PANDA RECORDINGS TOOLS: ILLUSTRATOR, PHOTOSHOP, MAC G4 MATERIALS: 180GSM XPACE TRANSLUCENT PAPER, FILEMASTER LAMINATED MANILLA BUFF 180GSM

Q
0471
ART DIRECTOR: LAURENZ NIELBOCK WRITER: CHRISTOPH KOHL CLIENT: ARJOWIGGINS GERMANY TOOLS: PHOTOSHOP, QUARK, MAC MATERIALS: VARIOUS

0479
ART DIRECTOR: THILO VON DEBSCHITZ DESIGNERS: TANJA MANN, DAVID BASCOM CLIENT: ARJOWIGGINS GERMANY TOOLS: FREEHAND, MAC MATERIALS: YEARLING CLASSIC/JAZZ

QUESTION DESIGN
0147
ART DIRECTOR: CHARLOTTE NORUZI CLIENT: STEVEN MADDEN, INC. TOOLS: QUARK, MAC MATERIALS: COTTON FABRIC, STITCHING

0586
ART DIRECTOR: CHARLOTTE NORUZI DESIGNER: CHARLOTTE NORUZI CLIENT: QUESTION DESIGN. TOOLS: QUARK, MAC MATERIALS: WOOD, PAPER, ROPE

0613
ART DIRECTOR: CHARLOTTE NORUZI DESIGNER: CHARLOTTE NORUZI CLIENT: QUESTION DESIGN TOOLS: QUARK, MAC MATERIALS: WOOD, PAPER, YARN

R2 DESIGN
0056, 0071
ART DIRECTORS: LIZA RAMALHO, ARTUR REBELO DESIGNERS: LIZÁ RAMALHO, ARTUR REBELO CLIENT: TEATRO BRUTO TOOLS: FREEHAND, MAC MATERIALS: MUNKEN COUCHÉ

0220
ART DIRECTORS: LIZÁ RAMALHO, ARTUR REBELO DESIGNERS: LIZA RAMALHO, ARTUR REBELO CLIENT: TEATRO BRUTO TOOLS: FREEHAND, MAC MATERIALS: MUNKEN COUCHE

0370, 0371, 0413
ART DIRECTORS: LIZÁ RAMALHO, ARTUR REBELO DESIGNERS: LIZÁ RAMALHO, ARTUR REBELO CLIENT: CASSIOPEIA TOOLS: FREEHAND, MAC MATERIALS: MUNKEN CÓUCHÉ, CLK

0575
ART DIRECTORS: LIZA RAMALHO, ARTUR REBELO DESIGNERS: LIZÁ RAMALHO, ARTUR REBELO CLIENT: MARTA + GIL TOOLS: FREEHAND, MAC MATERIALS: COUCHÉ CLK

RADFORD WALLIS
0481, 0750
ART DIRECTORS: STUART RADFORD, ANDREW WALLIS DESIGNERS: STUART RADFORD, LEE WILSON PHOTOGRAPHER: DUNCAN SMITH CLIENT: ARTS & BUSINESS TOOLS: QUARK MATERIALS: NEPTUNE UNIQUE 200GSM, LUC PRINT PVC

RADLEY YELDAR
0428, 0954
ART DIRECTOR: ROB RICHE DESIGNERS: ROB RICHE, NEIL LATMORE CLIENT: COMIC RELIEF TOOLS: PHOTOSHOP, QUARK

0512
ART DIRECTOR: ROB RICHE DESIGNER: DARREN BARBER CLIENT: MCNAUGHTON PAPER TOOLS: PHOTOSHOP, QUARK MATERIALS: COLOR IT

0518
ART DIRECTOR: ANDREW GORMAN DESIGNER: KEITH CULLEN CLIENT: RADLEY YELDAR TOOLS: ILLUSTRATOR, PHOTOSHOP, QUARK

0519, 0877
ART DIRECTOR: ANDREW GORMAN DESIGNER: JAMIE NEALE, KEITH CULLEN CLIENT: DIAGEO TOOLS: PHOTOSHOP, QUARK

0553
ART DIRECTOR: ADAM MILLS DESIGNER: ADAM MILLS CLIENT: MINERVA PLC TOOLS: PHOTOSHOP, QUARK

0669
ART DIRECTOR: ANDREW GORMAN DESIGNER: KEITH CULLEN CLIENT: RADLEY YELDAR TOOLS: QUARK, NEEDLE

0674
ART DIRECTOR: PHIL METSON DESIGNER: CHRISTIAN BATES CLIENT: UNIVERSITY OF PORTSMOUTH TOOLS: PHOTOSHOP, QUARK

0675
ART DIRECTOR: ROB RICHE DESIGNER: DARREN BARBER CLIENT: MCNAUGHTON PAPER TOOLS: ILLUSTRATOR, PHOTO-SHOP, QUARK MATERIALS: COLOR IT

0738
ART DIRECTOR: ANDREW GORMAN DESIGNER: ROB RICHE CLIENT: MCNAUGHTON PAPER TOOLS: PHOTOSHOP, QUARK MATERIALS: T2500, HANNO ART

REEBOK DESIGN SERVICES
0661, 0753
ART DIRECTOR: ELENI CHRONOPOULOS DESIGNERS: ELENI CHRONOPOULOS, VILISLAVA PETROVA CLIENT: REEBOK TOOLS: ILLUSTRATOR, PHOTOSHOP, QUARK, MAC MATERIALS: 3M REFLECTIVE MATERIAL, FIBERMARK TOUCHÉ, CURIOUS METALLICS

RICK JOHNSON & COMPANY
0583
ART DIRECTOR: TIM MCGRATH COPYWRITER: TOM PEGORS CLIENT: RICK JOHNSON & COMPANY TOOLS: ILLUSTRATOR, MAC MATERIALS: TAGS, RUBBER STAMP

RICKABAUGH GRAPHICS
0394
ART DIRECTOR: ERIC RICKABAUGH DESIGNER: ERIC RICKABAUGH CLIENT: THE COLUMBUS CREW, MLS TOOLS: FREEHAND, MAC MATERIALS: CENTURA GLOSS BLACK CORRUGATED

RINZEN
0238
CLIENT: FAMILY (CLUB) TOOLS: FREEHAND, MAC

0434
CLIENT: EDWARDS DUNLOP PAPER TOOLS: FREEHAND, MAC PRINTING: CHROMATICO, BOXBOARD, NEWSPRINT

RIORDON DESIGN
0055
ART DIRECTORS: RIC RIORDON, DAN WHEATON DESIGNER: SHIRLEY RIORDON CLIENT: SCOTIA CAPITAL TOOLS: QUARK, ILLUSTRATOR MATERIALS: SILK FABRIC, VELLUM

0237
ART DIRECTOR: RIC RIORDON DESIGNERS: DAN WHEATON, ALAN KAPAN CLIENT: RIORDON DESIGN TOOLS: ILLUSTRATOR, QUARK MATERIALS: BENEFIT TEXT AND COVER

0603, 0605
ART DIRECTOR: RIC RIORDON DESIGNERS: SHARON PELE, AMY MONTGOMERY CLIENT: RIORDON DESIGN TOOLS: ILLUSTRATOR, QUARK MATERIALS: NEENAH ENVIRONMENT

0656, 0785
ART DIRECTOR: SHIRLEY RIORDON DESIGNER: ALAN KAPAN CLIENT: RIORDON DESIGN TOOLS: ILLUSTRATOR, PHOTOSHOP, QUARK MATERIALS: CLASSIC LINEN, VELVET, SYNERGY

RIPE IN ASSOCIATION WITH ALCAN PRINT FINISHING
0120, 0126, 0560

ROBIN RAYNO
0578
ART DIRECTOR: ROBIN RAYNO DESIGNER: ROBIN RAYNO CLIENT: CHRISTABEL ROMANLIER TOOLS: ILLUSTRATOR, PC MATERIALS: WOOD, STARDREAM 150GSM, CONQUEROR 150GSM

ROSE DESIGN
0102
ART DIRECTOR: SIMON ELLIOTT DESIGNER: ESTHER KIRKPATRICK CLIENT: SPINE PUBLISHING TOOLS: ILLUSTRATOR, PHOTOSHOP, QUARK, MAC
0131
ART DIRECTOR: SIMON ELLIOTT DESIGNER: SIMON ELLIOTT CLIENT: WESTZONE PUBLISHING TOOLS: ILLUSTRATOR, PHOTOSHOP, QUARK, MAC MATERIALS: 350 NEPTUNE UNIQUE, 250 CHROMOMAT

0380
ART DIRECTOR: SIMON ELLIOTT DESIGNER: SIMON ELLIOTT CLIENT: WESTZONE PUBLISHING TOOLS: ILLUSTRATOR, PHOTOSHOP, QUARK, MAC MATERIALS: 250 CYCLUS, 120 FRENCH LEAVES HELLO SILK

ROUNDEL
0141
ART DIRECTOR: JOHN BATESON DESIGNER: PAUL INGLE CLIENT: ZANDERS FINEPAPER TOOLS: MAC MATERIALS: IKONO PAPER

0563
ART DIRECTOR: JOHN BATESON DESIGNER: PAUL INGLE CLIENT: ZANDERS FINEPAPER TOOLS: MAC MATERIALS: IKONO PAPER

0692
ART DIRECTOR: JOHN BATESON DESIGNER: KEELAN ROSS CLIENT: ZANDERS FINEPAPER TOOLS: MAC MATERIALS: SPECTRAL PAPER

ROYCROFT DESIGN
0121
ART DIRECTOR: JENNIFER ROYCROFT DESIGNER: JENNIFER ROYCROFT CLIENT: MOHAWK PAPERMILL TOOLS: QUARK, MAC MATERIALS: MOHAWK 50/10

0128
ART DIRECTOR: JENNIFER ROYCROFT DESIGNER: JENNIFER ROYCROFT CLIENT: MOHAWK PAPERMILL TOOLS: ILLUSTRATOR, QUARK, MAC MATERIALS: MOHAWK SUPERFINE

0920
ART DIRECTOR: JENNIFER ROYCROFT DESIGNER: JENNIFER ROYCROFT CLIENT: ROYCROFT DESIGN TOOLS: QUARK MATERIALS: FINCH FINE

SAGE COMMUNICATION
0528
ART DIRECTORS: KELSEY MCLACHLAN DESIGNER: CHRISTOPHER MCLACHLAN CLIENT: BRIAN SHARPE TOOLS: MAC MATERIALS: FOX RIVER

SALTERBAXTER
0313
ART DIRECTOR: PENNY BAXTER DESIGNER: ALAN DELGADO CLIENT: SALTERBAXTER & CONTEXT TOOLS: ILLUSTRATOR, QUARK, MAC MATERIALS: FLOCKAGE

0547
ART DIRECTORS: ALAN DELGADO DESIGNER: ROSE MCMULLAN CLIENT: DISCOVERY NETWORKS EUROPE TOOLS: ILLUSTRATOR, MAC MATERIALS: TYVEK

0559
ART DIRECTORS: ALAN DELGADO DESIGNER: ALAN DELGADO CLIENT: DISCOVERY NETWORKS EUROPE TOOLS: QUARK, MAC MATERIALS: PLASMA POLYCOAT CLEAR NATURAL

0881
ART DIRECTORS: ALAN DELGADO DESIGNERS: ALAN DELGADO, LINDSEY KELMAN CLIENT: DISCOVERY NETWORKS EUROPE TOOLS: QUARK, MAC MATERIALS: PRIPLAK CLEAR AND TRANSLUCENT RED SILK SCREEN

0883
ART DIRECTORS: PENNY BAXTER DESIGNER: PENNY BAXTER CLIENT: THE EMI GROUP TOOLS: QUARK, MAC MATERIALS: DISCARDED WASTE SHEETS

SAMPSONMAY
0022
ART DIRECTOR: RICKY SAMPSON DESIGNER: KATE MESSENGER CLIENT: SAMPSONMAY TOOLS: WOOD BLOCK MATERIALS: G.F. SMITH COLOURPLAN

0438
ART DIRECTOR: RICKY SAMPSON DESIGNER: RICKY SAMPSON CLIENT: SAMPSONMAY MATERIALS: G.F. SMITH COLOURPLAN

0681
ART DIRECTOR: RICKY SAMPSON DESIGNER: KATE MESSENGER CLIENT: ROLLS-ROYCE PLC

0906
ART DIRECTOR: RICKY SAMPSON DESIGNER: KATE MESSENGER CLIENT: SAMPSONMAY MATERIALS: NOVA SPACE INK TECHNIQUE

SAS
0065
ART DIRECTOR: DAVID STOCKS DESIGNER: MIKE HALL CLIENT: BBA TOOLS: QUARK, MAC MATERIALS: ZANDERS MEGA MATT

0354, 0733
ART DIRECTOR: DAVID STOCKS DESIGNER: MAREK GWLAZDA CLIENT: RADIO TAXIS TOOLS: ILLUSTRATOR, MAC MATERIALS: G.F. SMITH COLOURPLAN

0379
ART DIRECTOR: GILMAR WENDT DESIGNERS: CHRISTINE FENT, JOE MADEIRA, ANDY ROBINSON, BEN TOMLINSON CLIENT: BT TOOLS: QUARK, MAC MATERIALS: CONSORT ROYAL SILK, CONSORT ROYAL COMPLEMENT, HOWARD SMITH UNCOATED

0620, 0895
ART DIRECTORS: DAVID STOCKS, GILMAR WENDT DESIGNER: GILMAR WENDT CLIENT: SAS TOOLS: INDESIGN, MAC MATERIALS: PHOENIXMOTION, GLOW-EDGE POLYCARBONATE

0631
ART DIRECTOR: DAVID STOCKS DESIGNER: JAMES PARSONS CLIENT: HSBC TOOLS: QUARK, ILLUSTRATOR, MAC MATERIALS: JOB PARILUX MATT

0703
ART DIRECTORS: CHRISTINE FENT, GILMAR WENDT DESIGNERS: CHRISTINE FENT, GILMAR WENDT CLIENT: SAS TOOLS: ILLUSTRATOR, QUARK, MAC MATERIALS: PLANO PAK DÜNNDRUCK, SURBALIN MOIRÉ, CABRA

0797, 0856
ART DIRECTOR: GILMAR WENDT DESIGNERS: GILMAR WENDT, FRANKIE GOODWIN, MATT TOMLIN CLIENT: MAKINGSPACE PUBLISHERS TOOLS: MAC, ILLUSTRATOR MATERIALS: PHOENIXMOTION, VELBEC

0800
ART DIRECTOR: DAVID STOCKS DESIGNER: ALAN DELGADO CLIENT: BBA TOOLS: QUARK, MAC MATERIALS: ZANDERS MEGA MATT, MATERIAL FROM BBA NONVOWENS

0981
ART DIRECTOR: PENNY BAXTER DESIGNER: MIKE HALL CLIENT: NM ROTHSCHILD TOOLS: QUARK, MAC MATERIALS: G.F. SMITH COLOURPLAN, MUNKEDALS MUNKEN, FEDRIGONI PERGAMENATA

SCANDINAVIAN DESIGN GROUP
0005, 0059, 0103, 0521
ART DIRECTOR: MUGGIE RAMADANI DESIGNER: MUGGIE RAMADANI CLIENT: PRICEWATERHOUSECOOPERS COPYWRITER: SIGNE DUUS PHOTOGRAPHER: SIMON LADEFOGED DTP: CHRISTIAN BRÆNDER TOOLS: ILLUSTRATOR, PHOTOSHOP, QUARK, MAC

0006, 0473, 0706
ART DIRECTORS: MUGGIE RAMADANI, PER MADSEN DESIGNERS: PER MADSEN, MUGGIE RAMADANI CLIENT: MUNTHE PLUS SIMONSEN PHOTOGRAPHER: HENRIK BÜLOW FILM PHOTOGRAPHER: PHILIPPE KRESS IMAGE HANDLING: WERKSTETTE DTP: CHRISTIAN BRÆNDER TOOLS: ILLUSTRATOR, PHOTOSHOP, QUARK, MAC

0024, 0088, 0140, 0142, 0873
ART DIRECTORS: MUGGIE RAMADANI, PER MADSEN DESIGNERS: PER MADSEN, MUGGIE RAMADANI CLIENT: CREATIVE CIRCLE PHOTOGRAPHER: SIMON LADEFOGED PROJECT LEADER: JASPER VON WIEDING TOOLS: ILLUSTRATOR, PHOTOSHOP, QUARK, MAC

0249, 0261, 0280, 0476, 0477
ART DIRECTORS: MUGGIE RAMADANI, PER MADSEN DESIGNERS: PER MADSEN, MUGGIE RAMADANI CLIENT: PORTFOLIO—CPH DTP: CHRISTIAN BRÆNDER TOOLS: ILLUSTRATOR, PHOTOSHOP, QUARK, MAC

0342, 0343
ART DIRECTORS: MUGGIE RAMADANI, PER MADSEN DESIGNERS: PER MADSEN, MUGGIE RAMADANI CLIENT: MUNTHE PLUS SIMONSEN PHOTOGRAPHER: JETTE JØRS/6 AGENCY PAINTER: CATHRINE RABEN DAVIDSEN DTP: CHRISTIAN BRÆNDER TOOLS: ILLUSTRATOR, PHOTOSHOP, QUARK, MAC

0468, 0485, 0505, 0882
ART DIRECTORS: MUGGIE RAMADANI, PER MADSEN DESIGNERS: PER MADSEN, MUGGIE RAMADANI CLIENT: 6 AGENCY DTP: CHRISTIAN BRÆNDER TOOLS: ILLUSTRATOR, PHOTOSHOP, QUARK, MAC

0470, 0874
ART DIRECTOR: MUGGIE RAMADANI DESIGNER: MUGGIE RAMADANI CLIENT: PORTFOLIO—CPH/STYLE COUNSEL/UNIQUE LOOK TOOLS: ILLUSTRATOR, PHOTOSHOP, QUARK, MAC

0590, 0705
ART DIRECTOR: PER MADSEN DESIGNER: PER MADSEN CLIENT: NIGHTCLUB X-RAY TOOLS: ILLUSTRATOR, PHOTO-SHOP, QUARK, MAC

SEA DESIGN
0094
ART DIRECTOR: BRYAN GOMONOSON DESIGNER: CARSTEN KLEIN CLIENT: IDENTITY TOOLS: ILLUSTRATOR, PHOTOSHOP, QUARK, MAC G4 MATERIALS: ACCENT SMOOTH 115GSM PRINTING: 4-COLOR PROCESS LITHO, COPPER FOIL

SELTZER DESIGN
0439
ART DIRECTOR: ROCHELLE SELTZER DESIGNER: MEAGHAN O'KEEFE CLIENT: PARTNERS HEALTHCARE SYSTEM TOOLS: ILLUSTRATOR, QUARK, MAC MATERIALS: ROLAND MOTIF SCREENED, FRASER PEGASUS, FINCH OPAQUE

0676
ART DIRECTOR: ROCHELLE SELTZER DESIGNER: MEAGHAN O'KEEFE CLIENT: ANIMATION MD TOOLS: ILLUSTRATOR, QUARK, MAC MATERIALS: GILCLEAR WHITE HEAVY, CANSON SATIN 75LB CLEAR, MCCOY VELVET 180LB COVER, BUBBLEOPE, LION LABELS

0803
ART DIRECTOR: ROCHELLE SELTZER DESIGNER: MEAGHAN O'KEEFE CLIENT: SELTZER DESIGN TOOLS: QUARK, MAC MATERIALS: CURIOUS METALLIC ANODIZED

0999
ART DIRECTOR: ROCHELLE SELTZER DESIGNER: ANNIE SMIDT CLIENT: SELTZER DESIGN TOOLS: ILLUSTRATOR, INDESIGN, MAC MATERIALS: DOMTAR FELTWEAVE NATURAL, CURIOUS POISON IVORY

SHARP COMMUNICATIONS
0412
ART DIRECTOR: ANRI SEKI DESIGNER: ANRI SEKI CLIENT: NORDIC PARTNERS TOOLS: ILLUSTRATOR, QUARK

SHIH DESIGN
0032
ART DIRECTOR: GING-HUNG SHIH DESIGNER: GING-HUNG SHIH CLIENT: AUSPICE PAPER CO. LTD. TOOLS: ILLUSTRATOR, PHOTOSHOP MATERIALS: PHEONIXMOTION

SK VISUAL
0028, 0530
ART DIRECTORS: KATYA LYUMKIS, SPENCER LUM DESIGNERS: KATYA LYUMKIS, SPENCER LUM CLIENT: SK VISUAL TOOLS: ILLUSTRATOR MATERIALS: VELUM, LABEL TAGS, METAL CLIPS, STAMP

...,STAAT
0069
ART DIRECTOR: JOCHEM LEEGSTRA DESIGNER: YOURI KOERS CLIENT: BARTENDER NETWORK TOOLS: MAC, ILLUSTRATOR MATERIALS: PROMINENT 500GSM

0335
ART DIRECTOR: JOCHEM LEEGSTRA DESIGNER: YOURI KOERS CLIENT: CLUB JIMMY WOO TOOLS: ILLUSTRATOR, PHOTOSHOP, QUARK, MAC MATERIALS: CHROMOLUX

0714
ART DIRECTOR: JOCHEM LEEGSTRA DESIGNER: JARI VERSTEEGEN CLIENT: MOËT & CHANDON TOOLS: ILLUSTRATOR, QUARK, MAC MATERIALS: SILK SCARF AND POCHET, PACKAGING WITH FOILPRINT

0774
ART DIRECTOR: JOCHEM LEEGSTRA DESIGNER: YOURI KOERS CLIENT: CLUB JIMMY WOO TOOLS: ILLUSTRATOR, PHOTOSHOP, QUARK, MAC MATERIALS: PENCILS

0844
ART DIRECTOR: JOCHEM LEEGSTRA DESIGNER: ...,STAAT CLIENT: ...,STAAT TOOLS: ILLUSTRATOR, QUARK, MAC MATERIALS: CONQUEROR CX22, PLASTIC

0862
ART DIRECTORS: JOCHEM LEEGSTRA, STEF BAKKER DESIGNER: YOURI KOERS CLIENT: CAFÉ RESTAURANT MAMOUCHE TOOLS: ILLUSTRATOR, PHOTOSHOP, QUARK, MAC MATERIALS: PROOST & BRAND 50GSM HIGHSPEED ORANGE

STARSHOT
0026
ART DIRECTOR: LARS HARMSEN DESIGNERS: LARS HARMSEN, TINA WEISSER CLIENT: STARSHOT BYKE STYLE MAGAZINE TOOLS: PHOTOSHOP, FREEHAND, QUARK MATERIALS: GMUND BÜTENPAPIER (COVER), VIBE GENTLE ROSE (COLLECTION), HOT FOIL

0073, 0255
ART DIRECTOR: LARS HARMSEN DESIGNER: LARS HARMSEN CLIENT: STARSHOT BYKE STYLE MAGAZINE TOOLS: PHOTOSHOP, FREEHAND, QUARK MATERIALS: REFLECTING IMAGE

0164
ART DIRECTOR: LARS HARMSEN DESIGNERS: LARS HARMSEN, AXEL BRINKMANN, TINA WEISSER CLIENT: BERGWERK BIKES TOOLS: PHOTOSHOP, FREEHAND, QUARK MATERIALS: IVERCOTE

0751, 0848
ART DIRECTOR: LARS HARMSEN DESIGNERS: LARS HARMSEN, TINA WEISSER, CLAUDIA KLEIN CLIENT: STARSHOT TOOLS: PHOTOSHOP, FREEHAND, QUARK MATERIALS: GMUND BÜTENPAPIER, COLLECTION TREASURY

0851
ART DIRECTOR: LARS HARMSEN DESIGNER: LARS HARMSEN CLIENT: STARSHOT BYKE STYLE MAGAZINE TOOLS: PHOTOSHOP, FREEHAND, QUARK MATERIALS: REFLECTING IMAGE

STEERSMCGILLAN
0109, 0112
ART DIRECTOR: RICHARD MCGILLAN DESIGNER: CHLOE STEERS CLIENT: SPIKE ISLAND, BRISTOL TOOLS: QUARK, MAC

0146
ART DIRECTOR: RICHARD MCGILLAN DESIGNER: CHLOE STEERS CLIENT: CLORE DUFFED FOUNDATION TOOLS: QUARK, MAC MATERIALS: TRUCARD 1-COLOR PLUS FOIL

0628
ART DIRECTOR: CHLOE STEERS DESIGNER: RICHARD MCGILLAN CLIENT: DULWICH PICTURE GALLERY TOOLS: QUARK, MAC MATERIALS: ARCTIC VOLUME

0713
ART DIRECTOR: RICHARD MCGILLAN DESIGNER: PETER THOMPSON CLIENT: INSANELY GREAT TOOLS: MAC MATERIALS: PRIPLAK

0719
ART DIRECTOR: RICHARD MCGILLAN DESIGNER: CHLOE STEERS CLIENT: THE STUDY GALLERY, POOLE TOOLS: QUARK MAC MATERIALS: TINTED PRIPLAK, SCREEN PRINT

STOLTZE DESIGN
0107
ART DIRECTORS: CLIFFORD STOLTZE, ROY BURNS DESIGNER: ROY BURNS CLIENT: STOLTZE DESIGN

0358, 0872
ART DIRECTOR: CLIFFORD STOLTZE DESIGNER: CLIFFORD STOLTZE CLIENT: DOROTHEA VAN CAMP

0492
ART DIRECTOR: CLIFFORD STOLTZE DESIGNERS: BRANDON BLANGGER, CINDY PATTEN CLIENT: SIX RED MARBLES

STRICHPUNKT
0086
ART DIRECTORS: KIRSTEN DIETZ, JOCHEN RÄDEKER DESIGNERS: KIRSTEN DIETZ, FELIX WIDMAIER, TANJA GÜNTHER CLIENT: PAPIER-FABRIK SCHEUFELEN TOOLS: QUARK, MAC MATERIALS: PHOENIXMOTION/SCHEUFELEN

0089, 0861
ART DIRECTORS: KIRSTEN DIETZ, JOCHEN RÄDEKER DESIGNERS: KIRSTEN DIETZ, TANJA GÜNTHER CLIENT: PAPIERFABRIK SCHEUFELEN TOOLS: QUARK, MAC MATERIALS: PHOENIXMOTION/SCHEUFELEN

0267
ART DIRECTORS: KIRSTEN DIETZ, JOCHEN RÄDEKER DESIGNERS: KIRSTEN DIETZ CLIENT: 4MBO INTERNATIONAL ELECTRONIC AG TOOLS: QUARK, MAC MATERIALS: LUXOR STAIN (SCHNEIDER & SÖHNE), SHOPPING BAG

STRUKTUR DESIGN
0271, 0460, 0925
ART DIRECTOR: ROGER FAWCETT-TANG CLIENT: STRUKTUR DESIGN TOOLS: QUARK, MAC MATERIALS: STORA FINE

0346
ART DIRECTOR: ROGER FAWCETT-TANG DESIGNERS: ROGER FAWCETT-TANG, SANNE FAWCETT-TANG CLIENT: STRUKTUR DESIGN TOOLS: QUARK, MAC MATERIALS: STORA FINE

SUM DESIGN
0115
ART DIRECTOR: SIMON WOOLFORD DESIGNER: CAMERON LEADBETTER CLIENT: RIVER ISLAND TOOLS: PHOTOSHOP, QUARK MATERIALS: MIRROR BOARD

0133
ART DIRECTOR: SIMON WOOLFORD DESIGNER: LORINDA SMITH CLIENT: INCA PRODUCTIONS TOOLS: ILLUSTRATOR MATERIALS: CX22

0557
ART DIRECTOR: SIMON WOOLFORD DESIGNER: LORINDA SMITH CLIENT: BILLY BAG TOOLS: ILLUSTRATOR, PHOTOSHOP, QUARK MATERIALS: ESSENTIAL SILK

SUSSNER DESIGN COMPANY
0098, 0404
ART DIRECTOR: DEREK SUSSNER DESIGNERS: DEREK SUSSNER, RALPH SCHRADER, BRENT GALE, RYAN CARLSON CLIENT: SUSSNER DESIGN COMPANY COPYWRITER: JEFF MUELLER IS FLOATING HEAD PHOTOGRAPHER: ELLIE KINGSBURY TOOLS: ILLUSTRATOR, PHOTOSHOP, QUARK, MAC MATERIALS: 100LB NEKOOSA SOLUTIONS CARRARA WHITE SMOOTH COVER, 80LB FOX RIVER EVERGREEN HICKORY COVER, 80LB MCCOY SILK TEXT, 80LB NEKOOSA SOLUTIONS RECYCLED WHITE SMOOTH TEXT

TAXI STUDIO
0127
ART DIRECTOR: RYAN WILLS DESIGNER: OLLY GUISE CLIENT: CLARKS TOOLS: PHOTOSHOP, QUARK MATERIALS: ARCTIC VOLUME

0349
ART DIRECTORS: SPENCER BUCK, RYAN WILLS DESIGNER: ALEX BANE CLIENT: INTEGRALIS TOOLS: PHOTOSHOP, QUARK

0356
ART DIRECTOR: OLLY GUISE DESIGNER: OLLY GUISE CLIENT: CLARKS MATERIALS: CHALLENGER OFFSET

0921
ART DIRECTOR: RYAN WILLS DESIGNER: OLLY GUISE CLIENT: CLARKS TOOLS: PHOTOSHOP, QUARK MATERIALS: CHALLENGER OFFSET

TEMPLIN BRINK DESIGN
0002
ART DIRECTORS: GABY BRINK, JOEL TEMPLIN DESIGNERS: BRIAN GUNDERSON, GABY BRINK CLIENT: JANUS CAPITAL GROUP TOOLS: ILLUSTRATOR, PHOTOSHOP, QUARK, MAC

0016
ART DIRECTORS: GABY BRINK, JOEL TEMPLIN DESIGNERS: BRIAN GUNDERSON, GABY BRINK CLIENT: ORACLE TOOLS: ILLUSTRATOR, PHOTOSHOP, QUARK, MAC

0017, 0584
ART DIRECTORS: GABY BRINK, JOEL TEMPLIN DESIGNER: BRIAN GUNDERSON CLIENT: LEVI STRAUSS TOOLS: ILLUSTRATOR, PHOTOSHOP, QUARK, MAC

0037
ART DIRECTORS: GABY BRINK, JOEL TEMPLIN DESIGNER: BRIAN GUNDERSON CLIENT: OAKLAND A'S TOOLS: ILLUSTRATOR, PHOTOSHOP, QUARK, MAC

0038
ART DIRECTORS: GABY BRINK, JOEL TEMPLIN DESIGNERS: MARIUS GEDGAUDUS, GABY BRINK CLIENT: EDAW TOOLS: ILLUSTRATOR, PHOTOSHOP, QUARK, MAC

0161
ART DIRECTOR: JOEL TEMPLIN DESIGNER: JOEL TEMPLIN CLIENT: SHARPE + ASSOCIATES TOOLS: ILLUSTRATOR, PHOTOSHOP, QUARK, MAC

0165
ART DIRECTORS: GABY BRINK, JOEL TEMPLIN DESIGNER: GABY BRINK CLIENT: KELHAM MACLEAN TOOLS: ILLUSTRATOR, PHOTOSHOP, QUARK, MAC

0310, 0352, 0369, 0599
ART DIRECTORS: GABY BRINK, JOEL TEMPLIN DESIGNERS: BRIAN GUNDERSON, GABY BRINK CLIENT: TARGET TOOLS: ILLUSTRATOR, PHOTOSHOP, QUARK, MAC

0700
ART DIRECTORS: GABY BRINK, JOEL TEMPLIN DESIGNER: BRIAN GUNDERSON CLIENT: SAND STUDIO TOOLS: ILLUSTRATOR, PHOTOSHOP, QUARK, MAC

0979
ART DIRECTORS: GABY BRINK, JOEL TEMPLIN DESIGNER: BRIAN GUNDERSON CLIENT: LEO BURNETT TOOLS: ILLUSTRATOR, PHOTOSHOP, QUARK, MAC

THAT'S NICE LLC
0555
ART DIRECTOR: SCOTT ROBERTSON DESIGNER: ELAN HARRIS CLIENT: THAT'S NICE LLC TOOLS: ILLUSTRATOR MATERIALS: 120LB STROBE COVER

THIRTEEN
0230
ART DIRECTOR: JOHN UNDERWOOD DESIGNER: JOHN UNDERWOOD CLIENT: CENTRAL WORKSHOP TOOLS: ILLUSTRATOR, PHOTOSHOP, QUARK MATERIALS: WICOTEX CLOTH, MUNKEN LYNX, ARCTIC SILK

0447, 0451
ART DIRECTOR: JOHN UNDERWOOD DESIGNER: DANIELLE WAY CLIENT: BRISTOL REGENERATION TOOLS: PHOTOSHOP, QUARK MATERIALS: EUROCHIP ESSENTIAL OFFSET

0448
ART DIRECTOR: SUFFIA KHANAN DESIGNER: SUFFIA KHANAN CLIENT: WHITE DESIGN TOOLS: QUARK MATERIALS: G.F. SMITH COLOURPLAN

0453
ART DIRECTOR: DANNY JENKINS DESIGNER: DANNY JENKINS CLIENT: ARNOLFINI TOOLS: QUARK MATERIALS: REGENCY GLOSS, MUNCHEN LYNX

0472
ART DIRECTOR: DANNY JENKINS DESIGNER: DANNY JENKINS CLIENT: HITEC-LOTEC TOOLS: PHOTOSHOP, QUARK MATERIALS: INDUSTRIAL EPDM FOAM, ANTALIS PRINTSPEED

0568
ART DIRECTOR: NICK HAND DESIGNERS: NICK HAND, NEIL TINSON CLIENT: ORANGE TOOLS: PHOTOSHOP, QUARK MATERIALS: CONSORT ROYAL SILK

0632, 0977
ART DIRECTOR: DANNY JENKINS DESIGNER: DANNY JENKINS CLIENT: HITEC-LOTEC TOOLS: PHOTOSHOP, QUARK MATERIALS: PHOENIX MOTION

0985
ART DIRECTORS: DANNY JENKINS, SUFFIA KHANAN DESIGNER: SUFFIA KHANAN CLIENT: ORANGE TOOLS: ILLUSTRATOR, PHOTOSHOP, QUARK MATERIALS: DUTCHMAN

THOMPSON
0061, 0740, 0780
ART DIRECTOR: IAN THOMPSON DESIGNER: IAN THOMPSON CLIENT: THOMPSON TOOLS: QUARK MATERIALS: GRAPHIC TEXTURES

0425
ART DIRECTOR: IAN THOMPSON DESIGNER: IAN THOMPSON CLIENT: DESIGN YORKSHIRE TOOLS: QUARK MATERIALS: NEPTUNE UNIQUE

0426
ART DIRECTOR: IAN THOMPSON DESIGNER: IAN THOMPSON CLIENT: LEEDS METROPOLITAN UNIVERSITY/CHARLES QUICK TOOLS: QUARK MATERIALS: NEPTUNE UNIQUE

0480, 0871, 0911
ART DIRECTOR: IAN THOMPSON DESIGNER: IAN THOMPSON CLIENT: LEEDS METROPOLITAN UNIVERSITY/CHARLES QUICK TOOLS: QUARK MATERIALS: NEPTUNE UNIQUE

0622
ART DIRECTOR: IAN THOMPSON DESIGNER: IAN THOMPSON CLIENT: THOMPSON TOOLS: QUARK MATERIALS: NATIONAL VELVET, CRUSADE OFFSET

TONIC
0696
ART DIRECTOR: SIMON HEYS DESIGNERS: SIMON HEYS, JAY PRYNNE CLIENT: DOB INTERNATIONAL MATERIALS: THERMOCHROMIC INK

0775
ART DIRECTOR: JAY PRYNNE DESIGNERS: JAY PRYNNE, DANIEL HUTCHINSON CLIENT: TONIC MATERIALS: WOOD

TRACY DESIGN
0293
ART DIRECTOR: JAN TRACY DESIGNER: PATRICK SIMONE CLIENT: JENNIFER ANNE TOOLS: ILLUSTRATOR, MAC MATERIALS: CURIOUS METALLIC, ALUMINUM DISKS

0648, 0845, 0973
ART DIRECTOR: JAN TRACY DESIGNER: PATRICK SIMONE CLIENT: CERNER CORPORATION TOOLS: ILLUSTRATOR, MAC

TRICKETT & WEBB
0154, 0289, 0577
ART DIRECTOR: BRIAN WEBB DESIGNERS: BRIAN WEBB, KATJA THIELEN CLIENT: LONDON INSTITUTE TOOLS: QUARK MATERIALS: Z3 ACID FREE OFFSET (TEXT), FEDRIGONI SAVILE ROW (COVER)

TWELVE:TEN
0045, 0672, 0826, 0840
ART DIRECTOR: ALUN EDWARDS DESIGNERS: ALUN EDWARDS, SI BILLAM CLIENT: TWELVE:TEN TOOLS: FREEHAND, QUARK, MAC

TYLER MAGAZINE
0912, 0914, 0936, 0952
ART DIRECTOR: PHIL CAUBIT DESIGNER: PHIL CAUBIT CLIENT: TYLER MAGAZINE MATERIALS: CD

ULTRA DESIGN
0186
ART DIRECTOR: BRAULIO LACERDA CAROLLO DESIGNER: MARCO DURAN CLIENT: ULTRA DESIGN TOOLS: PHOTOSHOP, CORELDRAW, PC MATERIALS: MATTE COUCHÉ 340GSM, LAMINATION

UNA (AMSTERDAM) DESIGNERS
0283
DESIGNERS/TYPOGRAPHERS: UNA (AMSTERDAM), HANS BOCKTING, WILL DE L'ECLUSE, STEFAN HENGST CLIENT: VAN LANSCHOT GROUP COPYWRITER: PAUL GROOT TRANSLATOR: SHERRY MARX-MACDONALD TYPESETTER/ LITHOGRAPHER: BLOEM, ASSENDELFT

0582, 0591, 0607
DESIGNERS/TYPOGRAPHERS: UNA (AMSTERDAM), WILL DE L'ECLUSE CLIENT: VAN LANSCHOT GROUP

0680
DESIGNERS/TYPOGRAPHERS: UNA (AMSTERDAM), HANS BOCKTING, WILL DE L'ECLUSE CLIENT: ACF COPYWRITER: MORE THAN FINANCIALS TRANSLATOR: ANTHONY FUDGE PHOTOGRAPHER: FRISCO KEURIS

UNDERWARE/FAYDHERBE DE VRINGER
0079
ART DIRECTOR: WOUT DE VRINGER DESIGNER: WOUT DE VRINGER CLIENT: UNDERWARE TOOLS: QUARK, MAC MATERIALS: BIOSET

0416
ART DIRECTORS: UNDERWARE, PIET SCHREUDERS DESIGNERS: UNDERWARE, PIET SCHREUDERS CLIENT: UNDERWARE TOOLS: FREEHAND, QUARK, MAC MATERIALS: NEOBOND

UNTITLED
0021, 0811
ART DIRECTOR: ZOE SCUTTS DESIGNER: ZOE SCUTTS CLIENT: UNTITLED IMAGE LIBRARY TOOLS: ILLUSTRATOR, PHOTOSHOP, FREEHAND, QUARK MATERIALS: BOARD, PAPER, PLASTIC OUTER BAG

0641
ART DIRECTOR: ZOE SCUTTS DESIGNER: ZOE SCUTTS CLIENT: UNTITLED IMAGINE LIBRARY TOOLS: PHOTOSHOP, FREEHAND, QUARK MATERIALS: PAPER, PVC PLASTIC, PLASTIC OUTER COVER

0760
ART DIRECTOR: ZOE SCUTTS DESIGNER: ZOE SCUTTS CLIENT: NICK VEASEY TOOLS: PHOTOSHOP, QUARK MATERIALS: BOARD, PLASTIC, METAL

0769
ART DIRECTOR: ZOE SCUTTS
DESIGNER: ZOE SCUTTS
CLIENT: UNTITLED IMAGINE
LIBRARY TOOLS: PHOTOSHOP,
QUARK MATERIALS: PAPER,
PHARMACEUTICAL PLASTIC
PACKAGING

0948
ART DIRECTOR: ZOE SCUTTS
DESIGNER: ZOE SCUTTS
CLIENT: NICK VEASEY,
UNTITLED ORGANISATION
PHOTOLIBRARY TOOLS:
PHOTOSHOP, QUARK
MATERIALS: PAPER, BOARD,
GLOSS UV VARNISH

URBAN MAPPING
0129
ART DIRECTOR: CHRIS CANNON,
ISOTOPE 221 CLIENT: URBAN
MAPPING LLC, IAN WHITE
TECHNICAL CONSULTANT:
DAVID SANTUS
CARTOGRAPHER: DORIT
KRIESLER TOOLS: ILLUSTRA-
TOR, PHOTOSHOP, AVENZA
MAPPUBLISHER, SRI ARCVIEW,
QUARK, FUJISU C SERIES
LIFEBOOK, MAC G3 MATERIALS:
LENTICULAR POLYMER SUB-
STRATE, PAPER BACKING

VIVA DOLAN
COMMUNICATIONS & DESIGN
0081
ART DIRECTOR: FRANK VIVA
DESIGNER: TODD TEMPORALE
CLIENT: ARJOWIGGINS TOOLS:
ILLUSTRATOR, PHOTOSHOP,
QUARK, MAC MATERIALS:
CURIOUS COLLECTION

0500, 0504
ART DIRECTOR: FRANK VIVA
DESIGNERS: FRANK VIVA
CLIENT: ARJOWIGGINS
ILLUSTRATORS: SETH, FRANK
VIVA PHOTOGRAPHERS: RON
BAXTER SMITH TOOLS: ILLUS-
TRATOR, PHOTOSHOP, QUARK,
MAC MATERIALS: CURIOUS
COLLECTION

0503
ART DIRECTOR: FRANK VIVA
DESIGNER: SARAH WU CLIENT:
WORLD LITERACY OF CANADA
PHOTOGRAPHER: JEFFREY
GRAETSCH TOOLS: QUARK
MATERIALS: PRODUCTOLITH
MATTE COVER 100LB,
PRODUCTOLITH MATTE TEXT
80LB

0868
ART DIRECTOR: FRANK VIVA
DESIGNERS: FRANK VIVA,
FRANCE SIMARD, TODD
TEMPORALE, SARAH WU
CLIENT: VIVA DOLAN
COMMUNICATIONS & DESIGN
INC. TOOLS: QUARK MATERIALS:
60LB COATED PUBLICATION
STOCK

V06
0031
ART DIRECTOR: YOMAR
AUGUSTO DESIGNER: YOMAR
AUGUSTO CLIENT: MOV.
PRODUCTIONS TOOLS: CALLIG-
RAPHY MATERIALS: SOFT PAPER

0113
ART DIRECTOR: YOMAR
AUGUSTO DESIGNER: YOMAR
AUGUSTO CLIENT: EMI MUSIC
BRASIL TOOLS: ILLUSTRATOR,
QUARK

0117
ART DIRECTORS: YOMAR
AUGUSTO, CLAUDIO DESIGNERS:
YOMAR AUGUSTO, CLAUDIO GIL
CLIENT: V06 TOOLS:
ILLUSTRATOR, CALLIGRAPHY
MATERIALS: KRAFT PAPER,
SILK SCREEN

0721
ART DIRECTOR: YOMAR
AUGUSTO DESIGNER: YOMAR
AUGUSTO CLIENT: V06 TOOLS:
ILLUSTRATOR, MAC

0885
ART DIRECTOR: YOMAR
AUGUSTO DESIGNER: YOMAR
AUGUSTO CLIENT: MOV.
PRODUCTIONS TOOLS: ILLUS-
TRATOR, PHOTOSHOP, MAC

VOICE
0099
ART DIRECTOR: SCOTT
CARSLAKE DESIGNER: SCOTT
CARSLAKE CLIENT: LOTUS
TOOLS: PHOTOSHOP, FREEHAND,
MAC MATERIALS: TYVEK 1050

0913, 0956
ART DIRECTORS: ANTHONY DE
LEO, SCOTT CARSLAKE
DESIGNERS: ANTHONY DE LEO,
SCOTT CARSLAKE CLIENT:
COLOUR COSMETICA TOOLS:
PHOTOSHOP, FREEHAND, MAC
MATERIALS: PACESETTER

WAGNER DESIGN
0736
CREATIVE DIRECTOR: JILL
WAGNER ART DIRECTOR: AMY
CONSIGLIO CLIENT: PROQUEST
COMPANY TOOLS: PHOTOSHOP,
QUARK, MAC MATERIALS: 80LB
STERLING GLOSS TEXT,
CHARTHAM RED TRANSLUCENT,
80LB DULL STERLING COVER

WALLACE CHURCH, INC.
0015
ART DIRECTOR: STAN CHURCH
DESIGNER: LAWRENCE
HAGGERTY CLIENT: ICON
BRANDS TOOLS: ILLUSTRATOR,
PHOTOSHOP, MAC

0171, 0348
ART DIRECTOR: STAN CHURCH
DESIGNERS: STAN CHURCH,
WENDY CHURCH CLIENT:
WALLACE CHURCH, INC. TOOLS:
ILLUSTRATOR, PHOTOSHOP, MAC

0612
ART DIRECTOR: STAN CHURCH
DESIGNERS: LAWRENCE
HAGGERTY, CLAIRE REECE, RAY
BOULD CLIENT: WALLACE
CHURCH, INC. TOOLS: ILLUSTRA-
TOR, PHOTOSHOP, MAC
MATERIALS: PLASTIC
SHRINKWRAP, BASEBALL
STITCHING, RED THREAD, CD
WITH BASEBALL MUSIC

0683
ART DIRECTOR: STAN CHURCH
DESIGNER: NIN GLAISTER
CLIENT: WALLACE CHURCH, INC.
TOOLS: ILLUSTRATOR, PHOTO-
SHOP, MAC MATERIALS:
MOHAWK

0720
ART DIRECTOR: STAN CHURCH
DESIGNER: LAWRENCE
HAGGERTY CLIENT: WALLACE
CHURCH, INC. MATERIALS:
PAPER PLATE, RUBBER BAND

0884
ART DIRECTOR: STAN CHURCH
DESIGNERS: NIN GLAISTER,
LAWRENCE HAGGERTY CLIENT:
WALL CHURCH INC. TOOLS:
ILLUSTRATOR, PHOTOSHOP, MAC

WEBB & WEBB
0033
ART DIRECTOR: BRIAN WEBB
DESIGNERS: BRIAN WEBB,
CHRIS GLOSTER CLIENT:
LONDON INSTITUTE TOOLS:
PHOTOSHOP, QUARK, LETTER-
PRESS TYPOGRAPHY
MATERIALS: G.F. SMITH BRIGHT
WHITE 200GSM (JACKET),
GALLERY SILK 170GSM

0159, 0180, 0817
ART DIRECTOR: BRIAN WEBB
DESIGNERS: BRIAN WEBB,
CHRIS GLOSTER CLIENT: THE
ROYAL MAIL, 2003 TOOLS:
QUARK, LETTERPRESS TYPOG-
RAPHY MATERIALS:
HANDMADE CARTRIDGE

WILSON HARVEY
0063
ART DIRECTOR: PAUL BURGESS
DESIGNER: STEPHANIE
HARRISON CLIENT: PHILLIPS
GROUP

0152
ART DIRECTOR: PAUL BURGESS
DESIGNERS: BEN WOOD, PETE
USHER, PAUL BURGESS CLIENT:
LIBERTY

0190
ART DIRECTOR: PAUL BURGESS
DESIGNERS: BEN WOOD, PAUL
BURGESS CLIENT: LUKE AND
LIZA TOOLS: QUARK, MAC
MATERIALS: 35GSM OFFSET

0345
ART DIRECTOR: PAUL BURGESS
DESIGNER: GRAHAM FARR
CLIENT: WENNER-GREN

0366
ART DIRECTOR: PAUL BURGESS
DESIGNER: PAUL BURGESS
CLIENT: WILSON HARVEY

0396
ART DIRECTOR: PAUL BURGESS
DESIGNER: BEN WOOD CLIENT:
CCD

0418
ART DIRECTOR: PAUL BURGESS
DESIGNER: WAI LAU CLIENT:
CCD

0707
ART DIRECTOR: PAUL BURGESS
DESIGNER: DANIEL ELLIOTT
CLIENT: NET BENEFIT

0772
ART DIRECTOR: PAUL BURGESS
DESIGNERS: EMMA GARNSEY,
PAUL BURGESS CLIENT: PFIZER
MATERIALS: POLYPROPYLENE

0778
ART DIRECTOR: PAUL BURGESS
DESIGNER: PAUL BURGESS
CLIENT: MUTINY

0804
ART DIRECTOR: PAUL BURGESS
DESIGNERS: DAN ELLIOTT,
PAUL BURGESS CLIENT: OLWEN
DM MATERIALS: POLYPROPY-
LENE COVER

THE WORKS DESIGN
COMMUNICATIONS
0034, 0589
ART DIRECTOR: SCOTT
MCFARLAND DESIGNER: MIKE
REHDER CLIENT: UNISOURCE
TOOLS: ILLUSTRATOR, PHOTO-
SHOP, MAC MATERIALS:
NEENAH CLASSIC LINEN
DUPLEX

0333
DESIGNER: SCOTT MCFARLAND
DESIGNER: MIKE REHDER
CLIENT: THE WORKS DESIGN
TOOLS: ILLUSTRATOR, PHOTO-
SHOP, MAC MATERIALS: BLACK
KEAY KOLOUR HOPPER HOTS
RED

0399
DESIGNER: SCOTT MCFARLAND
DESIGNER: MIKE REHDER
CLIENT: GREATER TORONTO
AIRPORTS AUTHORITY TOOLS:
ILLUSTRATOR, PHOTOSHOP,
QUARK, MAC MATERIALS: MEAD
WESTRACO 100LB SIGNATURE

0815
DESIGNER: SCOTT MCFARLAND
DESIGNER: NELSON SILVA
CLIENT: ABER DIAMOND TOOLS:
ILLUSTRATOR, PHOTOSHOP,
QUARK, MAC MATERIALS:
SYNERGY FELT TEXT 100LB

XAX CREATIVE
0235
ART DIRECTOR: ZACK
SHUBKAGEL CLIENT: WORKING
SPACES TOOLS: ILLUSTRATOR,
INDESIGN, MAC MATERIALS:
COUGAR WHITE 80LB COVER

YAEL MILLER DESIGN
0075
ART DIRECTOR: YAEL MILLER
DESIGNER: YAEL MILLER
CLIENT: ASTOR
CHOCOLATE/VENETIAN HOTEL,
LAS VEGAS TOOLS:
ILLUSTRATOR MATERIALS:
COATED STOCK, FOIL STAMP

0666
ART DIRECTOR: YAEL MILLER
DESIGNER: YAEL MILLER
CLIENT: LE BELGE
CHOCOLATIER TOOLS:
ILLUSTRATOR MATERIALS:
UNCOATED COLORED TEXTURED
PAPER, HOTSTAMPED RIBBON

0768
ART DIRECTOR: YAEL MILLER
DESIGNER: YAEL MILLER
CLIENT: ASTOR CHOCOLATE
TOOLS: ILLUSTRATOR
MATERIALS: VELVET PAPER,
FINE GOLD CORD

ZIGZAG DESIGN
0520, 0614
ART DIRECTOR: RACHEL
KARACA DESIGNER: RACHEL
KARACA CLIENT: ZIGZAG
DESIGN TOOLS: ILLUSTRATOR,
MAC MATERIALS: RUBBER COV-
ERS, CLOTH RAG

ZIP DESIGN
0208
ART DIRECTOR: PETER
CHADWICK DESIGNER: PETER
CHADWICK CLIENT: SKINT
RECORDS TOOLS: PHOTOSHOP,
QUARK MATERIALS: DIE-CUT CD
WALLET

0440, 0822
ART DIRECTORS: PETER
CHADWICK, TIM DELUXE
DESIGNER: NEIL BOWEN
CLIENT: UNDERWATER
RECORDS TOOLS: PHOTOSHOP,
QUARK MATERIALS: SPIRO-
BOUND HARDBACK CD BOOKLET

0825
ART DIRECTOR: PETER
CHADWICK DESIGNERS:
CAROLINE MOORHOUSE, NEIL
BOWEN, DAVID BOWDEN
CLIENT: HED KANDI TOOLS:
ILLUSTRATOR, FREEHAND
MATERIALS: CARD DIGI PACK
AND CLEAR ACETATE SLIPCASE
0950
ART DIRECTOR: PETER
CHADWICK DESIGNERS:
CAROLINE MOORHOUSE,
HANNAH WOODCOCK CLIENT:
OBSESSIVE/BMG RECORDS
SCREEN PRINTER: MATT
WINGFIELD TOOLS:
PHOTOSHOP, QUARK
MATERIALS: DOUBLE WHITE
REVERSE BOARD

ZULVER & CO.
0336
ART DIRECTOR: DAVID KIMPTON
DESIGNER: LEON TORKA
CLIENT: REGALIAN
PROPERTIES MATERIALS: JOB
PAVILOX MATT WHITE 170GSM

0341, 0813
ART DIRECTOR: ANDREW
ZULVER DESIGNERS: DAVID
KIMPTON, GRAHAM BIRCH
CLIENT: GHM ROCK TOWNSEND
MATERIALS: SKY DXM XENON,
MUNKEN LYNX

0360
ART DIRECTOR: ANDREW
ZULVER DESIGNER: GRAHAM
BIRCH ILLUSTRATOR: GRAHAM
BIRCH CLIENT: REGALIAN
PROPERTIES MATERIALS: 300
GSM PARLUX SILK

ABOUT THE AUTHOR

+

WILSON HARVEY IS A LONDON-BASED INTEGRATED DESIGN AND MARKETING AGENCY WORKING ACROSS A WIDE RANGE OF DESIGN DISCIPLINES SUCH AS BRANDING, IDENTITY, COLLATERAL, ADVERTISING, DIRECT MARKETING, PUBLISHING, AND NEW MEDIA. COLLECTIVELY THEY HAVE DESIGNED MORE THAN 500 BOOKS FOR A VARIETY OF PUBLISHERS AND ARE THE AUTHOR/DESIGNERS OF *THE BEST OF BROCHURE DESIGN 7.* THEY HAVE RECENTLY JOINED FORCES WITH FIVE OTHER LEADING MEDIA AGENCIES UNDER THE BANNER OF THE LOEWY GROUP, CONTINUING THE LEGACY OF THE GREAT RAYMOND LOEWY.

PAUL BURGESS IS COFOUNDER AND CREATIVE DIRECTOR OF WILSON HARVEY. HE HAS BEEN WORKING AS A MULTIDISCIPLINED GRAPHIC DESIGNER FOR MORE THAN 14 YEARS WITH B2B AND B2C CLIENTS ALIKE. PAUL HAS BEEN PUBLISHED IN MORE THAN 20 DIFFERENT INDUSTRY TITLES.

BEN WOOD IS A SENIOR DESIGNER AT WILSON HARVEY. BEN'S WORK HAS BEEN RECOGNIZED BY THE DESIGN INDUSTRY, ACHIEVING A D+AD STUDENT GOLD AWARD.